P9-DNL-812

HARLEM WORLD

DOING RACE AND CLASS IN CONTEMPORARY BLACK AMERICA

JOHN L. JACKSON JR.

THE UNIVERSITY OF CHICAGO PRESS
CHICAGO AND LONDON

JOHN L. JACKSON JR. is a postdoctoral fellow in Harvard University's Society of Fellows.

The University of Chicago Press, Chicago 60637
The University of Chicago Press, Ltd., London
© 2001 by The University of Chicago
All rights reserved. Published 2001
Printed in the United States of America

10 09 08 07 06 05 04 03 02 01   1 2 3 4 5

ISBN: 0-226-38998-7 (cloth)

Library of Congress Cataloging-in-Publication Data

Jackson, John L., Jr.
 Harlemworld : doing race and class in contemporary black America / John
 L. Jackson, Jr.
     p. cm.
 Includes bibliographical references (p.) and index.
 ISBN 0-226-38998-7 (cloth : alk. paper)
 1. Harlem (New York, N.Y.)—Social life and customs. 2. Harlem (New
York, N.Y.)—Social conditions. 3. African Americans—New York
(State)—New York—Social life and customs. 4. African Americans—Race
identity—New York (State)—New York. 5. African Americans—New York
(State)—New York—Social conditions. 6. New York (N.Y.)—Social life
and customs. 7. New York (N.Y.)—Social conditions. 8. Social classes—
New York (State)—New York. I. Title: Harlem world. II. Title.

F128.68.H3 J33 2001
974.7'1—dc21

                                                    2001027871

♾ The paper used in this publication meets the minimum requirements of
the American National Standard for Information Sciences—Permanence of
Paper for Printed Library Materials, ANSI Z39.48-1992.

HARLEM WORLD

To the people I met in Harlem

For their guidance, love, and wisdom

Thank you beyond words

CONTENTS

PREFACE

This book serves as the first half of a two-part ethnographic field project in Harlem, New York. The second segment of this project places some of the theoretical claims I make here into more decidedly politicized contexts. As I write this preface, I am continuing my fieldwork in Harlem, charting how several local community organizers use what I describe in this book as "performative understandings of racial difference" to galvanize Harlem residents as political agents. Most specifically, I am examining the rhetoric and practice of neighborhood activists working to stave off low-income tenant dislocation in a post–empowerment zone Harlem. Recent changes in New York's rental laws have increased landlords' incentives to evict poorer long-term tenants in hopes of raising rental rates as high as a gentrifying housing market can bear. I want to see how definitions of racial belonging parsed through everyday actions are utilized in such political battles. The possibilities are hinted at in my discussion of the 1994 relocation of Harlem's street vendors in chapter 1, but the next half of this project looks more substantively at the political coefficients implicated by contemporary folk theories tethering race to actions. This second part of my larger Harlem project is still a work in progress, but the first half is finished in the form of this book. As a beginning to the beginning of the story it tells, let me backtrack a bit to talk just a little about how *Harlemworld: Doing Race and Class in Contemporary Black America* came into being.

My relatively short connection to Harlem as an ethnographic field site began when I was a graduate student in the Department of Anthropology at Columbia University in the 1990s. I spent more than two years "in the field" for this initial research project. One major component of my fieldwork was participant observation, with field notes written up on a daily basis. I also conducted ten in-depth interviews, the average length of which was six hours, the longest being eleven hours and taking several sittings to complete. Along with this, I carried out thirty-one shorter thematic interviews, specifically organized around issues of race and class and lasting an average of two hours each. I was interested in socioeconomic diversity within my research sample and within the social networks of the participants. This meant that I did two things. First,

I identified several Harlemites who seemed to represent different places along a socioeconomic continuum of employment, income, and education. Then, I plumbed their social networks for class diversity, using what I found to identify other potential candidates for inclusion. Still, the insights I gained from these contacts were based on participant observation as much as on formalized interviews—although I do draw quite heavily on these interviews throughout this book.

As a further note on methodological concerns, I should be clear about the fact that there is no quintessential Harlem subject, no single "informant" who will allow the well-intentioned anthropologist total access to an entire community's internal logic. Be this as it may, I do admit that I started out my days and nights in the field wishfully looking and longing for just such a person: some local resident who could speak for all of Harlem's heterogeneity. I wanted to find some special Harlemite whose life would exemplify the entire place. This person would be my "key informant," someone who would show me all that I needed to know about the neighborhood and its inhabitants.

Once I hit the pavement, however, I didn't find that person. Instead, I found folks who often wouldn't speak to me, didn't care what I was doing, didn't have the time to think about answering my silly little questions, and didn't necessarily seem to represent Harlem at all—at least not the Harlem I had in my mind or in my research proposal. This fact prompted me to walk Harlem's streets for weeks without a purpose or a clue long before I started my actual fieldwork.

To become better focused, I moved from a Columbia-owned building on 122nd Street and Morningside Drive to a five-story walk-up on Old Broadway and 125th Street, a main thoroughfare and commercial artery for the Harlem community. The rent was cheaper, and I no longer shared a building almost exclusively with Columbia students. For weeks, that move stood as the beginning and end of my ethnographic activities. I would go into my building, quickly say "hello" to the one or two neighbors I happened to pass in the hallways, and type feverishly on my computer, crafting what I believed to be carefully phrased open-ended questions—with no one to whom I could pose them. I was truly dumbfounded by how little my knowledge of "the literature" on Harlem and black America had prepared me to conduct actual fieldwork. Moreover, I had a specific and personal problem that—although undertheorized in anthropological discussions about fieldwork methodology—seemed to be my biggest ethnographic Achilles heel: I was terribly shy, and shyness is a self-inflected deathblow to any self-respecting anthropologist. A month after my move, I was shopping at Mart 125, seeing shows at the Apollo Theater, ordering beers at the Lenox Lounge, and walking diligently through every nook and cranny of Harlem. All the while, however, I had barely spoken to a single resident. I hardly felt comfortable going up to strangers and striking up conversations, and I wasn't sure how best to forge the kinds of relationships I needed to make my ethnographic work possible.

One newsworthy incident that took place in Harlem at around this time was the forced relocation of 125th Street's open-air vendors to an enclosed space on 116th Street. Many store owners in the area had complained for years that the street vendors were unfair competition; however, skeptics blamed the sudden enforcement of these antivendor mandates on the empowerment zone money designed to bring big businesses back to Harlem. That money—upward of $300,000,000 of federal, state, and city funds—has been a major issue of concern and contention throughout my time in the field. Pathmark's groundbreaking ceremony on 125th Street and Lexington Avenue in 1997 was attended by the community's elite, many of whom argued that this huge supermarket would go a long way toward helping rejuvenate the area and its residents. The on-again, off-again preparations for the multimillion-dollar, 275,000-square-foot "Harlem USA" mall at 125th between Frederick Douglass (Eighth Avenue) and St. Nicholas is the major empowerment zone effort that some see as the ultimate reason why the vendors were finally ousted.

This sudden removal of the 125th Street open-air vendors seemed to galvanize many activists in the community, temporarily changing the atmosphere of the place. And I could feel that change in the air. For me, the vendor controversy provided a perfect pretext for breaking out of my shell and engaging local residents. It would be another two and a half years before I would actually begin my formal fieldwork, but the vendor issue allowed me to get to know some of my neighbors, and these ties would pay off later. Here was an event that garnered massive amounts of media attention and encouraged the community to talk to strangers even more than usual—if only to lament how Harlem was being mistreated by City Hall. I made some of my first substantive social contacts in the field under the auspices of community activities organized around the vendor crisis. I had business cards made so that I could hand them out as I spoke to people. I would tell them who I was, that I lived up the street, and that I was interested in what they thought about the future of their community. Eventually, as I spoke to more and more residents, I gained confidence in my status as an ethnographer and my reasons for approaching people under the auspices of social research.

In February 1997, I finally began my fieldwork in a more formal way, and the contacts I had slowly begun cultivating three years earlier proved invaluable. A few of the Harlemites I met even seemed genuinely excited to talk to me, whether they agreed to sit for an interview or not. Sometimes we just hung out at a bar for a couple of hours (drinks on me, of course) or talked on the sidewalk for a few minutes before we parted ways. No matter what the case, the fact that I was a young black man living in Harlem and working on a Ph.D. from Columbia University usually meant that a few people would at least take a second to talk, if only to find out what I was really about, what I was really up to. Some folks I met on a whim—eating at a restaurant or just waiting in a check-out line at a local store. Other people were referred to me. Someone would say that if I was interested in Harlem, then so-and-so is a good person for me to talk to. I tried to meet people on their terms and at their convenience. For many of my earliest informants, formalized inter-views in their homes were the extent of our ethnographic exchange. For many others, these same interviews were only the tip of a larger interac-tional iceberg that consisted of a deeper kind of "hanging out," a kind that blurred the lines separating fieldwork from friendship. During this time, I spoke to people about their social networks, became a part of some of those same networks, and tried to get residents to explain how race, class, and the interconnections between them affected their every-day lives and their ideas about the social world.

This book comes out of those relationships, out of late-night conver-sations that took place from, say, someone's apartment building to the corner store—a trip for cigarettes, or baby formula, or beer, or whatever else an informant-friend happened to need as we spent time together. Some of our conversations were taped; others were not (and I'd have to reconstruct the conversation in my notes). Sometimes, I wouldn't see a particular individual for days on end, and other times we would be joined at the hip for weeks, spending day after day navigating the streets together and talking about what made us each tick. Most of this time, I wasn't even sure what kind of "ethnographic data" I was really collect-ing at all. I wasn't necessarily confident that I could piece my Harlem interviews, conversations, and experiences together into some kind of semicoherent whole. Fieldwork seemed a lot like living my life, only with a vaguely ethnographic agenda. Eventually, it was my closeness to these folks that forced me to purposely (and selfishly) disengage from them once it was time for me to start writing up my exchanges with them, and the arguments in this manuscript are what I came up with in terms of making sense of my time in the field. This is one story of race and class as seen through the prism of my fieldwork in Harlem. Of course, this is not the definitive word on the subject, and I have already returned to the field to retest, refine, and reformulate some of what is presented here.

I should not miss the opportunity to thank the many people who helped make this project possible. Katherine S. Newman, my dissertation advisor, has always provided endless amounts of guidance and shown great patience, without which this book absolutely could not have been completed. I am also indebted to Lee D. Baker for his generous feedback and effortless friendship. Elaine Combs-Schilling, Sherry Ortner, Steven Gregory, and Patricia J. Williams were gracious and critical dissertation committee members, each challenging my work in interesting and useful ways. I thank the rest of the people who were colleagues, friends, and mentors during my graduate stint at Columbia, especially Martha S. Jones, Prudence Carter, Deborah McCoy, Linda Green, Alex Alland, Manning Marable, Kate Ramsey, Anthony Browne, Roxanne Varzi, Kate Hoffman, J. R. Jarrod, Melissa Fisher, Daryl Scott, Roger Lancaster, Bayo Holsey, Curtis Stokes, Katherine Hoffman, Stanford Carpenter, Todd Ochoa, Linda Green, Travis Jackson, Robert Adams, Dora King, Carlyle Thompson, Elliot Skinner, Paulette Young, Michael Taussig, Ingrid Summers, Kate Ellis, Ana Ramos, Chauncy Lennon, Devin Fergus, Lucinda Holt, Cynthia Lee, Sasimar Sangchantr, Shawn Brown, and Khari Wyatt. This is only a partial list of the many people who offered support, read drafts, encouraged perseverance, and even provided distractions when necessary.

My Ford Fellow colleagues have always been inspirational, especially Heather Dash, Lawrence Jackson, Stephanie Curenton, Anna Scott, Celeste Milligan, Diana Paulin, Jennifer Brody, and Nicole Vaughn. Bambi Schieffelin offered a critical ear and a helping hand many times. Lucius Outlaw was a role model and an inspiration. Kathryn Dudley (who later revealed herself as one of the two critical and challenging anonymous readers at the University of Chicago Press) and Rosell Jeffries provided wonderfully compelling and convincing critiques of the manuscript in its penultimate form. I also am grateful for the freedom afforded me by a fellowship from Harvard University's Society of Fellows, as well as for the community of scholars and friends who made Cambridge sometimes feel like more than just a relatively short train ride away from New York City: Karyn Lacy, Salamishah Tillet, Scheherazade Tillet (who also took many of the still photographs for this book), Mario Small, James Dawes, Rava da Silveira, Eugene Demler, Sudhir Venkatesh, Jeff Dolven, William Julius Wilson, Lei Liang, Robert Travers, Nina Gouriani, Fiona Doetsch,

Tim McCarthy, Kim Gutschow, Jacob Hacker, Erika Naginski, Dimitri Leger, Robin Templeton, Adam Bradley, Rosemarie Bernard, Noah Feldman, Cathy Cohen, Celeste Watkins, Marcy Morgan, Skip Gates, Nur Yalman, and Raquel Hill. I thank my friends Larry Shields, Cora Daniels-Evans, and Marianne Manilov for support and encouragement. I thank Michelle Dent for soft words and a warm heart—and for seeing me through to the end of this project. Doug Mitchell and Robert Devens at the University of Chicago Press offered great advice and insight. Jane Zanichkowsky was a measured copyeditor.

I have promised to keep my Harlem respondents anonymous, but I should still thank every single person who trusted me with a portion of his or her personal story. I am awed by the lives of the Harlemites who have touched my own life so profoundly. And I dedicate this book to them. Thank you for your gifts. I thank Deborah Thomas for her beyond-the-call-of-duty engagements with my work and for teaching me about so much more than just anthropology (although she also taught me a great deal about this discipline as well). Finally, I also acknowledge my amazingly nurturing family of aunts, uncles, and cousins and especially my mom, dad, sister, and brother (Ethlyn Roberts, John Roberts, Arlene Roberts, and Jason Roberts). Thank you all for your love and support.

DOING HARLEM, TOURING HARLEMWORLD

Why Harlem Is Not Manhattan

Standing at the end of a too-long line of customers inside a too-crowded fast food restaurant in northern Manhattan, I listened attentively as Dexter, a twenty-three-year-old black man, argued across the shiny McDonald's countertop with the Dominican cashier who was trying patiently to take his order.[1] Dressed in white, gray, and black fatigues, with neatly coifed dreadlocks down to his shoulders and two-summers-old Air Jordans on his feet, Dexter held up that queue by waving a color-ful coupon in the palm of his right hand. Scissored out from an insert in that Sunday's local newspaper, the coupon redeemed a ninety-nine-cent Big Mac in every part of New York City (so read the fine print) "except the borough of Manhattan," where Big Macs, with this very same square of paper, were discounted to $1.39 instead. Well, hearing the cashier, Pam, make that borough-specific distinction several times, Dexter became increasingly annoyed. He crossed and uncrossed his arms with emphatic gestures. He sighed audibly and repeatedly. Squeezing a dollar bill and a dime in his outstretched left hand (the ten cents was "for tax," he declared numerous times), Dexter made his case: "This is Harlem," he stated with electrified finality, "not Manhattan! If they meant Harlem, if they meant Harlem, they should have written Harlem! Harlem is not Manhattan! So, I'm paying $1.10 for my Big Mac."

Once Dexter finished this spiel and dumped his change on the coun-tertop, several other customers in front of cash registers all around him joined the staff in chuckling and shaking their heads incredulously at his argument—an argument that, in its unabridged iteration, took more than ten full minutes to play out. But Dexter didn't mind their smirks.

He was adamant, determined, unflinching—even though his half-smirking face clearly indicated that he knew good and well that this Harlem neighborhood was located smack-dab in the middle of Manhattan, an island where Big Macs simply cost forty cents more than they did in any other part of the city. On this particular rainy day, however, Dexter would not and did not leave that crowded McDonald's restaurant until Pam, poised and patient behind her cash register, reluctantly snatched up his dollar and his dime, handing him a Big Mac sandwich to go. He munched heartily on the burger as I jogged out to catch up with his lengthier strides through the wet and slippery parking lot.

I open with this seemingly trivial transaction—a customer haggling over the cost of a specialty hamburger at an iconic fast food joint— because Dexter's geography-warping interpretation of Harlem's relation to the rest of New York City hints at something important about the place. His somewhat "infrapolitical" stand, aimed at saving just a little bit more money on a McDonald's sandwich, highlights the symbolic perimeter that subjectively cordons off the neighborhood he calls home.[2] Dexter's Harlem is geographically situated in Manhattan, but it is not quite bound there. And listening to him argue with Pam about the distinct and separate location of Harlem vis-à-vis Manhattan, of Harlem's irreducibility to its geographical position within the borough, opened my eyes to the first of many knotty issues of place and space that help constitute, ethnographically speaking, Harlem and its endpoints.[3] To do fieldwork in Harlem is to make sense of a place that somehow is and "is not Manhattan" at the same time. *Harlemworld: Doing Race and Class in Contemporary Black America* seeks to do just that, marshaling ethnographic evidence for a rendition of race and place that draws centrally on popular beliefs about race and class that defy our habit of safely depositing fraught identities into neat, discrete social boxes.

I am not a Harlem native. I grew up across the river in Brooklyn, rarely leaving the southernmost precincts of that borough save for sporadic weekend visits to relatives in the Bronx or in Spanish Harlem, vastly different places from the Canarsie community of my childhood. East Harlem seemed an especially different world, one with an unintelligibly foreign tongue. Long family treks on the L, the #4 and then the #6 trains are my earliest and most tactile memories of how I always ended up in Harlem, a wide-eyed kid, on not-quite-carefree Saturday afternoons following mornings of church worship in East Flatbush, Brooklyn. There was the dark rattle of lightning-fast metal. The hot, steamy, and never-ending subway platforms that reeked of an unholy mixture of grapefruit and urine. All that underground locomotion eventually spit us out into a land of merengue and jazz music at an aunt and uncle's two-bedroom apartment filled with canines scratching paws on front doors as we arrived, of fire-hydrant playgrounds where cousins joined me in scraping flesh from knobby knees on unmercifully concrete playgrounds, and of Grandma's double-decker chocolate cakes topped with ice-cold chocolate icing at the end of a long, hot summer day.

When I was a good deal older, my mother would oblige me sparingly with details of her own childhood in Harlem. As a teenager, newly arrived from the Caribbean island of Barbuda, she was responsible for shoveling coal into a fiery furnace and shuttling filled garbage bags to the curb for the five-story walk-up in which she lived with her aunt, the building's super. These are her earliest memories of life in Central Harlem during the turbulent 1950s and 1960s. But *my* formative years were spent in the county of Kings, which I disclose with all requisite and unjustifiable hubris. And Harlem always felt very, very far away from Jamaica Bay, Seaview Pier, and the Bay View housing project of my youth.[4] But there was also "something else" about Harlem, something that seemed inviting, even familiar. The place was subjectively both near and far.[5] A paradoxical intertwining of nearness with farness, literality with metaphor, familiarity with peculiarity, is at the core of a place like Harlem, a place where fame and infamy stubbornly cloud any attempt at seeing and knowing the actual community itself.

Doing Difference: Introductory Formulations

As a cultural anthropologist, I'm trained to speak as a social scientist, to describe contemporary society, almost by rote, as a time of elusive and emergent cosmopolitanized identities, of sweatshop- and shantytown-spawning multinational corporations, of entry-level, service-sector-only employment opportunities in deindustrialized urban America. These characterizations are useful shorthands for suggesting globalized occurrences that affect the tiniest crevices of people's lives and livelihoods— macrosociological phenomena that rev engines for change the world over. As such, their influence on the Harlemites in this book is unmistakable. These grand-scale themes emerge again and again in the pages that follow—sometimes quite explicitly, sometimes only implicitly. With all that said, however, my interpretive lens is focused on the micro level, on how some of the people I met in Harlem make sense of the many forces that disturb the small and discrete individualities of their everyday lives.

Through the qualitative data presented here I examine the contours of African Americans' theories of identity, a rather phenomenological study dressed up in ethnographic garb. I offer a fairly straightforward argument: many African Americans have decidedly performative notions of social identity. Class position is glimpsed through interpretations of everyday behaviors. Racial identity is predicated on perceptions of particular social actions and is shored up with recourse to specific kinds of activities. Racial "location" is not contingent solely on one-drop rules or degrees of skin pigmentation.[6] Socially meaningful identifications are partially derived from observable behaviors, practices, and social performances, and *Harlemworld* offers this specific conflation of identity and behavior as a potentially useful way of hewing antiessentialist social identities.[7]

Schematically speaking, contemporary social scientists working in urban U.S. communities tend to discuss race, class, and their links to people's everyday behaviors in at least one of four ways. First, there are the proverbial "culture of poverty" arguments, chalking up socioeconomic underachievement to pathological learned behaviors that inculcate failure.[8] This stance offers behavior as a lens through which we can decode the causes of poverty and its intergenerational transmission. These theorists believe that if poor people just behaved properly (worked harder, had fewer children, got married, and discontinued various other deviant actions said to perpetuate their own impoverishment), they would gain the necessary traction to climb the slippery rungs of America's social ladder. This usage of everyday behavior justifies a "tough love" approach to poverty, positing poor people's behavioral choices as primary explanations for their economic plight. Opponents of the culture of poverty approach tend to present these very same behaviors as ghetto-specific *responses* to poverty and not the causes thereof.[9]

Another popular approach to "behavior" and racialized social outcomes argues that so-called soft skills (for example, how one sits, gestures, and talks in an interview setting) have a considerable effect on occupational success in the contemporary job market.[10] Applicants who perform a certain brand of behavioral "middle-classness" have an advantage over those without such skill, affording themselves a decided leg up on equally low-skilled competition within a welfare-reformed labor market. These arguments owe much to the social theorist Pierre Bourdieu's definition of "cultural capital" as a mechanism for imbuing meaningful sociocultural distinctions with objective socioeconomic consequences.[11]

Yet a third major slant on behavior's connection to identity emphasizes the self-consciously mobilized behavioral cues that help people negotiate dangerously class-stratified inner-city sidewalks. For example, the sociologist Elijah Anderson argues that urbanites in certain communities use a carefully crafted "code of the streets" to avoid potential altercations, "streetwise" presentations of self that foreground an alternative repository of cultural capital (different from the cultural capital lauded by mainstream employers) to navigate the harsh streets of urban America.[12] This position can be made to privilege a kind of class-estrangement model of black America, where a bifurcated class structure creates two distant and decidedly noncommunicative social halves: a black underclass and a black middle class.[13]

Most directly related to my own interest in folk amalgamations of race and behavior, scholars of education emphasize black students' conceptions of blackness as purposeful underachievement, a blackness pitted against a whiteness posited as intellectual success and mainstream behavior.[14] These social analysts argue that black children's racialization of certain behavior adversely affects their academic and social accomplishments, forging "oppositional" notions of black behavioral specificity that function as reactionary and self-destructive authenticity tests. Black teens, they say, adhere to a prestige system that valorizes the assessments of their black peers over and against more mainstream calculations of proper behavior and legitimate achievement. This argument offers an often-invoked explanation for gaps in test scores and graduation rates between African Americans and other social groups.

My argument about the connections between race and behavior speaks to each of these behavioral stories but isn't quite reducible to any one of them. Folk theories of racial identity do link race and class to behavior, using that linkage as an explanation for iron-clad social differences: black people do things this way, white people do them that way, Asians do them this other way, and so on. However, these links from race to behavior are important not just because they explain who lands a good job, does well in school, or is branded inauthentic. Folk behavioral constructions of race are also sites for antiessentialist possibilities, for people to rethink their assumptions about racial differences. When racial authenticity is policed through the invocation of specific behavioral criteria, that very contrivance opens those premises to challenge. Once race is plucked from its safe exile within the exclusive physiological confines of phenotype and genotype, skin color and bloodlines, and once racial differences are tethered to behavioral differences (usually in support of xenophobic and exclusionary ideologies), that action-based racial difference is used either to justify discrimination *inter*racially or to disparage and censure behavioral misfits in more decidedly *intra*racial contexts.[15] However, this race-cum-behavior system also provides the preliminary opportunity for challenges to invocations of race as absolute difference. The arbitrariness of these racialized behaviors opens them up to critique and contradiction. For any racial group to be considered categorically different from (or superior to) any other group necessitates behaviorally observable pretexts for such social hierarchies. If race is a weighted scale, "a vertical system," the justification for that differential weighing demands measurable and observable criteria.[16] Blacks, say, are considered different from other social groups not solely based on skin tone but because they supposedly aren't as smart, don't perform as well in school, and lack self-control. I could go on ad infinitum with these behavioral linchpins for black inferiority, behavior-based differences that are made to index allegedly categorical disparities separating certain racial groups from their culturally or genetically determined betters.[17]

However, once the claim is made that the discreteness of racial groups can be seen in the things its members do and that racial difference is mirrored in behavioral difference, the lid falls from a Pandora's box of falsifiable claims and counterclaims. Any time a social group is categorized as such with respect to how that group supposedly behaves, this very move opens up space for exceptions to be made and stereotyped behaviors disproved. These exceptions, these breaches in the race-behavior matrix, must be explained—usually explained away—but doing so generates the kernels of an irreversible critique of all behaviorally anchored racial categories.[18] In this book, I use my ethnographic fieldwork among African Americans in Harlem to argue that race and class are often given emphatically behavioral glosses in contemporary folk analyses of identity. And these behavioral glosses can both underpin essentialist racial litmus tests, on one hand, and dispute the epistemological validity of those very same tests, on the other.

Harlemworld, the Place: A Primer

To explore these folk theories of race, class, and behavior, I could have chosen any number of geographical locales. So why Harlem? Or, more specifically still, why Harlemworld? And what do I mean by that term? Let me begin an answer to that question by admitting myself a thief. I swiped—let's say, "sampled"—the expression from contemporary hip-hop music and culture, a phrasing coined to emphasize, among other things, the extra-special significance Harlem holds for hip-hoppers who call that place home.[19] But this musical rendition of place also informs the ways in which some Harlem residents imagine the physical location itself. And Harlemworld starts there, with the actual geographical space sprawled out across the upper parts of Manhattan, only a short distance from some of the wealthiest census tracts in all of New York City. This is one layer of Harlemworld, perhaps the most obvious one, so it is where I'll start my discussion of place, taking a short detour through the where and what of Harlem's geographic and demographic specificities to arrive at a where and why of Harlemworld as ethnographic landscape—a discussion to be continued in the next chapter, and indeed the rest of this book.

New York City has a population of approximately 8 million people, and 1.5 million of them reside in the twelve community districts that make up the borough of Manhattan.[20] Of that number, more than 300,000 live in the section of northern Manhattan called Harlem, which consists of three formal community districts: West Harlem's district 9, East Harlem's district 11, and Central Harlem's district 10.

West Harlem, home to approximately 107,000 residents, stretches from the Hudson River on its west side to an eastern border that consists of Morningside, St. Nicholas, Bradhurst, and Edgecomb Avenues. West Harlem's northern boundary, porously separating it from the neighborhoods of Washington Heights and Inwood above, is 155th Street, and 110th Street's Cathedral Parkway marks off its southern limit. The 1.5 square miles of West Harlem land can be further subdivided into three distinct neighborhoods. From north to south, they are Hamilton Heights, Manhattanville, and Morningside Heights. Hamilton Heights, roughly 155th to 140th Streets, encompasses much of the black middle-class affluence and owner-occupied brownstones for which Harlem is partially known. Manhattanville reaches from 140th Street to 125th Street in West Harlem and includes City College as well as the infamous North River Pollution Control Plant, a waste disposal and treatment facility with the Riverbank State Park built on its roof as a concession to protesting community residents.[21] The institutions of Columbia University, Union Theological Seminary, The Jewish Theological Seminary, Bank Street College, and the Cathedral of Saint John the Divine dominate Morningside Heights from 125th to 110th Street.

West Harlem contains a pretty substantial amount of ethnic and racial diversity. Roughly 40 percent of the community is black, 38 percent Latino, and about 20 percent non-Latino white. This section of Harlem contained a lower proportion of residents receiving public assistance during my research stint than either of the two remaining Harlem districts, approximately 32 percent, still an undeniably high number given borough and city averages that hovered around 21 percent.[22]

East Harlem, which took form during the second half of the nineteenth century as a tenement community for consecutive waves of working-class European immigrants moving from downtown in New York's Lower East Side, consists of 2.2 square miles of land. It extends from 141st Street and Harlem River on its north side to 96th Street at its southernmost boundary. East to west, it reaches from the East River and the Harlem River Drive to Fifth Avenue. Of the approximately 110,000 people who live in East Harlem, 49 percent are classified as Latino, 46 percent as black, and 2 percent as white. East Harlem is one of the poorest communities in all of Manhattan. The median income is $12,000 a year, and more than 40.3 percent of its population received some form of public assistance when I was in the field, the second highest percent in the borough.[23]

Social scientists or politicians who rhetorically invoke the name "Harlem" are usually referring to Central Harlem. Roughly 92 percent of its 95,000 residents are black, with 5 percent Latino and less than 1 percent white.[24] Its 1.4-square-mile area extends from the Harlem River at its northernmost point to Central Park on its south and from Fifth Avenue on the east to St. Nicholas, Jackie Robinson, and Morningside parks on its border with West Harlem. More than 46 percent of its residents receive some form of government aid, allowing it to stand as one of the poorest areas in all of New York City. Average household incomes are steadily around $13,000, and about 32 percent of the residents in this area are making less than $6,000 per year. An equivalent number of people are making between $6,000 and $12,500. A slightly smaller number (27 percent) are making between $12,500 and $25,000 annually. Eight percent of Central Harlem's residents bring home more than $25,000 a year in reported income.[25] Recent gentrification has undoubtedly changed these estimates drastically over the past few years. Still, these are fairly close approximations of Harlem's demographic makeup during my time in the field.

As lopsided and dire as the numbers may appear, they still point to the fact that every single resident of Harlem is not an identical passenger on the exact same socioeconomic boat. Harlem contains a marked degree of social stratification. Moreover, although many of the poorer sections of Central Harlem are somewhat separated from the more affluent subsections by natural parks, hills, and so on, its residents still make use of those parks and pass through the permeable boundaries separating, say, the Ivy League halls of Columbia University from the other side of

Morningside Park, where the Morningside Park East Coalition works to clean up neighborhood stoops and streets.[26] I hiked to and from Dexter's home through that very park many times. He did the same—and had done so for years before I ever bumped into him on that rainy day inside that fast food restaurant. Places like Morningside Park (a huge and sprawling strip of greenery, basketball courts, and swings separating Columbia University's section of West Harlem from Central Harlem more than one hundred feet below) are often the fuzzy liminal spaces where tensions between wealth and poverty, the housed and the homeless, the black and the white, are rehearsed again and again in rumors and news stories about the palpable danger of these natural border areas. The simultaneity of proximity and distance, threat and safety, nearness and farness characterizes many people's definitions of contemporary Harlem and its relation to the rest of New York City.

But the Harlem of Harlemworld doesn't stop there, with census tracts and physical boundaries, with population rates and local landmarks. Harlem has several kinds of sites, demanding a different brand of "multi-sited ethnography" based not only on geographical distance but also on the complicated dynamics of what the historian Katherine Morrissey calls "mental territories," places where social, economic, political, and cognitive factors all have a part to play in the construction of spatial identity, in the creation of socially meaningful cartographies.[27] The term *Harlemworld* is intended to foreground Harlem's self-conscious place in the popular imagination, its ability to extend and exceed its geographical borders. Harlem is a symbolic center for African American culture, a key reference point for blacks who seek to define themselves in relation to a certain canonized version of African American tradition and history. Many locations in northern Manhattan carry this symbolic weight: the Audubon Ballroom, where Malcolm X was assassinated; the Hotel Theresa, where famous foreign dignitaries once stayed; the Apollo Theater, where many African American pop-cultural icons got their start. People from all over the country (and even the world) link their identities to Harlem and the notable landmarks within it. People cite Harlem's past as an iconic story, one of the quintessential stories of black American achievement.

Harlemworld is a word that highlights the area's own intertextuality (what might be called, in this instance, its own intergeographicality), predicated on the same recombinant properties of sampling, mixing, and scratching that define the musical genre from which I've pilfered the term. My field site is as much Harlemworld as Harlem because every single engagement with the place entails recognitions that stretch beyond its strict geographical boundaries. Harlem becomes Harlem-world as news articles, television shows, feature films, political pundits, cultural anthropologists, urban sociologists, city planners, neighborhood activists, community advocates, local leaders, national politicians, and international figures add more and more fodder to already overloaded representations of place, shadowy representations with a very real impact on the very real folks who live there. Dexter's Harlem is not Manhattan precisely because it is also Harlemworld, a singularly multiplicitous location seen by so many people as so much more than the literal place itself.

The hip-hop neologism *Harlemworld* has created and popularized a compound word that grammatically marks this location's inextricable embeddedness in global webs of signification and power, a Harlem that can only be explained in the worldwide context of shifting labor markets, multinational conglomerates, and immigration. This is a Harlem that is both a world unto itself and absolutely unintelligible without recourse to the outside world, from which it can never shake itself loose. Harlemworld as both spatially rooted and removed at the same time is less difficult to fathom once placed in the context of information-age "cyberian" electronic superhighways traversed by space and time travelers contacting places all around the globe simultaneously—and able to pass along all kinds of information as they go.[28] This state of affairs demands a peripatetic anthropology that attempts, however vainly, to keep up with the lightning-fast speed of cultural transmissions and transmutations at the very beginning of the twenty-first century, a peripatetic anthropology through which one can gain at least partial access to the complex realities of a late capitalist world.

Harlemworld, the Book

Obviously, race and class are highly contested social concepts. By unpacking the ways in which Harlemites theorize and practice them, we can gain an important understanding of contemporary black America that is often elided in academic and popular debates about the importance of race. Chapter 1, "Making Harlem Black: Race, Place, and History in 'African Americans' Africa,' " offers a brief account of Harlem's history and that history's relevance to the people who live there. I discuss Harlem's status as a quintessentially "black" community, the geographical apotheosis of categorical black difference. I also examine just how Harlem carries this exemplary blackness, arguing that it is Harlem's status as an essentially black space that makes it an interesting setting for discussions about class-related differences among African Americans—differences that add meat to the bones of behavioral mandates about black racial particularity.

In chapter 2, "Class Histories and Class Theories in a Raceful Social World," I argue that an underclass/middle-class model of black America as two geographically segregated and bifurcated communities does not necessarily work in a place like Harlem. Harlemites at various socioeconomic levels live and work right next to one another every single day, a point that becomes salient in several short biographies of a few of the people whose voices are heard and whose experiences are shared throughout these pages.[29] I discuss the varied lives led by some of the Harlemites I met: What kinds of jobs do they have? What kinds of life histories? What do they expect from their futures? These stories offer a picture of class diversity that I believe is yet another important piece to the puzzle of performative raciality, a partial answer to the question of how race is seen through social practices.

That all of these differently classed residents live in Harlem doesn't necessarily mean that they interact with one another. The next two chapters attempt to chart some of the specific ways in which black Harlemites theorize their social contacts across class lines. I use chapter 3, "Birthdays, Basketball, and Breaking Bread: Negotiating with Class in Contemporary Black America," to argue that many Harlemites have social relationships that extend across class lines. Here, I want to look at class-stratified relationships among family members and friends to examine just how class differences can inform and reshape important social contacts, sometimes ending friendships and straining familial ties, other times providing alternative spaces for mutually beneficial relationships to thrive despite class differences. In chapter 4, "Class(ed) Acts, or Class Is as Class Does," I argue that folk theories of identity recognize and describe class differences and their connections to behavior quite explicitly. I examine a few of the ways in which some Harlemites think about class and enact what they consider class differences to entail. How do black folks think up and down the class ladder to make sense of other blacks in different socioeconomic positions? Conservatives lament that African Americans fail to see beyond a "race card" they employ to trump all other forms of social differentiation. However, many of the folks I got to know in Harlem maintain that, on the contrary, only blacks can look at the black community and spot internal differences, differences that defy other people's monolithic notions of blackness. African Americans do clearly recognize class markers, and chapter 4 delineates the extent to which Harlemites theorize these class identities, transforming folk theories about class stratification into specific class-inflected practices that are often differently assessed.

Some social scientists still confidently talk about race as an "ascribed characteristic" and class as an "achieved" one. In chapter 5, "White Harlem: Toward the Performative Limits of Blackness," I argue that folk theories posit race as a kind of "achieved" characteristic, claiming that racial authenticity is often achieved through performances and practices—usually, although not exclusively, through class-marked performances and practices. Racial identity takes "work" (even hard work) and is therefore, in a sense, also achieved or not achieved based on one's actions and how they are interpreted. Folk theories of race discover race in the doing, arrived at through specific actions and not only anchored in one's epidermis and morphology.[30] This performative notion of race creates space for people to challenge arguments about what particular behaviors connect to which discrete races, potentially challenging all forms of "racial realism."[31]

Chapter 6, "Cinematicus Ethnographicus: Race and Class in an Ethnographic Land of Make-Believe," examines the multiple claims on race and class articulated in the mass media, specifically film. Here, it is most obvious that we have left Harlem proper for a kind of Baudrillardian Harlemworld of simulated realities.[32] Reading recent Hollywood depictions of Harlem (and of racial identity more generally), I argue that the mass media also offer up performative and practice-based notions of race, class, and their intersection—notions that often privilege a kind of fairytale voluntarism where interracial differences are easily transcended by classed behaviors. For example, in the motion picture *Hoodlum*, rival black and Italian mobsters, Bumpy Johnson and Lucky Luciano, form a secret alliance to kill fellow mob boss Dutch Schultz because he, unlike the two of them, doesn't properly perform middle-class gentility. Moreover, writer-director Quentin Tarantino can argue that he is justified in writing films with exorbitant usage of the word *nigger* because he grew up with poor blacks and was raised to act black, and therefore he is blacker than middle-class African Americans who have never been to the ghetto. These cinematic models start from the same premises that I highlight in folk theories about race but restrict these premises to a stubbornly make-believe reading of the social world where (1) classed behavior is a decidedly more powerful social glue than a still-extant racial difference, and (2) acting authentically black means being specifically classed. This is a perceptual schema wherein the same old-fashioned racial and ethnic hierarchies are simply hidden behind class proxies. I end this chapter with a specific nod to the hip-hop community's construction of Harlemworld, a multi-place where race and class are offered up in all their complicated and contradictory variety. Hip-hop's Harlemworld, I argue, is a useful model for talking about the complex relationship between race and class in the lives of all black Americans today—and for resignifying (that is, for signifyin') notions of racial identity predicated on interpretations of everyday social behaviors.[33]

Each of these chapters shuttles back and forth through discussions about the same few people, teasing out a singular argument about race and behavior, repeating similar points in slightly different ink: folk theories of race are inextricably grounded in readings of racialized behaviors, and these behaviors create not just normative policies for racial policing but also the possibility of escape from racial ideology's most reactionary directives. Constructing a definitively bifurcated and mutually exclusive contemporary black American class structure is not the analytical end point for discussions of how race and class intersect today. The popular categories "underclass" and "middle class" are not as easily and straightforwardly disconnected as social scientists might occasionally assume. Instead of starting there, we should take class and race seriously by examining them as mutually inclusive and reinforcing social realities that people constantly renegotiate and even perform regardless of their particular class positions.[34]

Introductory Conclusions

I want to end this introduction by admitting that there is no Game Room in *Harlemworld,* no Valois Diner or Talley's Corner to ground this study in its ethnographic place.[35] Before I entered the field, I formulated my project as one based on what I called "spaces of coalescence," class-based "contact zones" where people are forced to interact across class lines.[36] I wanted to find such a space and use that location as a kind of ethnographic home base. A particular church congregation could be a space of coalescence, or a specific soup kitchen, maybe even a class-stratified employment site where people are forced to deal with one another across class lines every day. There is a specificity to this kind of fieldwork, making sure that one doesn't float too far away from the particularities of place that make ethnographic field research, especially in contemporary urban American contexts, useful for in-depth qualitative analysis. I was going to find my space of coalescence and use it as a microcosmic exemplar of the kinds of cross-class dynamics I wanted to unpack.

The argument can probably be made that this kind of grounding is especially necessary in a place like Harlem, where powerful social currents can splash "vulnerable" observers all across an ethnographic landscape without the slightest chance of their regaining their anthropological bearings.[37] However, instead of one or two such spaces of coalescence, I found many, which is part of my overall point: African Americans are interacting across class lines all the time, in all kinds of social contexts, in various corners of their social lives, and constantly theorizing the significance of that cross-class contact for questions of racial identity and community. My decision, then, to forgo a single ethnographic site for a more peripatetic anthropological method should not just be interpreted as a flighty groundlessness. Following Harlemites around to their jobs, homes, friends' homes, family gatherings, parties, shopping trips, and so on, I realized that Harlemworld itself was my space of coalescence, a world with curving, shifting and pockmarked boundaries held together tenuously by the ways in which people who live there (and the many more who wouldn't dare) construct racial difference as a clear-cut ontological truism. We all think we know Harlem, and we do—in some ways. But what we really know, even more than Harlem itself, is Harlemworld, the presumptions of place we use to explain social difference and distance, the Harlem on our minds and in our minds. I have tried to study a bit of this Harlemworld and its connection to Harlem, New York. Along the way, I stopped off to find even smaller spaces where people peel away at the surfaces that bind them to some and supposedly seal them off from others.

Harlemworld starts with the people I met during my fieldwork stint and expands outward to include discussions that extend into other geographical communities and even into a cinematic landscape of racialized representations that fold back up into the lives of the residents themselves. In a sense, only a few hundred thousand people live in Harlem, but we all live in Harlemworld—some of us as raging and caged prisoners, others as contented inmates on their best behavior, and still others seeing ourselves as key-wielding wardens controlling the constrained movements of everyone else in the joint.

Every day, interactions in black America belie the popular proposition that black people live in absolutely class-isolated social worlds. Even if class-based isolationism were true for Harlem proper (which is not the case), it certainly doesn't hold in Harlemworld, where class stratification is constantly invoked and discussed in order to make practical sense of the place and its inhabitants. Dexter's Harlem is not Manhattan precisely because place is never determined wholesale by geographical fiat, especially a place so bound to race as one of its deciding variables in a racially segregated housing market. In utilizing data from my ethnographic field research in Harlem, I want to make a case for how identities work (and are put to work) in America more generally. By co-constructing our social spaces, we co-construct our social selves. Folk theories of racial difference are not simply given in totality by the cultural order and its taxonomic proclamations, but rather refashioned and fought for by the people who hold them dearest. This jostling over race's falsifiable projection onto the observable data of everyday behavior may serve as the interpretive beginning of the end for some of racial essentialism's most entrenched clichés.

CHAPTER 1

MAKING HARLEM BLACK: RACE, PLACE, AND HISTORY IN "AFRICAN AMERICANS' AFRICA"

History in a Quotation-Marked-Off Place

Harlem first suggested itself to me as a full-fledged field site in Jamaica, West Indies. It was there that Harlem jumped out at me in all of its imaginative grandeur—and not just through BET broadcasts of hip-hop music videos on local television sets or through cotton T-shirts emblazoned with Harlem's name neatly displayed in local tourist shops or even through the constant invocation of the term ("Yo, Harlem!") as some Islanders' synonym for my own given name.[1] Harlem congealed for me against the heat and sand of the Jamaican coastline because of how often and matter-of-factly many Jamaicans I met there purported to possess knowledge of that not-so-distant place. Some of them had actually been to Harlem. Many constantly wrote and telephoned relatives and friends who were still there. Others had never set foot in Harlem but spoke of its symbolic import for the black diaspora in seemingly heartfelt ways. Over and against my constant protestations (I preferred being associated more with the Brooklyn neighborhood of my childhood than the community where I lived as a graduate student), Harlem represented, even there, outside of a strictly American context, the quintessential black community. And I—as its living, breathing, embodied "Yankee" synecdoche—stood in for the place itself.[2]

Recent anthropological and geographical examinations of contemporary time-space compression predicated on technological advances in communication and transportation have offered useful analyses of the "traveling cultures" that link people in global networks of exchange and conversation.[3] My own decidedly nonsystematic interactions with several Jamaicans during that 1994 spring visit highlighted various sociopolitical dimensions of an imagined racial community unevenly connecting people across the permeable boundaries of nation-states. Most specifically, I faced several Jamaican men and women asking me to feel empathy for them and their families, newly homeless squatters whose shantytown had been razed that very morning, only moments before my plane touched down. I watched from my perch on the third floor of a two-star resort hotel as several young men I did not know beckoned from across the high cement gate for me to come down ("Come, come, Harlem, come!") and join their spontaneous march, to come down and hear them recount futile attempts at saving their homes from destruction. Critical issues of tourism, transnationalism, and global imperialism intermingled in that instant. I quizzically waved back at these people I did not know, who were invoking the name of the neighborhood where I lived without so much as having been introduced to me beforehand. Immediately identified as an outsider, a recognizable outsider, I slowly made my way out of the resort and into the teeming crowd below. Others could speak more directly to the many vectors of difference and commonality that explain both the initial call ("Come, come, Harlem, come!") and my cautious decision to heed it.[4] Suffice it to say here that after a week running around the island with my informal tour guides, I was struck by the extent to which these people knew Harlem, its history and the meaning it was supposed to hold for an African American on vacation in the Caribbean.[5]

All communities police the symbolic boundaries that surround them. Harlem's symbolic import is such, however, that even those who do not live within its ostensible borders can be heard invoking its social and symbolic significance—that is, more specifically speaking, invoking its racial significance. Harlem is often understood as a decidedly black space, as the home of African American cultural ferment and particularity, the "capital of Black America."[6] In this chapter I examine a bit of Harlem's commonsensical status as racialized social space par excellence.[7] These invocations of Harlem as a black space often assume a hermetically sealed-off social sphere easily vanquishing other potential trajectories of difference: class, gender, and so on. To call Harlem black, to understand it as such, is to join in popular presuppositions of that selfsame blackness as an ontological solution to vexing questions of race-based social interest. The political pundits on CNN or C-Span or any local six o'clock newscast who rhetorically ask, "What would people in Harlem think?" wield that place-name as if it served to signify an obvious racial difference geographied. I want to offer a historical, even ethnohistorical, rendering of Harlem as not just a black space but a blackened one, examining Harlem's axiomatic blackness as a contextually contingent racialization of place. As black as Harlem is imagined to be by those who invoke its name, this blackness requires more than exclusively racial criteria (that is, class differences, gender hierarchies, and ethnic particularities) to shore up its own uncertain spatial boundaries.

Even in Jamaica (or Rotterdam, Paris, London, or just about anywhere else I've had conversations with people about this project), Harlem operates as a kind of "quotation-marked-off place," paradoxically indexing "both absolute authenticity and veracity, on the one hand, and suspected inauthenticity, irony and doubt on the other."[8] Every application of the name supplies, implies, and applies oversaturated and highly charged assumptions about the neighborhood and its inhabitants as either the epitome of racial potentiality or the embodiment of squandered opportunities. The ethnographer Monique Michelle Taylor captures the bifurcated nature of this quotation-marking-off of place in her analysis of Harlem as both "Heaven and Hell" for those who invoke its name, a hypersymbolism that carries much more than lukewarm connotations when summoned to rhetorical duty.[9] According to the New York State Visitor and Convention Bureau, Harlem has the highest name recognition of any neighborhood in the entire state of New York.[10] And this tiny bit of trivia is quite important. The most famous neighborhood in what is arguably the nation's most famous city is Harlem! It is known the world over. But for those who live there, who live with (and benefit from) that notoriety, what does Harlem mean? What does a quotation-marked-off Harlem do? Where and how are its boundaries drawn? What categories and attributes of the place are used to make sense of its bigger-than-life hyperscape?[11]

To begin with, Harlem is a place set apart. It functions as a geographical space evoked for clear-cut racial distinction. Dexter's cartographic removal of Harlem from his mapping of Manhattan in this book's introduction literalizes that very distinction, and pundits and politicos who cite Harlem do so with Dexter's hard-and-fast referent in mind. It is Harlem's well-known and history-laden position as "the black Mecca," the "capital of black America," and "the queen of all black belts" that positions it snugly within the quotation-marked-off domain of stereotyped assumptions, both positive and negative. Moreover, this historic Harlem is important because it provides the constant and overstated symbolic backdrop for the very present Harlem one sees today. Walking through its streets, one sees conspicuous traces of Harlem history rather self-consciously and purposefully paraded before one's very eyes.[12] The

Harlemworld billboard
and boarded-up building
(photo by the author)

names of great Harlemites roll off residents'
tongues. Avenues are renamed for significant African Americans of the past. Pictures of Egyptian
ankhs and maps of the African continent (of various shapes and sizes—often red, black, and green
in color) adorn storefronts, posters, T-shirts, and
even the concrete street itself, offering a comfortable grounding for Harlem's assumed blackness,
a grounding that anchors racial particularity in a
different space and time entirely—across the Atlantic Ocean and in Egyptian antiquity.

Billboards intimating Harlem's central place in
the black world mask burned-down and hollowed-
out vacant buildings. Storefronts are draped with
Kente cloth that flutters majestically in the wind.
Framed posters of Roy De Carava's famous photo-
graph of jazzman Charlie "Bird" Parker playing
the saxophone—and the "sound" that was "seen"
when he did—hide tiny sections of off-white office walls. And one can, in fact, see that very
sound everywhere in Harlem. It is the syncopated
rhythm of a calculated historicizing that bellows
loudly above the present-day place, whose racial-

ized past rests lodged within its very real present. All of New York has such an ever-present history. For that matter, so does every other city in the world. The difference with Harlem, however, what over-determines its standing as Harlemworld, is the canonized, politicized and self-consciously recognized nature of that (usually half-hidden) modern history—as well as its decidedly blackened tint.[13]

The suspecting pedestrian bumps into racialized images of this past at every turn, images that are only there to evoke the past, that serve no other function but to call on history's authority and legitimacy. These historical images are from different time frames and refer to a variety of places and peoples, diverse black history moments that come together in Harlem's uncanny ability to encompass them all, to grasp any reference to blackness in its concrete and steel palms. And Harlem's history seeps through that concrete and steel, oozes from the cracks in local buildings—even necessitates those very cracks. Much of Harlem is famous today almost exclusively because the argument can be made that it (this store, this building, this brownstone) was famous in the past, way back "when Harlem was in vogue." This all *was* Harlem, a wasness that tethers Harlem to another time altogether.[14] The Cotton Club, the Lenox Lounge, the World Famous Apollo Theater, and other sites stake their notoriety as much on past acclaim and name recognition as on their contemporary realities. The Apollo Theater, for example, replicates Harlem's charm writ small, and its guardians know that, advertise that, construct that: the World Famous Apollo Theater. When one gets there for the first time, however, when one actually beholds that World Famous place, possibly with black letters dangling from a decidedly weathered marquee (some letters missing, all of different and haphazardly combined sizes), one might get the very same underwhelming sensation some feel the first time they slink their way through and around the crowded hallways of the Louvre to glimpse that small, framed painting called the *Mona Lisa*. "Is that it?" one might ask. "This little picture, this little frame?" The World Famous Apollo Theater is, in some ways, like Harlemworld's *Mona Lisa,* a Harlemworld offered up to tourists as a kind of lived-in Louvre, a living "colored museum."[15] It is perhaps less masterminded, one might argue, than the work done by 1970s social historians commissioned to re-historicize colonial Williamsburg, but no less museological—and certainly no less contentious.[16] The daily throng of international admirers and passersby snapping pictures in front of that Apollo marquee is itself a roadmap for the reading of contemporary Harlem as an inflatable past overstuffed into the topography of a seemingly deflated present.[17]

"Poetic battles" at the Apollo (photo by the author)

In a quotation-marked-off place like Harlem-world, the imaginative and symbolic components of its inflated past are just as palpable and meaningful as the physical concreteness of its nineteenth-century brownstones. And indeed those homes are important too.[18] This fetishized connection between Harlem and its past is the first point to stress about a location where notoriety is contingent on what the place used to be, on connections between the present and the once-glorious past. In that light, it is to some of this "history" that I will briefly turn.[19] This particular reflection on Harlem's history is warranted, I believe, by the seminal position granted a certain retelling of Harlem's past within the geographical community itself and within the community of scholars, activists, and politicians who control most terms of the debate on contemporary Harlem. After a brief historical discussion focused on some of the mascrostructural forces that colluded in the creation of Harlem as a black space, a space predominantly occupied by black people, I want to show how contemporary Harlemites use that same history to provide Harlem's blackness with a variety of different shadings.

Race, Class, and a History of Harlem

Manhattan's central business district and industrial hub started out at the southernmost tip of the island, and with the progressive and cumulative prodding of the Industrial Revolution, stretched its arms up and out across New York City. Factories grew and the workforce expanded while the city plodded its way uptown. As quintessentially black as Harlem is imagined to be today, it started out as Nieuw Haarlem in the 1650s, a Dutch settlement that was anything but a black enclave. After the English bought the area from the Dutch and turned greater New Amsterdam into New York, the same industrial advancements that transformed America's economy from agricultural exclusivity to industrial productivity helped spur urban growth throughout the eighteenth and early nineteenth centuries. New York City's ballooning industrial market pushed, pulled, and gnawed its way up the island, taking a growing city's population with it.

During that period Harlem was a place where people went to get away from the teeming city downtown—that is, if they could afford the relatively long horse and buggy ride away from the factory districts. Of course, if you were a member of the growing proletariat, you probably weren't able to engage in such leisurely excursions. During these early days of American industry, most workers resided, by necessity, close to their factories of employment, in the small industry-based communities that cropped up alongside them. The 1837 New York and Harlem railroad along present-day Park Avenue spurred the construction of small wooden homes throughout the eastern end of Harlem while the Irish were drawn to the western half. A good deal of Harlem was still fairly empty and open, however, often used as a premier location for picnics, retreats, and other recreational activities.

Black Manhattan during this time consisted of smaller strips of neighborhoods (no more than a couple of blocks in length) along the lowest end of the island where present-day City Hall and Wall Street are located. There, blacks "lived and congregated in the hovels along the wharves."[20] Slowly and collectively, black Manhattan moved northward with the rest of a quickly industrializing metropolis. From the start of the 1800s to the end of that century, blacks in Manhattan (from Little Africa and Five Points to Tenderloin and San Juan Hill, all geographical precursors to black Harlem) changed the location and size of their mostly small and segregated portions of the city, moving northward and growing larger with each relocation. These early black enclaves included tried and true black institutions (the black church, free black schools, YMCAs, Masonic lodges) and constituted a northern version of the formal and informal mechanisms of racial separation that had traditionally kept blacks of various classes and status positions connected to the same residential spaces.[21]

It was the Tenderloin–San Juan Hill area on the west side of mid-Manhattan that served as the last geographical pit stop at the turn of the twentieth century before blacks began entering Harlem by the droves. Originally, Harlem had been developed for a decidedly white middle-class population, the fairly well-to-do Manhattanites whose cash cow (a growing industrial economy) was still situated closer to the bottom of the island. These industrial elites actively sought opportunities to avoid the soot, danger, and disease of those factory-laden communities. As the industrial revolution caught its stride and advancements were made in locomotive technology, speculators realized that they could purchase, develop, and build on Harlem land that had been sorely underutilized. Before the construction of New York Railway lines (first in the 1870s and 1880s along Second and Eighth Avenues—and twenty years later along Lenox and Broadway Avenues), wealthier New Yorkers used Harlem as a getaway, a summer home, a way to take one's leave, however briefly, from the overflowing and diseased downtown areas. However, Harlem's distance had always mitigated any widespread migration of New Yorkers uptown. Advances in railway design and technology would eventually shorten the commute from the northern outskirts of the island to the central city. To speculators, this fact translated into the possibility of many more New Yorkers (that is, relatively wealthy and white New Yorkers) residing uptown. So industrious developers spent their capital building up the Harlem area and constructing homes for the white middle-class residents they were sure would move there.

Today, the decidedly middle-class edifices and tree-lined blocks on Striver's Row are indicative of the opulence and space that many Harlem homes were designed and built to offer.[22] Expensive and spacious tenement houses and apartment buildings were constructed so that white middle-class New Yorkers could obtain homes in the soon-to-be densely populated and racially segregated world of Harlem. And Harlem was specifically designed to be a white world. By the end of the nineteenth century, once the railways were finished and some Manhattanites had moved uptown, many white tenement residents and homeowners kept

African Americans out of the area through restricted covenants that barred whites from selling or renting across racial lines. Tenant associations such as the Property Owners' Protective Association of Harlem regulated prices beyond the reach of poorer blacks and blatantly discriminated against wealthier blacks who might otherwise have been able to afford the move.[23]

The Harlem developers and realtors, however, were faced with an inescapable problem. They had overspeculated, exaggerating the actual amount of interest in this newly built neighborhood. Furthermore, an economic recession coupled with competition from the newly annexed city of Brooklyn and other neighboring areas even further north (thanks, in part, to the same technological advances that made northern Manhattan more accessible) meant that Harlem could not attract the number of white middle-class residents that had initially been anticipated. Thus, either the speculators and realtors would take a financial loss and keep many of those homes unoccupied, or they could attempt to make back the money on their investments by exploiting black demand for housing.

Over the staunch protests of many tenant associations and Harlem homeowners, profit motives would dictate the next move. Black realty companies like Nail and Parker as well as white realtors (often called "white renegades" by many white Harlem activists mobilized against that "untoward circumstance" of black in-migration) began avidly renting and selling to blacks.[24] Farther south, Tenderloin and San Juan Hill were becoming prime real estate readily purchased from the black residents and institutions residing there, specifically black churches. The same black Manhattanites who sold relatively small tracts of land and modest-sized homes in Tenderloin were able to buy larger plots in the less-sought-after neighborhood of Harlem. Black churches (for example, St. Philip's Episcopal Church and the Abyssinian Baptist Church) used the depreciated housing market uptown to purchase a great deal of land in Harlem, land that panicking speculators were more than happy to sell.

Other black institutions followed the same "Sell Tenderloin, Buy Harlem" formula, relocating farther north in Manhattan than they had ever been before. *The New York Age,* the city's black weekly, encouraged Tenderloin blacks to move uptown to Harlem—that is, some of them. A clear distinction was made between the "civilized" blacks worthy of Harlem and the self-destructive riffraff who were not. Harlem was for black families with middle-class histories (or at least aspirations), a Protestant work ethic, and a Victorian value system. All other blacks, it was argued, would only destroy Harlem for those who really deserved it.

At this point, circa 1910, the pilgrimage was on to New York's version of the new black Promised Land. Concurrent with this influx of blacks into Harlem from lower Manhattan, the larger Great Migration was also in full swing, catalyzed by mechanical advances in industry, by southern droughts, floods, and boll weevils, and eventually by two world wars. This larger migration catapulted black southerners from the unfair and peonage-based sharecropper system in the South to wage labor in the industrialized north in places like Chicago, Detroit, and Harlem. According to many black New Yorkers living there at the time, these newest arrivals from the South were too uncivilized to live alongside the more highly cultured and cosmopolitan northern blacks, those who could truly take advantage of the better life that Harlem promised. The black Americans who had been in the North longer had already figured out how things worked in the big city. They were not as provincial, ignorant, and "backward" as the new arrivals, and this difference was often the seminal distinction on which blackness and community belonging hinged. These southern arrivals were seen as uncultured in a sense rife with class- and status-specific coatings, and black New Yorkers took this regional difference very seriously. Culture, class, and cosmopolitanism became linked with regionalism as blacks made their way into northern Manhattan. This regional difference was also inflected along decidedly gendered lines, as northern activists singled out black female migrants for paternalistic coddling and protection.[25]

Some of these black southerners were new to the demands of the city and therefore easily exploited, piled into small rooms of one-family homes partitioned by greedy realtors into smaller multifamily units that poorer blacks could more readily afford. These tactics quickly overpopulated Harlem. Particular class-based and racial concerns (providing the white middle class with a respite from the grime and danger found downtown near factories) had built Harlem architecturally, and a different set of class-based and racial issues (the inability of poorer blacks to afford the opulent homes initially built for wealthier whites, along with the realtors' need to turn a profit) overcrowded it.

White flight eventually took place once restricted covenants were broken, allowing more and more blacks into formerly nonblack sections of Harlem. White Harlemites who were at one time staunchly against other white neighbors selling or renting their homes to blacks quickly sold to realtors for relatively low prices once the first few blacks began to move in. These were the very same homes that realtors (black and white) carved up into multifamily units and resold to poor blacks at inflated prices. Landlords were rarely held accountable to their poorer black tenants, allowing their properties to fall into disrepair. Places weren't kept up to code. Some empty buildings were left to rot altogether, and this irresponsible guardianship of Harlem's housing stock helped speed along the neighborhood's deterioration. Indifference to the needs of the new black tenants combined with these poorer residents' own class-based vulnerabilities to quicken the creation of the racialized slum that captures many contemporary imaginings of Harlemworld's blackness.

Massive departures of white Harlemites did not spell the end of a healthy Harlem community. The Harlem Renaissance of the 1920s is the moment for which the neighborhood gained its greatest notoriety. Even after the depression, jazz music, imported from New Orleans by way of Chicago, was considered high art in a socially segregated Harlem where blacks enjoyed it at the Renaissance Ballroom as whites did the same at the Cotton Club or the Savoy. Moreover, Harlem helped revolutionize jazz by birthing a form of distinctly New York–style jazz called bebop, created in after-hours Harlem clubs by the likes of Dizzy Gillespie, Charlie Parker, and Thelonious Monk. If jazz was truly America's music— that is, created from its soil and not transplanted via the seas—bebop was Harlem's distinctive slant on Americana.

This Harlem of yore also received its reputation from the Harlem Renaissance poets, writers, and thinkers who made Harlem the cultural capital for Alaine Locke's New Negro, a decidedly learned and urbane black cosmopolitan who sought to change the way white Americans viewed black people. Countless names come to mind as one thinks of the artists, writers, entertainers, and entrepreneurs who made early twentieth-century Harlem famous all around the world. In many ways, the New York State Visitor and Convention Bureau's notion of Harlem's worldwide acclaim stems from this particular Harlem of yesteryear and is based on the popularity that Harlemites enjoyed among white Manhattanites at the time—before the great depression and massive structural transformations in the global economic system meant that much-needed jobs followed the white middle class out of the central cities.

Alongside urban growth in the North, migration from the South, and immigration from the Third World, Harlem changed from a white, suburban enclave into an overcrowded, underserved black slum—a neighborhood that solidified its status as a slum, many argue, once the black middle class was able to move away from poorer race-mates as a function of the legal and political gains of the 1960s.[26] With the advancements of the civil rights movement more generally, the black power movement of the late 1960s and early 1970s became synonymous with more radical demands for social change found in the urban North, especially after Malcolm X, minister of the Nation of Islam's Mosque 7 in Harlem, became the premier voice of black power politics in the United States. Some scholars argue that the black power movement spoke to the dispossessed urban poor much more than did the accommodationist rhetoric of the early civil rights movement.[27] Members of the ever-increasing urban poor were left to fend for themselves in once vibrant neighborhoods without the lifelines that stabilize community (businesses, public services, recreational facilities, and so on) and without the kinds of industrial job opportunities that had brought them north in the first place. New York's fiscal problems under Mayor Beame in the mid- to late 1970s only helped make a bad economic situation even worse.

Harlem's history of migration and mythification is part of the reason why the place stands as the "blackest" of American communities. Harlem is famous because of its history—a history that shows how today's Harlem was created through both race-specific actions (restricted covenants, white-flight, segregation) and class-inflected interests (of realtors, of the black press, and of northern blacks themselves) that materially and discursively constructed the black Harlem we know today from the many Harlems of yesteryear.[28] But it is not simply the migratory movements of black people that helped constitute Harlem's symbolic and racially charged significance. Blacks moved to many places besides Harlem during the Great Migration—and many blacks exited Harlem during the second half of the twentieth century for areas like Corona, Queens, and New Rochelle. Harlemworld's notoriety is a function of a temporally specific "wasness" of the Harlem Renaissance that foregrounds one moment in the neighborhood's past above all others, a moment when Harlem's black intelligentsia and literati were able to offer it up as the culmination of black racial civilization and achievement in America. It is that part of the history story that underpins Harlem's continued fame.[29] Today, many residents refer to Harlem and its past with a reverence inextricably linked to their sense of themselves and their social present. Let me briefly turn to some of the most salient comments several Harlemites have shared with me about their community's symbolic importance. These portrayals of Harlem's blackness leave a great deal to the community's collective imagination as class, ethnicity, and gender are all called on to outline the specific limits of this racialized space.

The Contemporary Meanings of Harlem

Paul is a thirty-something architect who recently moved to Harlem from Fort Greene, Brooklyn, where he was born and raised. I want to start with a comment from him, gathered during our very first sit-down, a six-hour life-history interview conducted at his circular kitchen table, because it provides a clear example of one of the most frequently offered motifs for framing the community's racialized and historical importance: the construction of Harlem as "home."

> **Paul:** I wanted to be someplace that was individual. Harlem is where my family is from. My mother was born here. My father lived here most of his life . . . so really, if you look at my family and not just me, it is home, you know, for me. But see, it is more than that. Even if, I, my family, was not from Harlem directly, Harlem is still the home of black America. It doesn't really matter where you're from. Harlem is home if you're black. ⊦

Paul's eyes darted suspiciously back and forth from the African masks and framed Billie Holiday poster on his living room wall to my Sony tape recorder on the table in front of him. He didn't enjoy doing these kinds of interviews, but his girlfriend had convinced him to sit down with me anyway. Paul showed me around his place a bit, and then we headed down the street to the local bar where he and some of his friends from work were going to have a get-together the next day. They'd usually held these events near the office, but he lobbied for one uptown, in his neck of the woods. Actually, he didn't have to lobby all that hard, he claims, because a lot of his white colleagues had been hearing the buzz about what was happening in Harlem and wanted to check the place out for themselves.

Once we finished walking around Harlem a bit, I traveled with him to the neighborhood where he grew up in Brooklyn. But even though Paul was raised across the bridge, he still lays claim to Harlem (and what he calls its "individual" nature) as an explanation for why it's a person's only natural home "if you're black." Paul feels that he has an individualized historical connection to the place because his parents used to live there, but he doesn't necessarily need such a direct link to call it home. "It doesn't really matter where you're from. Harlem is home if you're black." Unlike Paul's family members (who make the trip uptown to visit him every couple of months or so from their residences, mostly in Brooklyn), many people who call Harlem home have never left, and they often battle for the exclusive right to call Harlem "home" against those who once left for different pastures—or who never lived there in the first place.

"We've been robbed of our history, our real history," Dawn, a twenty-eight-year-old part-time college student from Central Harlem, says to me as we gaze at covers of books laid out on a fold-out vendor's table on 125th Street. The books are less about Harlem's history than about a kind of Africa-grounded ancient history surrounding it.[30] Dawn grew up in Harlem, but she spent her teenage years in Newark, New Jersey—only moving back here to live with her fiancé and attend college in the city. As we look over the books, she points out several she's already read and a few others she wants to buy when she gets some extra money. She has to purchase books for school, though, so she doesn't have much cash left over for her own personal reading enjoyment. Before we move on, I offered Dawn two gifts from among the vendor's hardbacks: Omar Tyree's "urban classic" novel *Flyy Girl* and Ivan Van Sertima's argument about African voyages to the new world before the European Age of Exploration, *They Came Before Columbus*. Dawn had talked about how much she wanted to read both of them, and so I figured that that was the least I could do, especially after she'd spent most of her afternoon traipsing with me around Harlem in search of a quirky orange, red, and black knitted checkerboard cotton cap that I had seen once before, only once, when I didn't have the cash on hand to buy it. That day I wanted to finally claim it. She and I never found anything close to the hat I wanted, but we did hang out for quite a bit, talking about her classes, her mother's recent heart operation, and her younger sister's feud with social services over benefits. After we left the vendor's table, she played with the two books' dust jackets as we walked the gauntlet of people whirling and swirling around us on the avenue, some snapping pictures of the Apollo, some selling watches and CDs from storefronts and portable briefcases, some just hanging out and watching people like us walk on by them. She continued:

> **Dawn:** We don't know it—who we are—so we hold on super tight, to like the little we do know that we got. We don't know what happened in Africa. We don't know none of that stuff. So we hold on to what we know—too tight, I think, sometimes. But that's why we love it. No one can take it away and say it doesn't exist. . . . Everyone knows Harlem. Everyone. But I grew up here. I lived here all my life. I'm not just fronting [faking it].[31]

"I don't think people realize what they got here," Dexter explains to me over French fries at a different McDonald's restaurant uptown, a store where crew members don nylon uniforms of Kente cloth design. Rhythm and blues crooner R. Kelly's latest music video plays on a TV monitor in the corner as Dexter elaborates. "I mean, they kind of think about this place, but they don't appreciate it right. A brother like me does, because I have to go downtown and deal with off-whites all the time, you know what I'm saying. And every day I do, every day, I'm like, 'shit, at least I can take my black ass back up here with my own people, where a brother belongs.'"

Such is the power of Harlem and its symbolism that it helps determine who "belongs" and who does not, and this issue of belonging begins to show rips, cracks, and holes in any ironclad notion of blackness, even one forced to "deal with off-whites."[32] The blackness of black Harlem has always been fought for and fought over: a blackness that was only for the civilized, well-to-do black northerners as opposed to the newly arriving southerners or for African Americans and not for West Indians criticized for stealing all the best jobs.[33] These understandings cloud any attempt at writing race, class, and culture in a deeply historicized area such as Harlemworld, where preconceived and continually reconfigured notions of the place and its people obscure yet illuminate what is most consequential about the neighborhood and its inhabitants.

Danielle is a thirty-seven-year-old elementary school teacher who lives on a tree-lined street off Adam Clayton Powell Boulevard, Seventh Avenue, just a few blocks from where she teaches third graders. She lives alone in a modest two-bedroom apartment, with a futon for a bed. Danielle claims that the Harlem she knows is home, but a very special kind:

> **Danielle:** Harlem is special. It is a special place. I've been here four-
> teen years, and I know that I am lucky to be here. Because there
> is only one Harlem in the whole entire world. There is just one.
> So I'm lucky to be here, you know, to be making a way here, be-
> cause it's easy not to make it. And there are plenty of people in
> Harlem who know that, you know, who live that. Who aren't as
> lucky as me. To be here and happy with their lives.

That Harlem is special doesn't mean it's problem-free. And Danielle knows that—if anything, the opposite might be true. As a schoolteacher, one case in point that she followed pretty closely was the closing of an-other public school in the area that was deemed contaminated by possi-bly cancer-causing chemicals. The building was formerly a commercial dry-cleaning establishment, but the overcrowded school district reno-vated it for much-needed extra space despite several protests from con-cerned members of the community about the possible lingering remains of the chemical perchloroethylene (perc) used for dry cleaning. After the academic year began, however, the school was finally tested, and ex-perts found dangerously high levels of perc on and around the school grounds. Officials closed the school immediately, but Danielle believes that the school should never have been opened in the first place. "Something like that wouldn't have happened any place but Harlem," she argues, a community that the rest of the city doesn't care about.

Asia, twenty-two, a third-generation Harlemite who lives on 104th and Lexington and works at another fast food restaurant on one of Harlem's main strips, offers a slightly different spin on Harlem's seemingly visceral particularity:

> **Asia:** Harlem to me is like the real nitty-gritty. Like hard and real and dangerous. I lived in Brooklyn before, for like two years, and my oldest sister lives in Long Island with her boyfriend, but none of those spots is like Harlem. They just don't feel like Harlem.
>
> **John:** What does Harlem feel like?
>
> **Asia:** I don't know, but no other spot feels like it. I could close my eyes and you could take me anywhere and if you bring me back to Harlem, I would say, I'm back home. 'Cause no place sounds and smells like here. Or is real and, I don't know, nitty-gritty, and rough and real like it. I can't really explain it. But I know I'm right.

Both Danielle's "special" Harlem, the only one of its kind in the whole entire world, and Asia's almost tactile "nitty-gritty" Harlem, a neighborhood that no other place quite "feels like," are significantly recurring strands of a common spatial argument running through contemporary discussions about Harlem's racial distinctiveness. There are, in fact, many people, even those who are not Harlem residents, with highly vested interests in what this peculiarly "special" and "nitty-gritty" place looks like and reads like, how it is to be seen and represented. People have a stake in this neighborhood's definition; they defend and police its meaning with a protective vengeance. Moreover, refracted through social hierarchies, this nitty-gritty place called Harlem can work as an important template for thinking not just about one's connections to place (and not just about one's sense of self) but also about one's relationships with others.

Charice, twenty-eight, is a part-time security guard for an office building on 125th and Frederick Douglass/Eighth Avenue. She was born in Virginia but has lived in New York City for the past twelve years—and in Harlem for the past eight. After Dexter introduced me, she agreed to let me hang around with her a bit on the job. Charice has a lot of freedom when she's at work, so she knew that no one would have a problem with my tagging along behind her. When they need her, she gets a walkie-talkie call. If not, she just watches the front door and makes sure that people sign in or show IDs as they enter. Charice lives with her little girl, Katrina, in a small one-bedroom apartment with sepia-toned pictures of relatives in an assortment of frames on three different end tables, on a glass and brass coffee table, and on a large oak-tiled wall unit. Some of the folks in the photos are still down south, others came north when she did, and still more are only "around in spirit." After Katrina goes to bed, we start our interview, and Charice immediately proffers a Harlem that looks quite specific—to her, even class-specific:

> **Charice:** When I see Harlem, you know, when I look at it, I don't see any welfare or crime or drugs. None of that nonsense. This is the Mecca. I mean, I don't see beggars and homeless people on the street. Or begging by the bank. When I see Harlem, I see, like, a perfect picture. It is just beautiful. That is Harlem.

Charice uses her "beautiful" and idealized version of Harlem to justify criticism of what the social science literature would call "the underclass"—a group that, according to Charice, tarnishes the shiny legacy of this "Mecca" of black America and, therefore, must be denied access (at least symbolically) to its most hollowed name. Charice's no-nonsense Harlem is asserted to the exclusion of stereotypical representations of urban America, stereotypes that would foreground poverty, criminality, and drug use as emblematic of the place itself. Contrary to these many negative images and depictions of urban America, Charice's Harlem is a place "where you can just have fun and feel free. No racism and things like that. No. Just good lives. Like what it used to be."

Carl, thirty-four, is a finance lawyer who has lived in Harlem for about fifteen years. He grew up with "dirt poor, broke parents" who moved here from the Caribbean in the 1950s, before he "was close to being born." Waving a waitress over as he whips out a credit card to cover our fried-chicken-with-all-the-fixins lunch at a new soul food spot in midtown Manhattan, Carl offers a picture of Harlem that locates its validity and reality even more specifically in the past:

> **Carl:** Harlem is history. And I don't know a lot about all of it. I'm just starting to really know it. I've been focusing on my stuff, you know. I've seen some tours. The [Hamilton] Grange. Not many, but that is Harlem. It is history, the history of an entire people. Sure there are bad things, but Harlem isn't just that. Troublemakers here are people who don't know what Harlem should be like.

That's all they've seen, you know, the nastiness, the poverty.
They haven't seen better and don't know no better. Maybe if
they knew more of that history, you know, they'd try to fly right.

Bernice is in her early forties. She's a community college graduate
with two high-school-aged kids, Salimah, seventeen, and Jason, sixteen.
Bernice only recently completed her undergraduate degree, and she's
still trying to figure out just what she wants to do with this new creden-
tial and may even go to graduate school for an advanced degree in social
work. When we sit down in her two-bedroom apartment for an interview, she launches right into her take on Harlem's history:

> **Bernice:** If you want to know where you came from and who you
> are, you need to start in Harlem. This is the backbone of black
> pride, black life. Right here in Harlem. You can't get the history
> of the black family in Brooklyn. You can get it but you won't
> get to feel it. Like you can walk to Marcus Garvey's house, you
> can walk to Striver's Row. You know. There are all these land-
> marks right here in Harlem you ain't gonna find nowhere else.
> There are landmarks in Brooklyn and everything but when I got
> up here in Harlem my first year it was like a totally different
> world. It was like I was someplace I ain't never been before
> where I had to take a trip and get on the bus or the plane and
> all night they were cooking their little food, they had their Bar-
> becues on the drop of a dime. They dressed totally different.
>
> **John:** How so? Tell me, what do you mean?
>
> **Bernice:** Okay, see the women of Harlem are more free to express
> themselves. You might say that they need to put on some more
> clothes. But it's evident that they have some love of self, self-
> pride, dignity, and exposing certain parts of their body, they
> have no problem with that. You go to Brooklyn, them girls say,
> "uh, unh, they too hoe-ish; they not dressing right; they're out
> of order." But these women are free. They're free spirited. And
> you can get that in Harlem. I love Harlem, myself. I would like
> to stay, I would stay, but not right here on Seventh Avenue.
>
> **John:** Why not? And where else would you go?
>
> **Bernice:** I want to go to a block where there are private houses.
> Where there's a little more organization amongst the people
> within that block. I would want to go where the people that's in
> the block have the same stance about illegal acts being acted on
> their block, on their corners, and they're willing to take some

stance. We could talk until next year. Talk done became very cheap recently.

Bernice's daughter is supposed to leave for the West Coast once she finishes high school, and Bernice wants to send Jason back down south to keep him out of trouble. There are days when Bernice threatens to leave Harlem herself, arguing that she needs to take her degree and parlay it into something substantial down in rural North Carolina, away from all the crime and craziness of the big city. Maybe if she could move to a Harlem block that has "a little more organization" she might have an incentive to stick around.

The internal divisions that carve Harlem into differently organized and understood neighborhoods also inform how people represent the place to outsiders. Janet, thirty-seven, who is working on a research project associated with a local hospital, talks about how these internal distinctions might work:

> **Janet:** I tell my friends who live downtown, like in the Village, about Harlem, and I have to convince them that it's not dangerous. So I tried to call where I live Hamilton Heights, you know, so it doesn't sound like Harlem, because then they think "Oh, where's that." And I say, "by City College." And they go, "oh that's in Harlem," and I know I'm done and I'm gonna have to spend hours trying to convince them that it's not bad.

Janet plays rather serious name games with her friends, invoking less-well-known designations of subsections of the infamous community to avoid assumptions intrinsic to many invocations of the term *Harlem*.[34]

Mary, a forty-four-year-old entrepreneur with a fluffy black cat named Langston (after Harlemite Langston Hughes), tries to talk about the Harlem of her childhood in similarly specific ways, to foreground the need to reconstruct that history:

> **Mary:** I didn't really remember. At least I felt as though I didn't remember, but what you do when you don't know something is you look it up. So I did. And I learned about Hamilton Heights and Striver's Row, and I just read up on the place because you can live somewhere all your life and never know anything about it except what you see. So I made sure I learned about Harlem because I wanted to.

Mary admits that her experiential knowledge of Harlem is supplemented by a rereading of its famous history. Just living in Harlem is not enough to really know it, or to remember it, so Mary forces herself to the archives.

Tamitha, thirty-nine, has been in Harlem for about six years. After a divorce, she left the South Bronx, where she was born, for Harlem and hasn't looked back:

> **Tamitha:** I feel more a part of Harlem. You know, I wasn't terribly unhappy in the Bronx, because, you know, you get into your certain section and you meet certain people and you get a feel of the place but, you know, I feel more connected here. I feel more like I'm home. This is like as close . . . I've never been to Africa or any stuff like that. But this feels like about as close to home until I can get there. And I'm comfortable with being here. I mean, like, I really love it here. It's like, you know, the black capital of America. It really is, yeah.

Ms. Joseph, fifty-five, a Seattle native who made postcollegiate stops in southern California and Omaha, Nebraska, before settling into a Harlem brownstone with her architect husband twenty years ago (in one of those private houses Bernice talks about), considers Harlem "the center of the world."[35] This "Harlemocentric" understanding of black America places an interesting spin on the same symbol of Africa that Tamitha summons:

> **John:** How would you describe Harlem to someone who'd never been here?
>
> **Ms. Joseph:** It is like African Americans' Africa. This is where it all is.
>
> **John:** Is it a bad place to live?
>
> **Ms. Joseph:** It ain't bad at all. I mean, no worse than any place else, right? The crime and stuff is not Harlem. If anything, that is gonna make Harlem not be Harlem anymore. You know?
>
> **John:** No. What do you mean?
>
> **Ms. Joseph:** More crime and violence and drugs and stuff, that stuff means we got less and less of Harlem every day. Every time somebody gets killed or something, Harlem is dying, too. That kind of thing is not Harlem. It's just killing Harlem—little by little, bit by bit. It takes away from Harlem, like as if one day we'll wake up and there won't be any Harlem any more and people would be looking around asking, "what happened, what happened to it." It would just be gone.

Tamitha is merely biding her time in Harlem until she makes her way "home" to Africa. For Ms. Joseph, Harlem is its own separate Africa. One might be tempted to wonder what Africa should mean to African Americans in a symbolic universe where Harlem can stand firmly and independently in its place. Furthermore, Ms. Joseph's Harlem, that "center of the world," that "African American's Africa," a place slowly but surely dying, constitutes and reinforces its borders at the very point where violent activities erupt, bracketing those eruptions out of her definition of the place. Ms. Joseph's Harlem, to be Harlem at all, presumes the exclusion of violent death and crime. It flies in the face of vicious murders and drug dealing, the kinds of actions that don't just kill people, she says, but kills place as well. In fact, when pressed, Ms. Joseph can look down the social ladder and see everything that, contrary to appearances, doesn't really belong to the Harlem she knows at all—things *in* Harlem, as it were, but not *of* it:

> **Ms. Joseph:** I just get tired of all of it. Like when, when, when Jeffrey's sister, my husband Jeffrey, got held up right around the corner that wasn't more than a month ago. I don't usually have no problems here. I see the people doing what they doing, but I usually just go about my business. I go right past them like they weren't there. Because for me, they are not there. I don't see them. They just like ghosts: you know, the drug dealers and, and, and things. These people aren't part of my community. They aren't from here.
>
> **John:** Where are they from, do you think?
>
> **Ms. Joseph:** I mean, maybe from the Bronx, or some other state, but even if not, they still ain't from Harlem. Even if they from here, if they live here. Maybe you could say they from upper Manhattan, or from 155th Street, but that don't mean they from Harlem. That just mean they live on 155th Street. Not Harlem. Not if they doing that kind of stuff. Harlem don't want them.

Ms. Joseph also has neighbors, like Charice's "beggars at the banks," who do not necessarily belong, who don't merit a place in her portrait of contemporary Harlem life. Hers is a lens through which one is able to peer down the social ladder at others who share the same physical surroundings but are excluded from a valid, socially recognized and sanctioned place in the peopled space. Here, a kind of folk analysis of socioeconomic differences functions as one of the nonracial criteria used to sift through the social landscape and separate legitimate citizenship from an illegitimate kind. However, just as Ms. Joseph, Charice, and many other Harlemites can mobilize the symbolic boundaries of Harlem to look down the socioeconomic ladder at undesirables (pan-handlers, according to Charice; drug dealers, says Ms. Joseph), some Harlemites (a designation that is obviously up for grabs) can invert that class-chiseled usage of this quotation-marked-off "Harlem" in order to challenge upper-class race-mates' right to call Harlem home.

Damon is a twenty-five-year-old native Harlemite who had been unemployed for more than a year by the time I met him. However, he had just come back from "a pretty good interview" for a "city job" on the day I sat down to speak with him at his step-sister's apartment. As we talked, Damon was clear about his belief that Harlem only belongs to certain set of black folks, a slightly different group from the one Ms. Joseph and Charice would argue for:

> **Damon:** We need Harlem. Poor people deserve Harlem. Not that it isn't nice to have good homes, and rich, like big homes and mansions and stuff, but Harlem belongs to us, to folks who are just regular.
>
> **John:** What do you mean, regular?
>
> **Damon:** Not big money and all that stuff. I'm barely making it. And most people I know is barely making it. That's what I'm talking about. Harlem is the place where you can not be ashamed and just feel proud.

To Damon, Harlem is potentially ruined by the wealthy. And this is a wealth that he can also link more explicitly to whiteness:

> **Damon:** I know why they want to live up here. Rich white folks. 'Cause they know this is like an island somewhere. They can tell. And they don't even want us to have anything, that is why they always coming up here and talking about what's going on on the news. They don't have a Harlem. Everything white folks got—money, diamonds, all of that—they don't have a Harlem anywhere. And you can't buy it, either—and they trying. But money can't make a Harlem, and that is why they will never get this place. It belongs to the same poor black people they trying to kill off and lock up. What they say about Harlem is they own lies.

Damon's invocations of what people are saying about Harlem is a direct indictment of the media's portrayal of this place: a crime-riddled, seething black slum that is the scapegoat for demagogues on all sides trying to leverage the rhetorical power of the symbolic black world. He would paint these one-sided views of Harlem as lies that need to be dispelled, lies offering up a black neighborhood as always already synonymous with an inherently bad neighborhood.

"Harlem is what I know," says Sheila, twenty-seven, unemployed and trying to get into a GED preparation program. We are walking and talking on Frederick Douglass Boulevard as she points out places she's lived in, or been to, or heard about—where her friend purchased a winning lottery ticket, where someone got stabbed three weeks ago, where "that crazy guy burned down the store and killed all those people."[36] Stories upon stories embedded in decades-old concrete. This, she says, is the "real" Harlem:

> **Sheila:** The people I know, the people who have to work and struggle to make it everyday, we here and we real. Real life. There are people who want to come in here and don't have a clue, but they come 'cause its cheap rents and stuff, and they want to be here and act like they better than any of us, but they really need to be some place else. They not from here, not belonging here. They the ones that think they can do whatever they want up here, that they can do whatever they want and won't nobody do nothing. But that ain't true. And most of them gonna learn too.

For Sheila, as for Charice and Ms. Joseph, there is a marked difference between living in Harlem and having Harlem living inside you. There is vast space separating mere residency from real belonging. Sheila's is an idealism that criticizes others' more utilitarian motives for moving to a place whose real importance, according to her, runs counter to exclusively pragmatic schemes for cheaper rents and lower mortgage payments. Just a few weeks after our interview, the *New York Times* published an article on the rising influx of middle-class blacks into Harlem. I photocopied the article for Sheila, and she scoffed at the title immediately, an "I told you so" look frozen to her face. David, Sheila's boyfriend, read the first paragraph or so and shook his head. He argued that all of the black middle-class people in the article think Harlem is what it's not. David even challenged some of Sheila's class-specific claims to place by talking about the Harlem community in a less idealistic tone:

> **David:** Harlem is from the left side to the right side of Manhattan. Uptown. Period. Good and bad. Take it or leave it. Harlem

is like a ghetto like everywhere else, where black people live and work and play and die. People kill each other and they go to church. And they, some times, some of them work, and some of them stay home and do drugs and wait for a welfare check and don't do nothing else except watch TV and movies. All of that is what is going on here every day. That's what's happening.

Listening to David capture the series of divergent experiences found on any average day in a Harlem "where black people live" in a "ghetto like anywhere else" (no more or less special and specific than any other neighborhood) makes this place's value as an anthropological field site that much more compelling. David's Harlem shows the ease with which a globally recognized Harlemworld (that most famous neighborhood in all of New York City) slides effortlessly back and forth between atypicality and stereotypicality. All of these understandings of Harlem speak to the ways in which any community and its residents, not just those of Harlem, apply the litmus test of desirability to define the residents who are thought to jeopardize the sanctity and solidity of the collective social space.[37] These specifications for belongingness in Harlem suggest that race does not simply trump other trajectories of difference for Harlem residents. The blackness of Harlem is often a class-inflected blackness, and its symbolic power stems from its ability to be both special and ordinary at the same time. But what do these two not quite mutually exclusive understandings of Harlem (as extra-special but also ordinary; as decidedly racialized but also resolutely classed) mean for attempts at making sense of this place? By way of fielding that query, it is important to remember that in a place like Harlemworld, what is "real" (what is Harlem, really?) becomes a tricky question indeed.

A Post-Afrocentric Black Harlem

Margaret, thirty-three, goes to school at City College, fifteen minutes south, by foot, from where she lives with her mother, three sisters, a brother, and two nephews in a three-bedroom apartment. Her place is always full of commotion, and so after several failed attempts at conducting an interview at her home, we decide to go to my office. Looking around at the dingy walls of my tiny office space, she offered her own fairly idealistic picture of Harlem:

> **Margaret:** Harlem is no poverty, no immigrants, no trash on streets. Harlem is not any of that. That is not what I think about [when I think about Harlem]. I don't. I don't at all. Harlem is

nothing bad. Nothing bad like that. And nobody can't tell me any different. Nobody.

Margaret doesn't want to hear stories of stereotyped poverty in Harlem. She's probably heard them all too many times. She prefers a more uplifting portraiture of her home. And she refuses to accept anybody telling her any different. Likewise, some of Dexter's usual references to Harlem often explicitly refer to a kind of overly imagined place, too: "Harlem is lights and glitz and glamour. Harlemworld, baby. The pimps and the players and the macks showing out." What people think about Harlem and its boundaries, whether true or not (even a Harlem unrealistically peopled, as Margaret asserts, without immigrants and the poor—or, according to Dexter, sounding as much like Rodeo Drive as an uptown exit off the Harlem River Drive), has true enough consequences, especially as they inform the decisions made by outside investors and the like, decisions that have specific consequences for the lives of Harlem's residents today. Furthermore, notions of Harlem that can preclude, in turn, the very poor and the very rich can also use other trajectories of difference as justification for exclusion. For instance, Harlem's blackness is often a decidedly African American blackness, foregrounding ties to the South and implying that other ethnic groups can be denied a right to belong.

"I don't live in Harlem, I live in the Dominican Republic," Tina, the twenty-seven-year-old mother of three, says, gesturing emphatically with both hands to the world behind her living room walls. Decorated with framed posters of Malcolm X and Marcus Garvey, bookshelves housing Langston Hughes paperbacks and Million Man March paraphernalia, Tina's home bespeaks the historical blackness that Harlem often represents. But Tina argues that so many of the residents in her section of West Harlem are Spanish-speaking foreigners that she doesn't necessarily feel as though she lives in Harlem at all:

> **Tina:** I swear to you, I think I'm not even in New York sometimes. I can't understand what people are saying. Not even just if they speaking Spanish. They'll be speaking English, and I don't know what they are talking about. This is Harlem and it's, like, a shame, that it is so different.

The foreign soundtrack provided by her Spanish-speaking neighbors seems to dilute the kind of blackness implied in the history pasted to her poster-covered walls. Similarly, Dexter argues that Harlem has very specific ethnic borders:

Dexter: Puerto Ricans live in Spanish Harlem, but that is different from Harlem. They have their own stuff, religion, cultures. That is Harlem, but it's not *Harlem* Harlem, like what most people thinking about when they just say Harlem. That's black people.

Sometimes linguistic and cultural difference between African Americans and other ethnic groups can cause misidentifications and the need to make adamant assertions about one's identity in such an ethnically diverse place.

Tamitha: You know, it's like how people think that I am from Harlem until I open my mouth and speak Spanish, 'cause I learned it in school. I speak it okay, and then they think I must be Dominican. . . . And I lived all over. Mostly Washington Heights or Spanish Harlem, but when I'm in Harlem here, they don't know what I am. Or they assume one thing or the other. That's the worst thing. People assuming. So I don't speak Spanish like I used to.

Ethnicity and race intersect in interesting ways in Harlem. Speaking Spanish can mean passing for Dominican, and not speaking Spanish can become a refusal to identify with a Latin American culture pounding against the off-white walls of black homogeneity. Spanish being spoken on the other side of a living room's plaster-filled barricade can mean "not even [being] in Harlem" at all. And people talk about such connections entangling race, ethnicity, and class all the time in Harlem. "That's what makes me different," Pam says. "Some of [these Latinos] swear they too good for everybody else. . . . They be thinking they white or something . . . I swear. They think that." It's not just thinking oneself white that challenges the blackness of black Harlem. There are sometimes important distinctions between blackness and brownness as well:

Dexter: Let me not even get into that [Latino issue], because that is a whole different thing. We have some of the same struggles, some of the same issues, but it's always different. I ain't got no beef with them, but they have a different thing altogether. Now I love a little "hay papi" [Puerto Rican women saying "Daddy" as a term of endearment] and all that, but I ain't gonna roll on 25th and Lex like I would on Powell. Totally different thing going on, different vibe. . . . Once you get past, like, Fifth, you are on the other side. It's still all good. I can still roll, but I ain't in my spot no more.

The Latino presence in Harlem is important because Harlem's lore is often offered up as a multicultural one, as a minoritarian community that easily accommodates other people of color within its diasporic folds. Botanicas and bodegas line the streets. Caribbean cuisine is bought and sold. Kente clothing adorns heads and shoulders. But Harlem can both use this ethnic diversity and disclaim it, remaining relatively strong as a racial space either way. Janet and I walk past 144th and Frederick Douglass, and there are guys on the sidewalk rolling up marijuana "blunts," sitting on bicycles, laughing and joking together. This scene makes Janet talk about sexual advances as a locus for discussing the connections between ethnicity and sexuality in contemporary Harlem:

> **Janet:** They can be so rude. These guys can be so rude. And it's mostly the black guys and the Latino guys, I guess Dominican. Calling you "mommy" and all of that. And talking about "Psst." What the hell is psst? I just try to keep walking because I know that I have nothing to say to them and they have nothing for me that I want.

Janet's friend, Paula, thirty-eight, agrees with her about the Dominican men ("as nasty as shit, I hate walking by them") but thinks the cultural gulf that is most difficult to cross is the one separating African Americans from continental Africans. "The worst thing," she claims, "is the Africans who come over here. You can't understand them. You don't know what they saying. Gonna stand over here and act like they, I don't know what, like they are royalty, like they African queens. They all nasty. [Laughing] I know you think I'm awful, but it's true."

Elisha, eighteen, "half African American, half Costa Rican," argues, "at least blacks and Latinos can chill. Hang out. Listen to the same music and whatnot. Africans want to be here in their African shit and act like they still in Africa. All they want us for is so they can braid our hair and give us extensions." Dexter also places Harlem's blackness in a specifically American context. "Blacks are mostly from the South," he says. "Most blacks in Harlem is from the South. They don't know a thing about Africa except that it is far and got trees and animals. They can deal with Puerto Ricans."

Elisha, Paula, and Dexter voice what I would like to label a kind of post-Afrocentric blackness, a black identity that does not need Africa to authenticate and ground its legitimacy. It is a blackness that can invoke the African continent as an icon of heritage and history in one context while disavowing personal connections to other parts of the African diaspora in another. When Ms. Joseph calls Harlem "African Americans'

Africa," it forces us to wonder what Africa, then, means to African Americans if Harlem can maintain its racial identity without it.[38]

Street Vending

There is a context-specific ethnic calculus at work within this historicized and racialized black Harlem that, using Dexter's language, can "deal with" certain ethnic differences at certain times and not others. As an example of how this calculus might work in more formally politicized contexts, let me turn briefly to the events of October 1994, events that offer a media-disseminated display of just how Harlem's assumed blackness can be made to operate—in this case, as an all-inclusive blackness bracketing out many of the ethnic differences described above. I am thinking of the attempt by African American, West Indian, and West African street vendors to challenge Mayor Rudolph Giuliani's decision to shut down the open-air street markets along one of Harlem's main thoroughfares, 125th Street.

Others have done a persuasive job of showing the international and ethnically diverse mixture of those thousand or so street vendors, charting the conflicts and animosities that sometimes distinguished, say, the African American vendors' interests from the West Africans' interests on certain key issues.[39] For example, religious and cultural differences positioned some West Africans very adamantly against a local Islamic group's backing of the vendor coalition—or against other African vendors from other African countries. However, coalition organizers and sympathizers (including coalition leader Morris Powell and community activist Reverend Al Sharpton) made every effort to mobilize a united front across ethnic lines. A City Hall–centered bureaucracy was pitted against a kind of catchall black difference, a difference admitting to few internal divisions within its strategically politicized identity.

The street vending controversy stands as an interesting moment when ethnic differences, some of the same ones that Elisha and Dexter would use to distinguish black Harlemites from Africans and Latinos, were downplayed so as to offer an ostensibly seamless black front against which Giuliani and his "police terrorists" could be juxtaposed in local rallies. Black leaders positioned against these street vendors' continued presence on 125th Street (city council members in particular) were read as "Headless Leaders" controlled by white leashes and outside interests. Moreover, it was the very history of Harlem that was often invoked to frame discussions of Giuliani's foreigner status during rallies and protest marches held by the vendors and community sympathizers. For many

Street vending (photo by
Scheherazade Tillet)

of the street vendors, the issue was simple and straightforward: moving from Harlem's main thoroughfare to an enclosed open-air market on an empty lot nine blocks south would mean less foot traffic and lower profits. Some vendors offered the already opened Mart 125 as a case in point.

Created in 1979 by a grant administered through the Harlem Urban Development Corporation as an attempt to move vendors from the same sidewalk strip on 125th, Mart 125 is a kind of indoor bazaar–flea market where vendors can rent stalls on a month-to-month basis and sell their goods.[40] On any given day, one could walk into the rectangular layout of the mart and purchase African masks, black-interest videos and books, cowry-shell jewelry, video games, hair-care products, clothing, health-food items, and much more. The second floor houses a food court where people can usually find vegetarian, Caribbean, and southern fare. Even though Mart 125 is located just across the street from the Apollo Theater, several vendors argue that profits were cut dramatically for those who left the sidewalk for stalls inside the mart—some estimating the profit drop-off at well over 50 percent. How much more of a loss would they take, many argued in 1994, if the proposed move would carry them even further away from the sidewalk space of 125th Street?

Most of the people to whom I spoke in Harlem were split on the vendor issue. Many were very suspicious of the move: Why now? And who is really getting hurt? Some residents thought of it as a very clear harbinger of future gentrification and residential dislocation. Others described it as a nice change and a way to ease some of the pedestrian traffic and congestion on 125th, suggesting that the 116th Street lot was still close enough to Harlem's main strip for most people to get there every now and then. Some residents took to the streets and protested the forced relocation (especially individuals with personal ties to the vendors); others unsympathetically wished them good riddance. A few of the women claimed that some of the mostly male vendors often spent as much time ogling them and trying to get phone numbers as they did actually selling merchandise.

The removal of the 125th Street vendors had been in the works for quite some time. Former mayors Koch and Dinkins both made attempts to relocate them. The vendors had rallied and protested against proposed moves each and every time they found themselves newly threatened by the prospect. In 1992, street vendors held a major protest march that so frightened many local store owners that they decided not to open that day for fear of reprisals and vandalism. Many local businesses had complained for years that the vendors were clogging up sidewalks and stealing potential customers. In 1994, the 125th Street Business Improvement District worked along with the local community boards and the Department of Business Services to prepare the neighborhood for the vendors' removal under Giuliani. Still, on the first day of the vendors' forced relocation, Harlem looked like a war zone and was likened to such by many residents. Local stores closed again in anticipation of trouble. Vendors marched down 125th Street and held a rally at the Adam Clayton Powell State Office Building, a rally that led to the arrest of several key vendor organizers. Most corners of the blocks on 125th, especially between St. Nicholas and Fifth Avenues, were filled with dozens of officers each, officers placed there to make sure that no vendor was able to set up shop on that fateful morning. This magnified police presence in the neighborhood lasted for many weeks, several residents comparing it to the military occupation of a hostile foreign land.

One flyer distributed to advertise a meeting to discuss the predicament serves as a good example of how blackness was used as a kind of monolithic nonwhite difference in attempts to organize against the vendors' displacement.[41] Playing on the meeting's proximity to Halloween,

In Anticipation of the Gloomy Night of Halloween
The Patrice Lumumba Coalition will present A Pre-Election
African Internationalist Forum

THE LEGEND OF SLEEPING HARLEM AND ITS HEADLESS LEADERS

A Horrifying, Haunting History--A Blood Sucking Tale!
Featuring Global Goblins, Imperialist Tricks and Threats, Wretched Witches, Capitalist Ghouls
and Vicious Vampires, Civil Rites Ghosts plus Spooks Who Sit By The Door!

FRIDAY, OCTOBER 28TH, 1994
6:30 p.m. Until 10 p.m.
HARRIET TUBMAN SCHOOL

A haunting history (flyer from rally)

Giuliani's vampiric image, sporting a black cape and ominous shadow, was headlined as explanation for the vendors' "Horrifying, Haunting History—A Blood Sucking Tale." Several speakers at the rally actually referred to the mayor as "Ghouliani" all night long. The piece used a doctored image of Giuliani as goblin to frame the issues at hand in unequivocally racial terms: Giuliani sent in police to harass black businessmen as he smiled and shook hands with the white constituents he really cared about. This gambit, linking Halloween to the racialization of community, was extended even further by the cover art of a packet distributed during the meeting. The handout outlined New York Police Department goals, objectives, and tactics for crowd control and dispersal during acts of public protest such as the ones this

Black cats and white rats
(flyer from rally)

vendor group staged over the next few days. The handout's frontispiece contained a drawing of the Harlem community depicted as a black cat (with musculature reminiscent of 1970s Black Panther iconography) doing battle with a white rat in a top hat of stars and stripes.[42] On the sidewalk, well after the gathering had been completed, a local "old head" schooled some younger heads (including myself) about how important the community's history is to its struggles against insensitive outside forces.[43] In fact, he argued that that racialized history is the ultimate reason why the mayor picked on the vendors in the first place: the mayor was sending a message to all blacks in the city, he argued, a message about who will have the final say on Harlem's immediate future. Before our small group dispersed, he informed us of our duty to help our "vendor brothers" as they fight not just for their own livelihoods but also for the right to determine the fate of what he called "the most important black community in the world." For both that particular community elder and the activists who organized that day's meeting, there was an explicit appreciation of Harlem's dependence on its history, on its self-conscious and racialized historicity. In the context of that vendor-support meeting, such an appreciation was coupled with a campfire ghost story motif to reinforce the meeting's symbolic importance for the African American, Caribbean, and West African supporters who attended. And the organizers were quite right to invoke this history. It is truly a harrowing history that haunts each and every invocation of blackness in contemporary debates about the place and what it represents.

A Million Youth March

In front of the school building where the above-mentioned protesters organized their Halloween meeting in 1994, I waited patiently to rendez-vous with Dexter on my way to the Million Youth March four years later. Both the vendors' removal and that 1998 march serve as very rough bookends around my ethnographic field research. In 1994, even though I hadn't yet started my fieldwork proper, the vendor controversy was a good excuse to talk to neighbors about the issues at hand, to get to know them and understand where they stood on the whole matter. It was an event that garnered massive amounts of media attention and encouraged community members to talk with one another even more than usual—if only to lament the way Harlem was being mistreated again by the government folk downtown. The Million Youth March created an even greater public spectacle than the vendor relocation, and both events functioned as prime examples of how Harlem's history gets utilized in citywide displays organized around issues of identity and difference.

The theme of the 1998 Million Youth March was "Black Power into the 21st Century," and the issues on the table included empowering youth, freeing political prisoners, and lobbying for slavery reparations. The mostly youth-led organizing committee was backed by former Nation of Islam spokesperson Khallid Abdul Muhammad, infamous for anti-Semitic college speeches and his New Black Panther Party, which captured national headlines by wielding shotguns against a Ku Klux Klan threat in Jasper, Texas.[44] Mayor Giuliani minced no words about his disdain for Muhammad, continually referring to the proposed gathering as "a hate march." New York City's police chief labeled Muhammad a "black Hitler." At the other end of this dispute, Khallid Muhammad had his own part to play in catalyzing debate along decidedly racial fault lines, variously labeling Giuliani a "racist," a "devil," and a "cracker" who was never going to stop black people from marching in their own neighborhood. The march organizers had always wanted the event to take place on Malcolm X Boulevard/Lenox Avenue in Harlem, but the city was unwilling to issue a permit for that particular location. Instead, they offered permission for the rally to be held either in the Bronx's Van Cortland Park or across the river on Randall's Island. Neither site was acceptable to march organizers, who called on Harlem's rich history as explanation enough for why the rally could have no other legitimate location. The organizers eventually took the city to court on the matter and won. The Federal District Court judge for the case explicitly based his ruling on Harlem's racialized lore, calling Harlem "the most appropriate venue" because of its standing as "an international Mecca for the black community."[45] Harlem's history was called upon to justify his decision. With this judicial decree, the Harlem march was on, but instead of a twelve-hour event stretching twenty blocks along Malcolm X Boulevard, as the organizers had requested, they were given just a six-block strip and a four-hour time frame—as well as an unhappy mayor's office.

Many of the Harlem residents I knew were split on the march. Dexter, for example, was excited about it, arguing that there was no reason why the city shouldn't leave black folk alone and let them do what they wanted to do in their own neighborhood. He was glad the march was on and so agreed to meet me there that morning. Charice, Paul, Ms. Joseph, and others were worried about the potential threat of violence—either from Muhammad's fiery rhetoric or from police hostility toward the black community.[46] Local leaders held meetings with black police officers focused on important safety issues. There were concerns about logistics and community cooperation. Some residents backed the idea of a rally but argued that such a project should have been channeled through local political figures. Some people critiqued Muhammad for his supposed outsider status. He wasn't actually a Harlemite, they said, and so he had no business disrupting and endangering the community.[47] "Khallid Muhammad doesn't care [about Harlem]," one reporter for the *New York Post* wrote, challenging his rightful place in the community. "He lives in New Jersey and commutes to the city by baby-blue Rolls."[48] However, others thought that Harlem needed a shot of new blood to challenge the older community's leadership—and for some, Muhammad and Million Youth March organizers represented just that.

The New York Metro Organizing Committee of the Black Radical Congress was one of many organizations that distributed flyers during the days leading up to the march. One particular handout implored local residents not to "let the racist mayor intimidate and divide our community." This invocation was to be read as a twofold proclamation including both the Harlem community in a geographical sense and the more mythical "black community" as its dual referents.[49] Dexter ended up with some copies of these flyers and gave me several of them in the days leading up to the Harlem showdown. His favorite flyer criticized Giuliani's race baiting and insisted that "people of Harlem as well as progressive people and organizations" support and attend the Million Youth March. It went on: "Our Youth are suffering because our families have been destroyed and many of our women in particular are damaged by welfare/WEP worker slavery which undermines us and sets us working people against one another. Our youth and their families are ground under by abuses in foster care, governmental inaction against the rampant drug trade, and the cynical juvenile system and its institutions. Our youth are suffering because of the billions of dollars diverted into the prison-industrial complex, monies which should be returned to our communities in the form of training, education, better housing, and Jobs not Jail!" Dexter had held on to that particular flyer because he felt that it put the march into its fullest political context—and he liked the way the issues were framed.

I had actually brought some of these flyers with me on the day of the march, reading through them as I waited for Dexter on the corner of 127th and Adam Clayton Powell. That morning, local church doors stayed open as rest areas and relief centers providing assistance to participants in need. Volunteers shuttled around handing out safety tips for youth, insisting that they follow certain general guidelines for their own physical safety: "Have a picture ID. Don't carry any weapons (real or fake).[50] Don't bring alcohol or illegal drugs." "Don't wear expensive jewelry." "Try to leave babies, toddlers, and strollers at home." "Avoid Confrontations. If stopped by police officers, don't panic, stay calm and be polite; do not run, no matter the reason." "Keep your hands where the police can see them. Don't touch any police officer and do not resist even if you're innocent." "Remember all police badges, names, and patrol car numbers." "Don't get in the way or obstruct the police, because you can be arrested for obstructing justice." "Make sure you ask for medical attention if you are hurt while in police custody." "If you feel your rights have been violated, there will be a team of legal observers to help you."

Supporters were also out in full force to register potential voters and keep people's spirits up. In the days leading up to the march, several local black leaders had come out against the march because of Muhammad's involvement, and many of the march's backers were unforgiving about that lack of support. An underlying rhetoric of "vote the bums out" served as subtext for some of the pleas for voter registration and participation. Again, much of this internal debate was organized with an eye to invoking outside white interests to whom some of these same black leaders were said to be answerable. Community belonging became predicated on backing the rally against the racist wishes of the mayor's office.

After giving up on Dexter and being unable to find his cell-phone number, I slowly made my way to Lenox Ave. En route, I bumped into Bernice and her daughter Salimah. Bernice laughed at seeing me out there and wanted to know my take on the entire affair. As we compared positions on the event, all three of us tried to negotiate the elaborate maze of police barricades and one-way pedestrian traffic that had been conceived to keep the marchers orderly and controlled. Bernice analogized the entire setup to lambs being herded for the slaughter, and I couldn't help but agree. Along 124th, between Lenox and Adam Clayton Powell, Bernice and I watched as Salimah gave a public access television show several quick sound bites about why she was there and what the Million Youth March meant for her as a young black woman in Harlem. She was confident and sure. The cameraman was obviously impressed. He took back his microphone, thanked her for her articulate comments, and moved on through the crowd. Bernice beamed with pride at Salimah's eloquence. She was obviously happy to be out amid the energy and activity of the crowd, but Bernice was also a little worried about the threat of violence from police. She and her daughter headed for a friend's front stoop within earshot of the podium. Eventually, I separated from them to cope with the pedestrian traffic alone.

By the time I made it through the circuitous and police-regulated ebb and flow to Lenox Avenue, I was completely exhausted. A few blocks away from the main stage and platform, I listened to several of the speakers as I felt the pulse and breath of that crowd. I saw baby carriages folded up as parents held babies against their chests or piggy-backed around their necks. People hawked and wore Million Youth March stickers, T-shirts, and buttons. There were framed plaques and posters commemorating the event. People sold water and soda out of coolers hoisted above their shoulder. The tricolored African flag could be bought in various sizes—with or without a wooden handle.[51] A framed re-creation of the Last Supper placed Ethiopian Haile Selassie, Jamaican Marcus Garvey, Martin Luther King, and Malcolm X among the black dignitaries positioned around an oblong table. Here again, as attendees listened to the speeches through towering loudspeakers, African flags and intercontinental dinner parties framed a multiethnic rendering of place with links across the Atlantic Ocean.

After an hour or so of looking around and listening to speakers, I decided to head home, needing a respite from the heaving crowd. I retraced my steps through the obstacle course of police officers and equipment, beneath a blue and white sky noisy and darkened with helicopter blades. Eventually, I made it home and immediately turned on the television, figuring that I'd watch the rest of the march on a local all-news station. And what happened at 4:00 P.M. (the hour at which that march was ordered to end) was truly high drama meriting televisual mediation.

Just as the court-imposed deadline approached, police stormed the stage and those sky-darkening helicopters swooped down even lower than they'd been flying all day. Muhammad, the last speaker of the afternoon, had been talking about "self-defense" by telling the crowd to beat the police with their own nightsticks and guns if they tried to attack. A brouhaha developed as bottles and trashcans were thrown at the police officers in riot gear who were taking over the stage and confronting the nearest members of the crowd. Muhammad was quickly whisked off the stage by some of his handlers while much of the antsy audience pushed and pulled a bit in collective frustration.[52] Calm quickly prevailed as residents reminded one another what they were there for—and of the need to keep the younger attendees out of harm's way. People went home offended and upset by the way the police officers handled the situation, but most of them did get out of there unharmed. The actual police-protesters confrontation lasted only a few short minutes, but it created a citywide controversy that enlivened commentary and debate from New Yorkers for many months to come.

Not long after I had had my fill of television news coverage, the phone rang, and on the other end of the line an excited Dexter jumped into his analysis of the entire day's events. "Khallid was playing with fire," he said, "but it was still all good. He can say whatever he wants, people don't gotta do it." Dexter asked me if I was out there, and I told him that I had been but made it back home before any of the ridiculousness started. He cursed the police for their insensitivity and racism. As many residents maintained, he too argued that the police wouldn't have done that any place but Harlem. I interrupted.

"Hey, what happened to you, D?" I asked, "You were supposed to meet me out there. I wondered if I just missed you or something."

"Nah, man," he replied nonchalantly. "This is gonna make history, so I stayed home and taped it. So I have it, you know what I mean. This gonna be a one for the kids, man."

And, of course, Dexter was right. It was a historic story—a historic story in service to very present concerns. All history works just that way.[53] So why would Harlemworld's be any different? And how better to get a front-row seat for such a historic viewing than through the media-saturated close-ups and multi-camera setups that provide visual specificity and immediate rewind capabilities?

Harlem History

A certain reading of Harlem's past is often utilized to create a teleological and naturalized tale of how Harlem became black Harlem. However, the very same "blackness" that frames representations of Harlem and its history is tied up with other than specifically racial forms of difference, tied up with various sites of social hierarchization hardly reducible to strict racial distinctions. Harlem as a social and symbolic space was formed out of historical connections between racial and class-based interests, and these issues continue to inform how residents make sense of Harlem today.

To create a black Harlem of the past or the present always entails examining other trajectories of difference besides racial ones. Many residents employ class and ethnicity as constitutive elements in the creation of a racialized space to which, they claim, only some can rightfully belong. Some residents can highlight distinctions between African Americans and other residents who are not necessarily granted a legitimate place in the community. Sometimes, Africans, Latinos, and West Indians can be placed well outside the boundaries of valid citizenship, other times, safely within it. Class-specific differences—often translated through obvious extremes of poverty and wealth, membership in the proverbial underclass or middle class—can also be mobilized to determine degrees of community belonging.

Moreover, public events like the Million Youth March and the relocation of 125th Street's outdoor vendors provide insight into how this same blackness gets activated in specifically politicized contexts. In the vendor controversy, African American and West African differences of opinion could be downplayed in favor of a united black front against ghoulish white interlopers. In both events, ideational differences between middle-class community leaders and an assumed working-class constituency were sometimes rewired to the very same black-white matrix, black leaders holding the place for the white interests posited as controlling them. With all of this jostling for space within an ever-shifting racial expanse, the blackness of black Harlem should not be too quickly assumed. It is a contested blackness that can bend, shift, and change to either include or exclude depending on need and context, on situation and state of mind. With such a backdrop in place, it behooves us all to remember that calling Harlem a "black community" is not the end of a closed and obvious discussion predicated on transparent historical facts, but rather the beginning rhetorical salvo in a much longer and contested debate about identity, community, and solidarity in contemporary America.

CHAPTER 2

CLASS HISTORIES AND CLASS THEORIES
IN A RACEFUL SOCIAL WORLD

David's Past and Present

The first time I walked with David along 137th Street in Harlem, I listened attentively as he pointed out personal and public landmarks, waving at neighbors and acquaintances, reminiscing and complaining about his "old stomping grounds" just twenty-five minutes' walk from where he currently resides with his girlfriend Louise and her two little girls. David, the most natural of storytellers, was in his early forties, slender, and about six feet tall. We walked and talked together under overcast skies, a bitter November breeze stubbornly jostling its way up and under our winter coats.

That day, he made a point of stopping at one particularly dingy white-brick apartment building in hopes of introducing me to Harold. David and Harold "go way back—way, way back," as David put it, blowing ferociously into the palms of his wrinkled and chapped brown hands. He rubbed them together rather purposefully before ringing the street-level buzzer to Harold's fourth-floor apartment. By "way, way back," David meant that the two men have shared a variety of life-altering experiences and life-defining moments, everything from singing alto together in the church choir during their junior high school years to smoking crack cocaine and robbing unsuspecting pedestrians to pay for that drug habit in their late twenties and early thirties.

David and I stood for what seemed like forever in that cold air, each of us shifting our weight from leg to leg in vain attempts at shaking some heat into otherwise cold bones. Eventually Harold's muffled voice barked out unintelligibly from behind the rusted metal slivers of the building's intercom system. David responded with a yell. The door buzzed; he pushed it in, nodded for me to enter the vestibule, and then followed slowly, the heavy metal and bulletproof glass door closing behind us.

"If you had seen him two years ago," David offered as a kind of preparatory story to our visit, "you wouldn't have been able to recognize him now. You probably wouldn't have thought he'd been around now. He was in some bad shape; both of us, really messed up, messed up." The elevator arrived at the fourth floor, and David led me down a rather narrow beige-colored corridor to the last apartment at the end of the hallway. Before we reached the door, Harold, an equally tall and slim black man in his mid-forties, opened it, offered a broad smile, and warmly invited us inside.

Harold and David embraced heartily before we all finally sat down on the plastic-covered sofa set. After hugging a second and third time, David diverted their conversation from how mutual acquaintances were doing to the specific reasons for our visit. David told Harold that I was "a good kid" and an anthropology student, and that I was doing work "about people who live in Harlem." David recounted how he and I had spent the day going through various parts of the neighborhood. I was trying to get a sense of David's connection to the place and its people by hanging out a bit with him on his day off. I sat uncomfortably in Harold's living room thinking about this explanation of our expedition and wishing that it didn't sound so casual and unscientific. "So, of course, *you* gotta have come up," David assured Harold. "So I figured we should come by and check you a little. Maybe you can speak to him, you know, about Harlem and things—our mess." As if on cue, Harold rose from his seat on the sofa, a glass of soda in his hand, and immediately launched into a description of the two men's sordid, yet redeemed, history.

Harold unabashedly explained that, of the two men, he had been an addict first. They'd become addicted separately and for the longest time didn't own up to it, not even with one another. Before they knew it, they were doing drugs together. Periodically, Harold paused his autobiography to punctuate it with evaluative commentary. For instance, he assured me that he had never expected something like that (drug addiction) to happen to them. They both came from two-parent homes with consistently employed and present fathers ("better than most," Harold recognized), but they still "got caught up in all that craziness and shit." Harold's father actually moved out on the family by the time he was a senior in high school, but he kept in touch with his children—an important point, as Harold sees it, because "a lot of black children don't even get that."

The men admitted that they felt ashamed to be on drugs. They knew it was physically and emotionally harmful, but the worst thing about it was the shame. "To look around," Harold averred, "at my mother and my friends and know, you know, they knew I was fucking up like that, I couldn't deal with that. It made me feel bad about myself more than anything." The men revealed embarrassing incidents from their pasts, uncovering detail after detail (Harold running from the housing police "butt naked" in the middle of the winter, David spending night after night sleeping "in the street, broke and fiending"), only to end in a resounding crescendo of joy at the fact that they are no longer traveling recklessly down that slippery slope of addiction and sporadic homelessness. And their lives are very different—in only five years' time—from that drug-filled past that they so easily recollected. Both men work full-time (Harold in security, David as a substance abuse counselor), and David seriously contemplates going back to school and getting "some degrees." He feels financially secure enough to begin discussing marriage with Louise, and Harold has held down a job in the same company (with a couple of internal promotions) for more than three years now. The two men are experiencing a degree of stability in their lives that would have been unimaginable half a decade ago.

These kinds of life changes signal an important reminder: that despite patterned structural realities variously constraining the life chances of different categories of persons, class position is sometimes not a dead end. Important arguments about social mobility can get displaced in favor of sensationalist rhetoric of "underclass" imprisonment and "middle-class" alienation. Besides widely disseminated rags-to-riches autobiographies about Horatio and Horatia Algers moving up from projects to penthouses, less pronounced socioeconomic movements are often bracketed out of discussions about people's places in the social hierarchy.[1] The changes that mark David and Harold's lives challenge reified popular and social scientific categories that allow black folks little temporal wiggle room within seemingly ironclad and overly discrete classifications.

Looking around Harold's spotless apartment, I marveled at how much his present life differed from the stories he told. In the span of just a few years, he went from living on the streets, with nothing but the clothes on his back, to a warm apartment that was plush and polished by most reasonable standards: newly painted sky-blue walls with white ceilings; a dustless glass coffee table with a crystal motif; wood- and metal-framed artwork hung just so; stained-wood bookshelves filled with yellowing texts—each element combined with what seemed like almost an interior designer's trained sensibilities. Moreover, Harold was earning "a good bit of change" at his job, more than enough to pay his rent and other bills—and to even save up some rainy-day money on the side. David went from being a crack addict and criminal to being a drug counselor with a hankering for a B.S. degree in psychology. Those are surely class-inflected kinds of life changes that place these two men on slightly different rungs of the social ladder than just a few short years ago—and without any of the fanfare (and high-price book deals) that come with more remarkable leaps into the cultural and social elite from the depths of utter poverty. They are not overnight (or overlife, or over-generation) sensations—the tales that keep Americans dreaming.[2] They just made a few short and solid strides in the general direction of eco-nomic stability. These are strides that the men themselves recognize and emphasize.

Several weeks later, David and I were walking together again—this time along Adam Clayton Powell Boulevard a little north of 125th Street. I taught a class around the corner, and David met me for a Caribbean lunch on a relatively mild December afternoon rife with Kwanzaa and Christmas cheer. Our bellies full, we exited the four-tabled Jamaican eat-ery, crossed Martin Luther King Blvd., and passed a homeless person stretched out in the heatless sun, a disheveled man with plastic bags tied to his ankles and belt buckle loops, layer upon layer of musty clothing on his back, and humongously contorted laceless shoes over tongueless Reebok sneakers. As the man sat up quietly against the African-mask-shaped Adam Clayton Powell State Office building, David used this un-housed person's presence as a reason to revisit his own former lifestyle. "Man, I swear to you," he offered, "we were right there, man, right there. We were right the fuck there." David's voice seemed to quiver a bit as he spoke, gesturing to the "dirty gentleman over up against the side there."[3] Shaking his head back and forth, David kept stressing how lucky he felt about his life trajectory. "Me, I am thankful to God that I made it from there. We were there. Right there. . . . I like to see him [Harold], keep in touch, you know, because it keeps me honest. I know where the hell we been. I look at him and still see where we used to be getting high and all of that. He helps me not forget. . . . I don't want none of that again." Reminiscing with Harold (or spying a "dirty gentleman") re-minds David about both his troubled past and his more stable present. David shakes one of the man's hands and tells him to "stay strong." Knowing first-hand what it's like on the other side of that exchange, David thinks that even "a little hello . . . just talk" brings people some of the way back from the brink of self-destruction.

Adam Clayton Powell Building (photo by Scheherazade Tillet)

In a study of the interconnections between race and class in contemporary black America, certain things should not be assumed. For example, class categories must be examined concretely, not just presumed or taken for granted. The challenge is to think critically about how we classify, placing people into what we consider heuristically useful social groupings. In some ways, this text is an attempt to define the terms of social identity vis-à-vis race and class in ethnographic ways, arguing that black people often theorize class as always already articulated with race. These are notions of class identity understood as part and parcel of a racialized place like Harlem, a social world filled to the brim with the significances of race, a raceful and classful Harlemworld. I use this chapter to briefly ponder issues of class categorization and class-consciousness in light of the thoughts and lives of several Harlemites, highlighting the theoretical and discursive underpinnings of both popular and scholarly understandings of class.

Class is often invoked in discussions of contemporary black America as a hard and fast fact of social transparency; however, that is not necessarily what class looks like when mapped onto the lives of everyday people. In the case of David and Harold, relatively small (seemingly less-than-newsworthy) changes in their everyday realties have important implications for how they see themselves and their connection to others. The people I know in Harlem have lived lives that often cut across rigid class categories. Some of these same folks talk quite explicitly about class—not with an impoverished vocabulary incapable of speaking to the truths of economic inequality but with an understanding of the complicated connections that link any invocation of class to other forms of social differentiation, a notion of class as always articulated with race, gender, ethnicity, and so on.

Class Theories

Marxists have long argued for the recognition of "class" as the most salient aspect of an individual's sociopolitical identity.[4] In some versions of this argument, race, ethnicity, gender, and sexuality (big-ticket items in a long list of potentially meaningful social identities) are little more than ideological false-consciousness and superstructure, prompting many to debate the usefulness of class analyses that elide alternative explanatory models of the social world and its divisions.[5] So-called vulgar Marxists have been challenged by race and gender theorists who argue that gender, race, and ethnicity are not only epiphenomena of truer class realities but important life-structuring social variables in their own rights, variables that help organize people's everyday lives and group affiliations in fundamental ways.[6] Social identities are fluid and shouldn't be reduced to easy one-upmanships and reifications that certain versions of economic reductionism are prone to underscore. Feminist scholars have long argued that conventional Marxism's emphasis on the traditional workforce (a preoccupation indifferent to the jobs performed by women outside of the workplace and that also downplays the differences between men and women on the job) ignores important gender-based realities that problematize single-minded arguments about class as the premier organizing principle of contemporary society.[7] They argue that any brand of economic determinism privileging class over other forms of difference loses sight of the many complicated ways in which noneconomic factors have profound influences on people's everyday lives and life chances.[8]

Another compelling argument against certain varieties of Marxism and their conceptual underpinnings maintains that Karl Marx might have gotten capitalism wrong—or, at least, that his categories for unpacking and explaining capitalism as a social formation are not up to the challenge of explaining contemporary, information-age global forces.[9] Marx's pronouncements about the inevitability of communist revolution are dismissed by some political scientists and economists who see communism, that threat to the West, as less an *inevitability* than an *impossibility*—especially in the wake of recent political and economic changes in eastern Europe and in Asia. Capitalism, they argue, has globalized the reach of the free market into all four corners of the earth, and that same free market has proved to be the planet's only truly globalizing force—not an unstoppable communist threat or any of socialism's potential challenges to a market-driven economy.

Karl Marx offered a notion of class that he believed would serve as the very motor for historical change. The workers who sell their labor are destined to strike a blow for revolution the world over. Nation-state boundaries would prove inconsequential in light of class-based solidarities demanding that all the world's workers unite as victims of capitalist exploitation. At the throat of these workers, those who own the means of production purchase workers' labor power and exploit it for surplus value and profits, a surplus at least partially created through the fetishized imbuing of commodities with the congealed labor power of their true manufacturers. For Marx, class conflicts were at the heart of the capitalist order and were the inherent roots for the system's preordained destruction. However, with the changes in the communist bloc during the second half of the twentieth century, the classical Marxist model of clear-cut and inevitable class structures, class interests, and class conflicts simply does not hold in this moment of the-market-can-do-no-wrong late capitalism.

The other side of this critique emphasizes that what we have at the turn of the twenty-first century is a lone superpower with an avowedly capitalist economy that is also, at least partially, a decidedly planned one as well. The government of the world's most powerful capitalist nation taxes its populace to provide at least the minimum kinds of protections for owners, workers, and nonworkers.[10] The unchecked power of capital and the unfettered hands of the market are not so unchecked and unfettered after all. This is a kind of social democratic equilibrium that Marx's notions of class struggle did not necessarily privilege as a potentially successful means of staving off the creation of a communist reality in some postcapitalist future. Those exploited urban workers could be accommodationist and reformist, not just revolutionary.[11] The industrialized workforce of the United States has been called the least militant in the world, some going so far as to label the United States classless.[12] Others maintain that the argument about America's classless-ness is function of spuriously broad notions of the middle class that use the term in analytically suspect ways, including nearly every American under its ever-flexible rubric.[13]

Many Marxists contend, however, that class-based factors, regardless of quibbles about how one categorizes them, are still the operative as-pects of people's everyday lives. It is one's relation to the means of pro-duction that is most pivotal in discussions of life chances and social identity, whether or not the workers are deluded by the power of capital-ism and the ideology of the owning class, whether or not race, gender, and ethnicity are used as mobilizing rubrics for political activity, and whether or not a global class revolution seems remotely possible in the political present. These issues, they maintain, do not change people's objective conditions, do not alter the nature of their relation to capital, to owners, and to their own alienated labor power—no matter how much people may be fooled by the smoke and mirrors of bourgeois ideol-ogy into misunderstanding the most important aspects of their own so-cial identities. Others suggest, to the contrary, that we live in a post-industrial world full of splintered and fractured categories of working and owning classes, begging the question of what kinds of economic differences and designations are significant enough to merit sociological distinction in a world shot through with overlapping and fractal identi-ties—with gradational and relational notions of class difference.[14]

Occupation, income, and education are all used as quick indexes for class difference. However, social scientists often use these markers dif-ferently. Some privilege income as the central defining variable for assigning people class identities.[15] When necessary, education can be mobilized as a research-based proxy. Others argue that net worth and wealth are the most important variables in the determination of sub-stantive class differences—and for understanding persistent urban black poverty in the Unites States.[16] For the scholars who focus on occupation as the key indicator of class-based distinctions, which occupations are linked to which classes can sometimes appear arbitrary. Is occupational authority the key variable in determining class position? Someone who is a manager, controlling the working lives of people under his supervi-sion, might very well be meaningfully and categorically distinct in im-portant socioeconomic and sociopolitical ways from the nonmanage-ment workers under his charge. But is that enough of a difference to justify thinking about those individuals as separate social classes? How much more different are they if that manager is a she and not a he? Does it matter how much that management job is valued by society?

Moreover, how does one even begin to measure such societal valuation?[17] Few would argue that a medical doctor shouldn't be considered middle-class, but some occupations aren't as clear-cut. For example, some Ph.D.s are jobless while other university professors draw six-figure salaries.[18] There is the notion in some circles that anyone with a white-collar job is middle-class—especially in discussions about African American employees: black social workers, teachers, secretaries, cashiers, and others are all given access to a certain kind of "middle-classness." But what actually links such occupations class-wise—especially when the lack of unionization in certain service industries translates into markedly lower incomes and employee benefits than are often received on a factory's unionized shop floor? Maybe income is the bottom-line variable to think about when separating people into classes. At the very least, income-based categorizations clear the way for seemingly objective markers of class that are necessary in social scientific studies.

It is not just education or occupation, income or wealth, but lifestyles—skills and cultural practices—that distinguish and determine classes.[19] There is a culture of the middle class, which is not reducible to annual income and other easily quantifiable variables. But then what do you do with, say, the oft-disparaged wealthy "white trash" (popularized by everything from *The Beverly Hillbillies* to the last season of *Roseanne*) or with a homeless man turned lottery winner—that is, besides just invoking notions of "status inconsistency" and laughing heartily at how such inconsistency is lampooned on network television? These are whites with money and resources but little of the cultural capital equated with the middle class.

Talk of lifestyles easily bleeds into discussions of status and its difference from class per se. Status is supposed to be more subjective, individualized, and variegated than the harder and surer objective category of class.[20] The status ladder goes from the most esteemed to the most denigrated, sometimes for other than strictly economic reasons. So a high school teacher and a garbage collector might bring home identical wages, but by most standards the teacher's occupation is deemed higher on most status scales. Highlighting the fault line between status and class, some scholars have argued that blacks are more status-conscious than class-conscious.[21] Other researchers argue that white racism proletarianizes the entire black community regardless of class- and status-consciousness.[22] Many dispute the claim that blacks have discarded class-consciousness for either an exclusively status-based or race-based consciousness, arguing that working-class African Americans have a class-consciousness that is even more pronounced than that of their working-class white counterparts.[23] Part of this argument about classlessness in the United States stems from the belief that Americans have inherited a Lockian tradition of individualism. Hence, class interests are sacrificed for the sake of individual advancement.[24] Whereas the class-conscious worker would look to other workers for solidarity against the exploitative owners of production, in an individualistic tradition, workers size one another up as competitors rather than comrades. One looks at one's position vis-à-vis co-workers to place oneself slightly higher up a more variegated social scale. Instead of toppling the capitalist system in favor of a communist space wherein all have access to wealth, the goal becomes "moving on up" the system as an individual, improving one's status and position in the current scheme as opposed to overthrowing it altogether.

Powerful social movements organized around race, gender, and sexuality problematize overly simplistic arguments about the transparency of class-based interests over and against other potentially galvanizing social concerns. Likewise, people's socioeconomic lives change over time in ways that inherently critique notions of class difference that only highlight sensationalized depictions of utter poverty or elitist privilege—or a leapfrog from one state to the other. I want to look at some of the more ordinary socioeconomic changes in the everyday lives of people who do not stand as demonized representations of pathetic poverty or as propagandist icons of crème-rises-to-the-top meritocracy. The people I've met in Harlem have personal histories that would be unremarkable were it not for the degree to which their representative ordinariness goes so generally unrecognized by those seduced into fashioning contemporary black America as a diametrically divided social space of intergenerational welfare queendoms and the estranged suburban black sellouts moated off from them. I want to use this chapter to take a slightly closer look at the life histories of several Harlemites in this study, people whose lives aren't reducible to easy racial stereotyping or knee-jerk class categorizations. As a kind of primer for the next two chapters on intraracial class negotiations and definitions, I integrate the brief personal biographies with some of the subjects' own comments about class as a meaningful trajectory of social difference connected to other aspects of their identities.

Class Biographies

Brandi, twenty-four, was born and raised in North Carolina, part of a relatively large family that included four brothers and an older sister.

She now lives in Harlem, following her dream of being an accomplished dancer. Her mother and father are professionals in the medical and legal fields, respectively. They owned and paid off their home before Brandi was born, but she never thought that that was a significant fact until she left North Carolina and moved to the harsher streets of New York City. "My parents always said 'you do what you enjoy.' Don't worry about making money. Just do what you like."[25]

Brandi didn't like the South; it was too slow for her taste. She wanted "more pep, action." That is why she chose New York; however, her parents didn't want her to leave and made the move even harder for her than it would have been ordinarily. She's still angry at them for withholding financial support once she got to the city, though that strategy of nonassistance didn't dissuade her. If anything, it made her redouble her efforts to succeed here on her own, "with or without their money." She soon moved in with her cousin Lisa, who was born and raised in New York. Lisa, who was studying for a degree in English at the time, served as a role model for Brandi "because she is also following what she wants to do and working hard. . . . I look up to her, like, a lot."

Brandi met a cold and seemingly impenetrable city when she got here, and she wasn't really ready for it. She was pregnant within a few months of arriving and had an abortion. She knew what her parents would say— "that is just what they were talking about, why they didn't want me to go in the first place"—so instead of hearing all of that, she decided not to have the baby and not to tell them what happened. "That was the hardest thing, because I felt like a liar, like, with a secret. But they would have died, so I didn't. I couldn't. . . . They know now, but it took me a long time to tell my mom. And it really hurt her a lot."

Brandi can recount one mishap after another since her arrival in New York. "I got really low." She didn't want to go back to the South a failure, but she didn't want to stay in New York, either. Her cousin Lisa eventually finished school, got married, and moved to New Jersey, so Brandi was stuck with a two-bedroom apartment in uptown Manhattan with no really stable way to pay the rent over the long term. At that point, she hooked up with her boyfriend, Timothy, and the two of them got her "back on track." Working full-time and providing for her as she continues her dancing, Tim is her "inspiration." Brandi has also "been blessed" lately with some dancing opportunities and connections that have meant the two of them are able to pay rent—"usually on time." They are thinking about what life is going to look like several years from now, and they are trying to put money away to buy a house. They've even begun to work on a government-sponsored home-loan assistance program recommended by another one of her cousins. Brandi sees the two of them in that house within five years, a house with "a front yard, a swing, and all the things I had when I was growing up down South."

Brandi has a fairly standard notion of class achievement as concretized in owning a home. She also has a strong sense of what she considers her own present class position to be:

> **John:** If somebody asked you what class you were, not that anybody would but me [laughing], how would you answer? What would you say?
>
> **Brandi:** Now it's like I'm on my own, kind of. Not that [Tim] doesn't help, he does, but we still struggling by in here. But we used to it by now. We used to that. Just working, working and struggling. Nothing's easy. It's like you just trying to eat everyday and keep the light on, and the phone on and things. Not poor, but you can see it, you can smell it. You know. It ain't that far away, you know.
>
> **John:** Working like your parents worked?
>
> **Brandi:** Yeah, but they are chillin' compared. We don't got what we need. We can go to the movies on the weekend and things, but we want to do that so we do. You know, they [her parents] have a different, they are at a different place. They work, but not like us. They got savings. I could give you my bank card and keep on stepping. There's nothing in there for me to be scared to lose from that.

Brandi speaks clearly about the socioeconomic realities that constrain and define the life she shares with Tim. She knows they aren't "poor" (they have enough disposable income to, say, go to the movies together at least once a week), but they are a far cry from where they want to be—or from having the economic resources at her parents' disposal. The swing and front yard she offers as synecdoches for the middle-class life of her childhood, a life her parents still experience, are recognizably absent from her present situation in Harlem. Brandi is cognizant of that absence and longs for a future of home ownership.

Daniel, two years older than Brandi, has a very different kind of class history. He isn't ashamed to admit that he is the son of a welfare mother and has a "crack addict for a father." He never really knew his dad and isn't sure "if the man is live or dead." He and his three siblings were born out of wedlock—each with different fathers. "Childhood was tough," and Daniel's earliest memory of his first apartment was a one-bedroom home with so little space that they would "hold pictures up against the walls when we walked by them or else we'd knock up on them and they'd fall and break." Sitting with me at the coffee table in the living room of the apartment he shares with a younger brother, Ralph, he shakes his head and laughs at this particular memory.

Daniel's mother never married and was the victim of a series of abusive relationships. As far as he remembers, she never held down a job, either. "Not once. She would watch people's kids like, but nothing real. I don't even know if she got money for it." That was a big deal for Daniel. As the oldest boy left in the house once his big brother Jay moved out, he felt compelled to earn some money and help support his mom and siblings.

He never did particularly well in school as a kid, and he didn't like going. Now he realizes that lots of kids must have had his less-than-adequate experiences with public education, but he didn't know that at the time. He spent more energy "in the street and getting into mischief than worrying about school. That's for damn sure." He always liked the flashy clothes and other expensive things, and he had very little sense of deferred gratification. "Don't tell me wait, I want it now." That, he claims, was one of his main problems, and it got him in trouble with the law by the time he was twenty-two.

Daniel eventually stopped drinking, stopped hanging out, stopped most of "my fucking up, basically." All of Daniel's friends were doing the same exact things, "the same kind of bullshit, so we got into that bullshit together." They didn't let anyone else tell them anything. They wanted "to party and have fun all the time instead of working on anything productive." That, he says, is his oldest brother Jay's biggest problem, and he uses his unemployed brother as an example of what he doesn't want his life to look like:

> **Daniel:** Some people just don't have nothing to go with. He rather talk shit and scratch hisself than anything. And you can't say nothing either before he all up on your face and shit. I stopped trying to talk to that nigger long time. It just ain't worth it. He don't want to hear nothing. So let him do whatever. I just shake my head and do what I gotta do. I ain't gonna worry about his ass. He ain't worry about my ass. Shit, he ain't even worry about his ass.

Daniel says that he really started to get into trouble when he began hanging out with Diana, the mother of his baby boy. They met when he was only sixteen and the two of them acted like "it wasn't nothing but a thing. I guess that is how kids will be, but we was two nuts in the same thing. She got me in with that [drug dealing] and shit for her ass, so she'd have money to take care of the baby. But that wasn't it. She really wanted to sport her gold and whatnot too, and I was the dumb nigger risking my balls to get her that shit."

He started to get deep into selling marijuana and "fucking up all while I was doing that shit." After he ended up behind bars again, Daniel decided to use his time productively, "to read, get myself a little education. Learn some knowledge. Find out some things I didn't know," and that is when he began to change, when he decided that he should even want to change. Though his mother didn't finish high school, Daniel remembered how excited she got when he read Sunday school verses in church as a child. He remembered how much he enjoyed "standing up there, in my little suit, with the microphone. I know people must've thought I wanted to be a preacher." Those images helped to spur him on in his mission to reeducate himself and become a more "positive black man doing positive shit."

Nowadays Daniel is learning electronics part-time at a technical school in the city and taking it very seriously. He's also trying to find more financial aid so that he doesn't have to drop out. Although he's working hard, Daniel knows he's not yet where he needs to be. For example, he still has to sell a little weed to make ends meet. "I ain't up in the game the way I used to be, not like that," and everyone knows he's trying to stay "positive, but I need to eat, you know what I'm saying." Moreover, he wants to be a "real" father to his two kids, to be around and help take care of them. "I just want to make sure that I got my own shit locked down and sewn up." And he may be on the right track. Daniel just started a new job. He also has been writing a diary that he wants me to help him turn into a book of essays about his life. I've promised to help him get it published. "When all kinds of shit are going on in your life," he states calmly, sitting in my office and explaining his writerly motivation as I look over some of the pages he's dropped off, "you gotta let it out. . . . You gotta let it out and get rid of that negative shit or it will eat you the fuck up." That is why he writes. He's now trying to self-publish some of this material, looking to sell it through his contacts with a few of the book vendors on 125th Street.

Daniel and I were drinking Heinekens in his living room at about 10:00 on a Wednesday night, a Wu-Tang Clan CD supplying not-too-loud ambiance for our drinking. The television screen jumped with a bootlegged copy of *Why Do Fools Fall in Love?*[26] I simply sat there, taking in the film and his apartment simultaneously. I'd been there many days and nights before, a small one-bedroom dwelling in a five-story walk-up. A little dusty and dank, but larger and cleaner than my two-bedroom apartment six blocks west. As if seeing into my brain and catching me as I compared our homes in my head, Daniel looked around his apartment and began to nod. He spoke slowly, ironic laughter peppering his monologue:

> **Daniel:** I ain't got shit [laughing]. I know that. I don't know all of what you got, but I know what I got and it ain't shit. One of them have-not motherfuckers. [He laughs.] I know I'm gonna get shit, but I ain't got it now. [He pauses for a drink.] Being poor ain't fun, dog. Sometimes, I just wanna break shit. And I ain't said shit about white supremacy yet and these [people] wanting to make sure niggers ain't got nothing.

Although "have-not motherfuckers" are part of an easy binary with "haves" and can be read in strictly Marxist ways, Daniel puts a racial spin to his analysis by offering an equation of haves and have-nots that is further complicated by a color-coded logic, a logic wherein race lines up alongside class as an important component of the definitional distinction between those who have and those who have not. Still, that night Daniel's words seemed saturated with class-specific considerations and understandings—his invocation of white supremacy notwithstanding. Of course, Daniel recognizes that race does not define class, and on another day, during a non-liquor-induced conversation in my office, he says as much:

> **Daniel:** There are poor whites, true. White trash, living in trailers and whatnot. No doubt. No doubt. I mean they ain't living in New York, though. They on the farm, in the country and shit. But you don't need much there, you know what I'm saying. You don't need a lot of cheese you gonna live in the country. You need like a cow and animals and shit, but here, you need cheese here, though.

Daniel understands that race and class are inextricably linked. He also can look at regional, geographical, and residential differences as equally important for determining life chances and class position as any strict "cheese" (income) scale. Daniel and Brandi have had very different personal paths so far, but they share an understanding of class that places each one of them at the relatively disadvantaged end of a class-based relational dyad (Brandi vis-à-vis her parents; Daniel in relation to the more amorphously designated and partially racialized "haves" of this world).

Zelda, thirty-three, also has a decidedly relational view of class. She has always been a New Yorker—the only thing that has changed with time is the borough she calls home. Her father and mother emigrated from the Caribbean to the United States in the 1940s and 1950s, respectively. They were "those hard working, I guess, Jamaican types that people think about. They always worked hard. And I had, usually, what I wanted because they earned enough money to afford it. Maybe I didn't get it as soon as I wanted it, but eventually." Her mom worked as a home attendant. Her dad "always went to work in a suit and tie. I don't think I ever knew what he did for a living, but he always worked." Zelda doesn't remember either of them ever getting laid off or fired. At this point in their lives, "getting up there" in age, the two are about to pack up and head back to the West Indies. "They want to go back. This isn't home for them. It is more for me, but not them."

Zelda thinks of her parents as extremely strict and serious disciplinarians. Both her mother and her father would beat her if she didn't perform well in school, if she didn't do what she was supposed to as a student, if she didn't do her chores around the house. That strictness is part of why she couldn't wait to get old enough to move out of their Crown Heights apartment and get a place of her own. "They love me, and I love them. But it was either shoot them dead or move out. So I left."

As a young girl, Zelda was very active. "I was a Girl Scout and a cheerleader and everything else." From the time she started grade school, she took part in various extracurricular activities: glee clubs, karate classes, dancing troupes, and so on. She was always particularly athletic, "a runner, a jumper, physical," so she got into sports at an early age. She had two sisters, both older, also born in New York, with whom she shared bunk beds, church clothes, dress shoes, and the same small black and white television set for most of their childhood. Even though she was the youngest, Zelda was always the most responsible. Denise, the middle sister, got pregnant at fifteen and left for Washington, D.C., with her baby's father—or rather, was thrown out. "Our father was like, good riddance." Karla, the oldest, "just sits her ass home and don't do nothing. No work, nothing."

Zelda grew up in "a mostly West Indian neighborhood" in Brooklyn where everyone traced his or her lineage back to Caribbean islands. Most of her childhood friends were either immigrants or first-generation Americans like herself. "I always thought of myself as both. African American and Jamaican. I know both."[27] After she moved out of her parents' home at sixteen, having dropped out of high school before graduation, Zelda lived with the man who would eventually become the father of her two children, Tony, in his parents' two-story Browns-ville home. Tony's mother and father were able to afford them, and "put food out for us and helped with clothes for the kids after they came." However, living in Tony's parent's house didn't work out for long. To-ny's mother was "just evil, the devil evil," and Zelda eventually started to resent the way they treated her. "Nothing I can really put a finger on," but being there started to make Zelda "feel bad, small. I couldn't take that. That's all." Her children's grandfather, a unionized city em-ployee for three decades, "was okay, but I still wanted to leave, get on my own." Eventually, her relationship with Tony became strained. She admits that she allowed the stress and strain to get her hooked on drugs. After three difficult years, she moved out of Tony's family's home and wound up in a one-bedroom apartment with her cousin Melanie, an-other single parent who worked for the Department of Corrections. Zelda spent over a year trying to get off drugs and get clean in a drug-treatment program.

After being clean for a year and a half, Zelda entered a special program to work on her GED and even landed a job at her drug treatment pro-gram as a kind of drug counselor. Everything was looking up. With that job, she felt comfortable leaving Harlem for an apartment in Queens with her new boyfriend, someone she met at one of her GED classes. "He was about something. You don't see men, not black men, going back to school like that." However, Zelda and Melanie "fell out" over her departure. Melanie thought it was immature and irresponsible for Zelda to move her young children out to Queens with a man she hadn't known all that long. Zelda didn't want to listen to Melanie at the time, but now she thinks that Melanie was right. She's back in Harlem.

In addition to finishing GED preparation, Zelda is trying to meet more of her educational goals. She expects a great deal from herself. "I know I can do better, and my children need better. And I keep hearing my parents' voice in my head. They always worked and saved and got their lives straight, and I don't know how to think about all they did, if I don't do what I need to do." With her GED in sight, Zelda plans to get her B.A. and a job "downtown somewhere, in a high building, the higher the better." She smiles broadly when she says this. "You're probably get-ting some at least decent money in a place like that. You probably gotta be making more than I'm getting now."

My chance to further inquire about Zelda's beliefs about social iden-tity and class achievement came when we walked together down Broad-way Avenue near Columbia University. She intermittently pulled out change from her pants pocket, giving a few coins to only some of the many homeless people we passed on the street. I asked her to tell me how she decided who to ply with her quarters, nickels, and dimes, and her answer was very cognizant of class—but a notion of class situated squarely in a race-filled social world:

> **Zelda:** If I got a little more than my brother, I'll try to spread the wealth, you know. It makes me feel bad to see people struggling. I mean, not that I'm not too. But you know, worse off than me. I know that a quarter isn't all of that, but it's something. When you give, it comes back to you.
>
> **John:** When you don't give, I mean you haven't given to some people or maybe I'm wrong, but how do you decide who gets and who, like, doesn't get?
>
> **Zelda:** White people own the world. It's their world, so usually I'm like, they should be giving me money, you know. They own the world. How you gonna be homeless and be white? That means you must've really messed up. White people ain't got no excuse. We been through all kinds of stuff if you just see history.

Zelda invokes an easily viewed "history" to vouchsafe her racialized position on homelessness and class-based underachievement. Zelda is obviously cognizant of her higher social standing vis-à-vis those living on the streets, but she links that recognition to a specific reading of America's racial caste system, a reading that makes any homeless white person a different brand of "the undeserving poor."[28] They have access to a racial capital, Zelda argues, that blacks do not share, and that means that they are better protected against the slings and arrows of outrageous misfortune. They have no excuse for failure.

Like Zelda, Daniel, and Brandi, many Harlemites recognize and discuss class-based differences, but that does not mean they are willing to reduce all socially meaningful differences to strictly color-blind class analyses. They constantly theorize class distinctions as coexisting with other forms of difference and domination. Janet, thirty-seven, talks quite specifically about the quotidian differences between the rich and the poor:

> **Janet:** When you just walk, go right outside here and go down to 135th, you can tell what people are doing with their lives. I can see that a lot of the people around here probably don't make as much money as me, don't have the same kind of bank accounts, you know, saving money, that I have. I can see that, what else, that I'm doing better off than a lot of people. You can tell those

kinds of things. But that doesn't make me any better than anyone. It just means I went to school longer, and I didn't have some of the problems that they had. I just have had a different life, a more middle-class one, I guess, if you want to say that. But that is the world.

Janet makes a distinction between herself and the other people "around here" (and around her) in Harlem who don't occupy the same class position she does because of educational and experiential differences. She hedgingly sees herself as more middle-class (putting the onus on me for such a definition: "if you want to say that").

Janet first stepped foot in Harlem only four years ago, landing a lucrative job opportunity that would house her at a major New York City research institution, "not nearly enough to survive, but more money than a lot of other people here are getting. That always puts it kind of in perspective." Money issues notwithstanding, Janet decided to jump at the chance of living and working in New York City.

She had made short visits to the Big Apple before, but Janet had never spent any extended period of time in Harlem before moving here. She had heard all the frightening tales of New York crime and danger, but she didn't let that stop her—even though she knew that this city was a far cry from the suburban Ohio community where she was raised. The daughter of a lawyer and teacher, Janet recognizes that her early years with her mother and father are easily assimilated into models of the black middle class. The family owned their home and periodically rented out summer houses in fairly exclusive areas. "We are pretty straight middle class, I guess. Whatever that means."

Janet grew up in an "all-white neighborhood, with all white students, all white friends. Pretty much white all around me." She never thought about race that much growing up, though, and she didn't feel ostracized or ridiculed because she was black. Janet attended exclusive private schools and always felt like she fit right in. "My parents instilled a sense of pride in me. I never felt inadequate and inferior just because I was black. They didn't give me any of that thing to carry."

Janet looks back fondly on her time as a young child with relatively young parents. They were a beautiful couple, she offers, but their love affair didn't last forever. Janet remembers the break-up and how much it changed her life and altered her teenage world. "For the longest time, that was the worst thing that ever happened to me. It still might be. That might still be the most major experience of my life. Up until then I was living a pretty fairy-tale life, in some ways it is still pretty much a fairy tale compared to some other people, how they have it, but that was when my fairy tale, at least with my family, my mom and dad, ended." As tragic as the break-up was, both parents decided to stay in communication and to raise their daughter as best they could:

> **Janet:** I always felt like they were being phony. Smiling and act-ing cordial and stuff. I know they probably hated each another, but they never really let me see any of that. I almost felt like they were lying to me; they were so nice to each other after di-vorcing. Like they thought I'd break if they went at it or some-thing.

Janet's mother moved from the suburbs of Ohio to a job near down-town Cleveland, the place where she was born and raised before college took her to Pittsburgh, where she met Janet's father. Janet, all of fifteen at the time, was now in a different part of Ohio. "It wasn't all black, and it wasn't the ghetto, but it was, like, a whole lot of black people and it blew my mind."

She and her mom were also able to spend more time with family members they had only seen on special occasions and holidays. These were extended family members (cousins, aunts, and uncles) who had never left urban areas and were having a harder time struggling to sur-vive than Janet and her nuclear family ever had. At a little past seventeen years of age, Janet left Cleveland for college, to get the education she needed to become a teacher. Her mother is a teacher, so that is what she figured she would be as well. It was a foregone conclusion. "I never agonized over that. I just knew I was supposed to do it." Midway through college Janet became attracted to law and dreamed about earning a doc-torate. She graduated from college, entered law school, and hated it. After that first difficult year, Janet dropped out and decided to work on a master's degree instead, which she enjoyed a great deal more. That led to a Ph.D. program, and she had found her calling.

Now Janet is in Harlem, "a different experience entirely from any place I've been before." While in New York, she has worked to make sense of her life and where she wants the future to take her. "I want to stop running and start living. I feel like I'm doing too much running and not enough living." She is working on a research project and finding extra time to research some of Harlem's history for her own enjoyment and edification. She never thought she'd end up in Harlem, but she did, and she plans "to stay until Harlem doesn't want me anymore."

A few minutes after our first formal interview, Oprah Winfrey's syndi-cated television show began on the muted living-room television. Janet is never home in the afternoon, so she made a point of turning on the television "to see what Oprah's been up to" since Janet hadn't found time to watch the show in months. I ask her how she'd describe Oprah in class terms:

> **Janet:** Oprah is rich. She is, she would look at all of us and be like, "poor people, please." We are all struggling compared to Oprah, but she is rich. She owns a big corporation, her own business, Harpo Entertainment, and she runs it. She is on a different planet from you and me.

Janet is quick to point out her own differences from poorer blacks in Harlem (folks without "the same kind of bank accounts" or schooling), but she is also able to fit herself into a similar boat with these same neighbors when compared to the likes of Oprah Winfrey. The Oprah Winfreys versus the rest of us "poor people" on one scale of analysis, and Janet versus poorer Harlemites on another. One equation is a class argument that adds someone with a Ph.D. to everyone else in terms of a larger class picture that includes corporate tycoons. The other highlights differences between her life and the lives of Harlemites she sees on 135th Street. Being class-conscious doesn't necessarily entail a negation of one's abilities to see more nuanced and variegated forms of difference. Moreover, that individuals see class differences that separate them from others in one context doesn't mean they can't invoke class to form bonds of solidarity with those individuals. People are working with different measuring scales at one and the same time.

Another Harlem resident, Carl, a thirty-four-year-old lawyer, offers a similar reading of how and why one can, as Janet did, shift economies of scale and comparability in discussions about class position:

> **Carl:** I got some money. I know I'm pulling in more than a lot of people, but I have a lot less than a whole bunch of other people. It depends on where you're looking and who you look at. To me, I'm really just trying to make it, too. I'm really just trying to survive, and it's dog-eat-dog. To others, I might be, I don't know, like in the land of milk and honey. And I guess I am, from one point.

Carl has a six-figure salary, a 1994 Audi, and well over one hundred thousand frequent flyer miles. Still, he can see "a whole bunch of people" who are doing better than he is and counts himself among those just "trying to make it"—even though it may look like he is "in the land of milk and honey" from a lower rung of the socioeconomic ladder.

Three blocks northwest of Zelda's rent-stabilized apartment, one of Carl's close friends, Kirk, thirty, lives alone in his "bachelor's pad," the basement apartment of a newly renovated brownstone. Kirk "really never saw poverty," he claims, "except on television and what have you." He feels that he may have just been unable to see poverty (even though "it must have been there") because he was somehow "immune to it. . . . Maybe I just never thought about it." But the Queens neighborhood he called home as a child kind of kept him out of harm's way. "Queens was cool. We lived on a smooth block, suburbs all the way."

His mother was a social worker and then a teacher and his dad was an electrical engineer who ran his own business. He and his younger sister were good about school. "She was always better than me, grade-wise, but I was on honor roll, that kind of thing; she was always scoring higher than me though." He and his sister went to public schools, but they were always "integrated, really mostly white, I think. So the education was good, but it seemed the black kids were smarter than the white ones to me, at least in our schools." Kirk was always in the gifted classes and went to college straight out of high school. As was the case with Janet, not going was hardly an option.

After college, Kirk decided to head back to New York from Philadelphia so that he could start his own business. "I just want to get a slice of the pie and live comfortably." He has always had a one-track mind about running a business and thinks it's his father's influence. Kirk's business, however, will be entertainment—not wires and outlets. His days are spent in artist development meetings and exclusive late-night galas. All he's ever really known is that he always wanted to be doing exactly what he's doing. "It was never about maybe, or can I do it. Not to be cocky, or sound cocky, but I was always sure." Kirk admits that straight out of college, when he tried to get his company off the ground in Philadelphia, he had to struggle for a while, "eating popcorn and grits and avoiding my landlord 'cause I wasn't making money, and the little I had I was like, fuck it, I'm gonna invest this in me. So it was tight for a while." It got so tight that Kirk was sued and evicted by his landlord. His business was foundering, and he owed "like two thousand dollars in rent that I didn't have."

Kirk eventually left Philadelphia "kind of a failure," feeling as if he was going to have to think about doing something else before continuing with his business dreams. He teamed up with one of his "boys from undergrad," Don, and the two of them started to work as a pair. That was three years ago, and although they have a few glossy photos of up-and-coming recording artists already in the fold and a business plan for what they want their company to look like in five years, they are still not making the kind of money they would like to be making. Kirk does temp work sometimes, during dry spells, and Don is a full-time paralegal. Moreover, Kirk is only able to afford his apartment because his parents are willing to help him out when he can't cover the rent. "If not for them, I'd be in trouble. But that won't last forever." Kirk's sister, a lawyer who lives in Colorado, also helps her brother out from time to time financially. "But you know, pride and all, sometimes I'm like, I don't want to take it. We are like competitors a little. I don't want to seem like the black sheep who is feeding off his family like that. But if it's between that and moving in with moms and pops, I'll just have to suck it up and be like, 'thanks sis, you know I love you, and I'll get this back to you when the next check comes in.'"

Kirk has seen the many successes of his father as a businessperson. He also notices the economic achievements of other people in his social network, of people like Carl, who are part of his everyday world. Moreover, he uses these bits of information to create self-confidence regarding his own future exploits and his sense of middle-class belonging. His college degree and early career cycle mean that he expects a certain payoff on these investments. This network also means a safety net for any somersault into debt and hard times—for instance, a sister who can help out until "the next check comes in." But he ties this kind of class achievement to a specifically collective racial achievement as well:

> **Kirk:** We [African Americans] need more people doing this business thing. You know. Not just to get paid. You know, as role models and that kind of thing. We need that kind of thing. For the kids coming up to see. That's why it's important for us to do what we are supposed to do on our side. It's not just wanting to get paid only.

Kirk's professional aspirations pivot on an expressed connection between individual class achievement and the collective progress of a black community in need of "role models and that kind of thing." Class achievement is highlighted, but not at the expense of notions of race. In this instance, racial consciousness inflects class-consciousness.

The reverse is also possible. Dexter explores the class-inflected ways in which he marks his own differences from other racial have-nots:

> **Dexter:** I just feel like you gotta know what is right and what is wrong. And you gotta work to do right. I ain't never done drugs. All I smoke is weed. I work hard. I take care of my girl. I ain't

living lovely, but I ain't one of these knuckleheads on the street just not doing shit for themselves, but trying to take somebody else's shit.

Dexter can talk class and status at one and the same time (invoking employment, familial performance, illegal activities, and "lovely" amounts of money) as a means of thinking about class and race and status all at once. Dexter uses the fact that he "work[s] hard" (an occupational distinction) and "take[s] care of [his] girl" (a familial obligation) to argue that he is different from the "knuckleheads on the street" who don't perform such class-coded tasks. Here, Dexter is making behavioral distinctions loaded with class-inflected markers, but he can also invoke class-inflected markers to identify with those aforementioned "knuckleheads":

> **Dexter:** We all catching hell up in this piece. Everybody. We all getting it. I don't care if you got a nicer crib, a little more money than somebody or something, unless you Donald Trump or some shit, you got the same shit I got, basically. Maybe you got sugar on top of your shit, but it's still shit.

Dexter seems to distance himself from these "knuckleheads" in one class-coded instance and identify with them (as non–Donald Trumps) in another. His life history may explain both moves.

A native New Yorker born in Bedford-Stuyvesant, Brooklyn, Dexter spent most of his early years in the first floor apartment of a five-story building with his mother, Madeline, and father, Porter. Madeline was seventeen when she had Dexter, only a year after she finished up her final semester of high school in Manhattan and moved with Dexter's father into a one-bedroom apartment in a six-story building in Flatbush, Brooklyn. Porter, about sixteen years older than his new bride, was employed as a part-time construction worker in his brother's construction firm in Brooklyn by the time Dexter could walk. "We didn't have much," he remembers, "but I don't think we were dirt poor. We were all right. Not poor, not rich. Just all right."

When Dexter's father left, his mother hit hard times. The age difference and the incessant verbal abuse were finally too much for Madeline, and the two separated on less-than-amicable terms. During those days, Dexter was at his mother's side incessantly, a "mama's boy like you wouldn't believe. People couldn't get me away from her. Not me." There were frequent trips to family members' homes to spend the night as well as hand-me-down clothes from well-meaning folks. "I don't even think we even knew some of them," he confesses, "but I was wearing people's pants, hats, everything, whatever." Madeline's oldest sister, Dexter's aunt Clare, was a nurse and her husband was a teacher, and the two had a little space in their Harlem apartment for the single mother and her son to rest their heads from time to time. Sometimes Dexter's mother would leave him there "for weeks, I think" and he'd commute across boroughs to his elementary school in Bed-Stuy, well over an hour's travel time each way. Once Madeline could no longer survive on the charity of friends and relatives throughout the city, she went on welfare and that, Dexter thinks, really demoralized her, "broke her spirit in a way. She is prideful like that."

They were now a pregnant mother and prepubescent son living the proverbial, poverty-stricken American Nightmare. "We was hand-to-mouth, just trying to survive." Madeline was not only an out-of-wedlock welfare mother, she was also about to have another baby, Dexter's sister Sherry—all without a spouse's help, a steady job, or any serious prospects for obtaining either. It was at this point that Dexter remembers his first encounters with the criminal justice system, from truant officers to misdemeanors and court appearances for "stupid pranks, running around trying to be a tough-guy kind of stuff, stupid."

While his mother was rededicating her life to God and the church, Dexter was running around in the streets. "I didn't want to hear none of that Jesus stuff. That wasn't me." Dexter's not sure whether it was her own pride, family frustration, or some mixture of the two, but eventually Madeline, who was able to market her high school diploma, got off welfare and found a job cleaning houses—using that money to land a small one-bedroom apartment for her, her son, and her newborn daughter.

As his mother worked, Dexter went to public school. He wasn't a particularly good student and maintained a C average throughout his entire educational career. But even before graduation, Dexter had entered the workforce with part-time positions in the service economy. Pizza shops, fast food restaurants, grocery stores, all within a few blocks of his mom's apartment building, were the places where Dexter first whet his whistle as a service worker. "I was, like, the man, you know. No pops around, so that's that. You the man. And you got to do it." Admittedly, most of his wages went to "sneakers and my own gear," but there was something about being the man of the house that had less to do with the percentage of one's earnings earmarked for household bills than with the fact that one was working at all.

It was in the ninth grade that Dexter stopped commuting to schools in Brooklyn. Instead his mother enrolled him in a Manhattan high school. Still, he kept in touch with some of the friends he ran around with in Brooklyn during his earlier years. Dexter admits dabbling in drug dealing during high school, and he respects the difficulty of that hustle, but it wasn't for him. "I'd take four and change an hour and a stupid-ass uniform over mad loot and a bullet in my dome all day." Dexter considers himself a good worker, one who doesn't "have a hard time working my ass off." And he has always worked, starting once he was old enough to get paid under the table to sweep the fronts of stores or carry groceries to shoppers' cars.

But everything hasn't been rosy for this hardworking Harlemite. His mom, Madeline, got hooked on drugs about four years ago and is still fighting to stay clean. He hasn't seen or heard from his father in more than ten years. And Dexter himself got caught for selling marijuana about two and a half years ago and has a criminal record because of it.

Dexter really didn't have any idea what he wanted to do when he got out of high school—except more of what he'd been doing: working. He's never had a job he was particularly proud of, but he has always worked. At most of these jobs he would read comic books and magazines and newspapers "and just try to work on my reading and stuff, get stronger." He loves reading (and even writing poetry) because he has seen so much, "you know, with my moms and the drugs and all of that shit." His love of writing convinced him to go back to school, and he is currently juggling a job and an undergraduate schedule at a small community college. He lives with his mom, his sister, and his baby nephew, Lawrence, in a one-bedroom apartment. Dexter sleeps in the living room on a fold-out sofa, and Sherry, when she's not at her boyfriend's family's apartment, sleeps in a queen-size bed in the bedroom with their mother and Lawrence. Dexter plans to find his own place once he saves enough cash for the move.

Although Dexter is going to college, he isn't attending a prestigious Ivy League school. And that is an important distinction in his mind—at least when he's talking to me. On several occasions (at my teaching job in Harlem, at his house, on trips downtown) he has playfully sprinkled his sentences every so often with the sound effect "ca-ching" or calls me "Mr. Jackson" or "Mr. Money" to highlight my relatively higher social position. He's teasing, but he is also very serious. He readily admits that for some of his peers, the fact that he's going to college at all, even a community college, is enough to place him in a class/status boat right along with me in terms of educational achievements and life chances. Whenever Dexter and I have hung out with his friends, he has always introduced me as an anthropologist studying at Columbia University, providing people with a clear sense of how much status I should have in their eyes—and maybe, by association, how much he should have, too. I made a point of asking him about this and doing my best to get across to him how seriously I take his intellectual pursuits. "Folks need to hear that we have young black men doing the things that you're doing," he offered, sitting in my office. That, he explained, is why he stresses where I go to school.

I told him that I appreciated what he was saying, but that he shouldn't underestimate his own college experience and how it can potentially model a lifestyle to the young black men coming up behind him. He nodded his head affirmatively:

> **Dexter:** True, but I ain't where you are at. I'm on the outside of the window looking in at you. I want to get in. And I will, 'cause I'm gonna put my mind on it, but I am not there yet. I'm just a minute from the street up in here. Straight up. But if I did ever fuck up and slip, I'll land on my feet. That is what separates the men from the boys. Do you land on your feet after shit gets crazy? Can you work it? A lot of these people around here ain't about nothing. . . . Or they can't see that where you are at school is better than where I'm at. That's their thing, but I ain't gonna let that stop me from doing my own thing. I wanna be where you at.

Dexter sees a transparent yet very real "window" that separates the two of us educationally. He believes in his ability to pass through that glass, but he also recognizes that he has not yet successfully and completely done so—even if his friends don't necessarily see things the same way. Dexter views education's connection to class difference as a many-sided thing—some sides separating him from an Ivy League graduate student, others linking us in a common quest for higher educational achievement.

Charice, twenty-six, who lives four blocks from Dexter, had a slightly different experience with the offerings of college life. She lives in the same middle-income building that her mother moved into nearly twenty years ago. Less than a year and a half away from receiving a B.A. from a small northeastern college three hours outside of New York City, she left before graduation because she "didn't like being there and the people there." Now Charice works as an assistant to a radio producer on a New York City radio station. She has lived in Harlem all of her twenty-six years (except for her stint as an undergrad) and loves it. "It sounds like a commercial," she says, "but Harlem is it. The people, the sense of community, the music." In her years in Harlem, she has seen it "go through cycles." Sometimes it looked like her block was getting worse, with more crime and poverty; other times, it looked like it was getting better.

Her father was born in South Carolina to parents who worked with their hands, "farmers and things like that, on the land, with nature." He migrated to New York when he was in his twenties, struggling to survive in a harsh northern city with little in the way of formal education, only a strong work ethic. Charice's mother, also born and raised in the South, brought her own brand of southern assiduousness and hospitality up north with her to the streets of Harlem. Charice grew up with her mother, and though her parents never married, Charice has always kept in contact with her dad, someone who's been an important influence on her life.

Raised in the church, Charice was always "a pretty good girl, I guess" as a child. She never ran with the wrong crowd or got into any serious trouble. "I didn't want my mom to do loco on me, so I drew a line with that stuff so she didn't have to whip my butt, which she would have had no problem with doing; she had no problem with that." Although Charice's mom never graduated from high school and spent all of her New York years making "like under minimum wage," she made sure that her daughter took school seriously and performed well in her classes. When her friends from the building were out playing and running around in the streets, Charice and her older brother Kenneth had to be home, "and mom wasn't messing around about no parts of that at all." Her mother was a champion of education as a tool for upward social mobility, and that focus on educational achievement paid off. Charice was always at or near the top of her class from as far back as she can remember.

When Charice turned seventeen, she spent her afternoons taking orders and cleaning dishes at a takeout place in mid-Manhattan. That was her first taste of the work world, but her mother made her quit after only a few months because Charice's grades started to slip in school. "She was wrong, but she thought it was going to mess me up in school. We could have used the money, but she wasn't trying to hear that." Charice's mom took on second jobs and various odd jobs instead of allowing Charice to split time between work and school. Her mother didn't have a great deal of money or resources, but she taught Charice the value of educational achievement. "She was always about putting the books first. I wouldn't be where I am without that, her saying that."

Charice's closest aunt and uncle on her mother's side live only three blocks away and started taking care of Charice after her mother passed away several years ago. Both were struggling themselves and had their own children to deal with (one son in prison, a daughter pregnant at fifteen), but they were family, so there was no question that they'd take her in:

> **Charice:** Family is supposed to do that kind of thing. Besides they were proud of me and happy that I wasn't pregnant or doped up or anything like that. I think they wanted to see a success; they thought I would be a success, I think. And I didn't want to disappoint them with that.

Her stint in college implied more opportunity for success than did some of her cousins' choices.

At about the same time, another cousin, Leslie, was sent up from down South and began to get into all kinds of mischief. Leslie was hanging with the worst crowds. Moreover, they were now six people crammed into a two-bedroom apartment, and Charice felt like the world was closing in on her. She decided to go away to school. "I wanted to live on my own, get out on my own and get away from there." College wasn't easy for Charice, especially in terms of finances. All in all, her grades were respectable, so she took out a few loans and received some need- and merit-based scholarships. The classes were okay, but she felt out of place and found it increasingly difficult to return to school after summer and winter breaks. Eventually, Charice landed a "skimpy" paying job at a radio station in New York and decided to stay in Harlem—thinking that she'd eventually go back to school in the city on a part-time basis. Since starting her radio job, however, Charice hasn't had the time to complete her degree. Still, she thinks that her mother would be proud of her if she were alive to see her baby girl today—working hard, close to finishing school, and living on her own in the big city. Charice confesses that it was the white people at that small New England school who made her feel out of place and uncomfortable. Harlem, she says, is a much better fit for her; it's where she grew up.

Diedra, a thirty-five-year-old social worker, lives in New Rochelle but works in Harlem. Unlike Charice, she talks about feeling uncomfortable and out of place around the blacks in this community:

> **Diedra:** Sometimes I feel like I'm a misfit. Because people, I'm talking about black people now, will laugh or look at me like I'm crazy when you haven't been poor and on welfare and food stamps all your life. When I say my father was a lawyer and

owned a restaurant and my mom was a nurse and teacher, and got her doctorate, and that I grew up in Connecticut and take the Metro North into work, people can start to act like "oh, what could you ever tell me about anything." Sometimes I lie or try to just be quiet. I just try to keep quiet, but sometimes it makes me upset that people think that they are the only ones who can say something because they are poor like that. Not to say that people on welfare are stupid, but you don't have to be dirt poor to be a good person or to deserve to be listened to by people.

According to Diedra, class differences can be used to silence or challenge those higher up the pecking order, and she's referring specifically to "black people now." When race informs understandings of status and class that fact does not necessarily mean that class is ignored completely. It simply gets rethought as integral to any and all understandings of racial authenticity, an authenticity that can, in Diedra's example, confer speaking authority upon certain classes of black people and not others. It means homelessness can be a socioeconomic state that is racialized in ways that exclude whites from valid claims to assistance (as Zelda maintains)—or that ground a certain kind of cross-class bonding (à la David and the "homeless gentleman") as a function of past experiences across class lines. Class markers can also be used to both identify with and distinguish oneself from the same group of individuals, as Dexter does. As important as race is in Harlem, as important as racial differences are to many of the people who live there, its importance does not mean that class and status differences are taken lightly or dismissed out of hand. Racial identity does not simply trump class consciousness or concerns. In Harlem, people are thinking about racial difference as they theorize class and status differences simultaneously: class invoked to talk about the economic ramifications of the racial order, race as an important social identifier that gets trucked, unsolicited, into discussions of class-based differences. As I pointed out in chapter 1, class-inflected differences are often used to separate the community members who truly belong from those who do not, regardless of race and residency, using class as a prism through which to make sense of racial community and commonality.

Class Summaries

People's actual life trajectories don't necessarily make sense in terms of middle classes, underclasses, or even carefully measured working classes.

Harlem, as a social space, is full of socioeconomic diversity—which may not be representative of every single majority-black neighborhood in America but still points to fertile ground for analyses of race and class today.[29] People with different economic realities live next to one another, work next to one another, and otherwise share the same public space. The people whose lives and words are highlighted here come from different places, earn incomes all along the socioeconomic spectrum, and will probably have very different future trajectories. What brings them together in this ethnographic work is the fact that they all call Harlem home. They have different family histories, present socioeconomic realities, and future socioeconomic expectations, but they all share the same neighborhood—everyone, save Diedra, residing within seven square blocks of one another, and even Diedra works within that geographical area. These folks don't necessarily enjoy or suffer identical day-to-day experiences, but they do walk the same streets and navigate the same public spaces. Moreover, each one's life speaks to the protean nature of people's social positions. Dexter has had some serious bouts with the criminal justice system and spent most of his youth on welfare, but he has also worked for a good portion of his life, is putting himself through school, and has been a responsible son who takes care of an ailing mother. Zelda has spent portions of her life as both an unemployed drug addict in need of counseling and as a full-time drug counselor paid to help others. Daniel, for one, is the proverbial illegitimate offspring of a crack-head father and welfare-queen mother. He's also been incarcerated. But Daniel has refused to remain trapped in anybody's criminalized underclass—choosing instead to cultivate a love for writing as he clocks time at a new job replete with medical benefits, not a trivial fact within Harlem's highly competitive entry-level, service-sector labor market.[30]

All of these people have lives that seem to curve around both sides of the black underclass/middle class divide. Even Kirk, who claims to have never seen poverty, had a spell when he wasn't working and wasn't able to pay his rent. Quick and easy uses of class labels don't necessarily tell you all you need to know about people's socioeconomic lives, about who is a member of which class category, and what makes her or him a member—about what criteria are used to freeze changing life stories into specific and often resolutely immutable class boxes. For example, what are the class positions of the people just highlighted? Are some decidedly middle-class, maybe Janet the Ph.D. researcher or Kirk, the would-be entrepreneur? Possibly, but even Janet admits that she is "not nearly making enough money to survive" and Kirk confessed to me that he still wakes up in cold sweats some nights, dreaming that he'll be broke again.

Very often, black middle-classness is a wide-open field.[31] The "black middle class" becomes a catch-all phrase that can expand to capture, say, Janet and Zelda for their occupations, Kirk for his aspirations, Brandi, Kirk, and Janet for different parts of their familial histories, and maybe even Daniel and Dexter for their writing pursuits—all depending, of course, on what slice of these people's lives one focuses on. Daniel's biography can be read as a rags-to-riches narrative of personal fortitude, perseverance, and achievement. He is finishing trade school and thinking seriously about getting a liberal arts degree, but he still is not in a place he's proud of or that makes him comfortable—and he sometimes has to resort to the underground economy, however grudgingly, to make ends meet. Moreover, many of these same individuals who can be seen as middle-class in the senses mentioned above might just as quickly get connected to notions of working-classness or even underclassness: Dexter's life with a mother recovering from drug addiction, Zelda's status as an unwed mother, Kirk's bouts with eviction and popcorn for dinner, even Janet's life after her parents' divorce—when she finally realized how poor her extended family had always been.

The black people I met in Harlem (as much as people anywhere else in the United States) have lives that shoot through overly rigid, static, either-or designations of class. They have juggled college education with welfare, homelessness with unionized jobs, drug dealing with steady service-sector employment.[32] Harlem may be atypical of black urban communities in terms of the degree of class stratification found there, but that does not mean that social scientific investigations of other black communities will not benefit from careful self-scrutiny about class categories and their social applications.

Most black communities are not merely irredeemable slums peopled by poor blacks champing at the bit to play the race card as a trump for all other forms of social difference. There are businessmen, teachers, crack addicts, security guards, welfare recipients, students, doctors, and drug counselors all within a stone's throw of one another, sharing the same community and conversing with one another about the ways in which that racialized community should be understood. However, the fact that people share the same neighborhoods doesn't necessarily mean that they have serious and substantive social interactions that transcend class-inflected differences linked to income, occupation, education, wealth, and so on. It doesn't mean that they have meaningful social bonds across class lines. I will use the next chapter to examine social contacts between people who would be considered to represent markedly different class-based social positions and realities. These same interactions are often downplayed or ignored in discussions about the connections between race and class in contemporary black America, discussions premised on class isolation and estrangement between two supposedly discrete and noncommunicating classes of black Americans. Highlighting class estrangement is not the only way to take class variety in black America seriously as an analytical starting point for discussions about what race and class actually mean (and do) in the lives of black people in the twenty-first century.

BIRTHDAYS, BASKETBALL, AND BREAKING BREAD: NEGOTIATING WITH CLASS IN CONTEMPORARY BLACK AMERICA

Party Politics, or the Two-Party System

On a particularly hot and humid summer day, Paul, an African American architect living and working in New York City, celebrated his thirty-first birthday with an extravagant party. In fact, he had two of them: the first with old friends and family members in his mother's Bedford-Stuyvesant apartment that afternoon; the second inside his friend Wilson's plush Harlem brownstone and lasting well into the wee hours of the morning. Paul scheduled these two separate parties (replete with distinct guest lists) because, as he puts it, "it's really like I have two lives." Today, he is an up-and-coming professional who hobnobs with other six-figure-salaried black Americans from across the country and jet-sets to Caribbean Islands for occasional attempts at rest and relaxation. However, before his five-year sojourn at a southern university and his well-paying position in a small architectural firm, Paul was born in a lower-income housing project, attended city public schools through twelfth grade, and spent most of his teenage years with a single mother, older sister, and younger brother in a one-bedroom apartment not more than twenty minutes away from the block where he was born and raised.

Paul's life story could easily make sense as a rags-to-riches tale of upward social mobility, one of those tales that continue to keep Americans dreaming. But what stands out about Paul's story is its interesting concretization into two separate birthday fêtes—along with his specific explanations for that double bash: "It's like I have to be two different people," he offers, shaking his head as he briskly rakes five short, stubby fingers over and through his recently trimmed, tightly curled black hair. The fingers of his other hand steady a cigarette between his lips. We're sitting across a dining room table in his girlfriend Laura's place, a nicely furnished condo just outside of the city, one of those relatively close parts of New Jersey that just seem to get more and more expensive every housing market year. Paul sits up purposefully as he speaks, checking his watch periodically for Laura's imminent return from the store.

> **Paul:** So, it can just be easier to let my two parts stay apart, you know. I don't want people feeling uncomfortable around other people because they don't talk the same language, or do the same things or anything like that, so I'd just as soon keep them apart. That cuts down on the drama. It cuts down on the drama for everybody—especially myself. . . . I got my peers from work and that environment, business and professional, the movers and the shakers, and my peops from way back when I used to run around in the streets like a wild man. Now and then.

Paul's is an almost proverbial tale of the black middle class, ever positioned betwixt and between seemingly discrete and easily separable social worlds: the rich and the poor, the black and the white. Today many people are taking a renewed interest in the trials and tribulations of these relatively well-off African Americans.[1] Recent literature on the black middle class has been both quantitative and qualitative, charting the group's condition (in terms of occupation, residency, education, and income) vis-à-vis the white middle class, chronicling some of its members' often arduous journeys from socioeconomic slavery to freedom, and describing the cumulative impact that racism has had on even African Americans who have achieved a modicum of economic success.[2]

The black middle-class experience has received a great deal of critical attention lately. Traditionally, poor (and usually minority) communities have served as the most frequent and fecund sites for social scientific research—either because the poor are often powerless to protest or because policy makers and politicians have been preoccupied with explaining the causes of perpetual urban poverty. Anthropologists were once major players in the academic and popular discourse on the black underclass, introducing the notion of "culture" into the debates and helping to solidify (sometimes inadvertently) or challenge the "culture of poverty" and its assertion about poor people's pathological and ghetto-specific behaviors as ultimate explanation for what keeps them trapped below the poverty line.[3]

Even with the growing interest in black middle-class lives, a good deal of important information is sometimes left out of discussions about how class affects the daily experiences of black citizens. Many people give the same party line, arguing that with affirmative action and 1960s anti-discrimination legislation, the contemporary black middle class has exercised an unprecedented residential freedom, leaving the black poor behind to fend for themselves—with little or no social interaction between the two groups. Studies based on this premise downplay the black middle class's continued relationships with lower-classed African Americans, foregrounding their estrangement as one of the major reasons for many poor blacks' inability to escape poverty. I want to focus a bit on the intraracial, class-stratified contexts wherein African Americans are forced to negotiate class differences in their everyday lives.[4] Harlem residents not only have life histories that transcend the discrete categories of "black underclass" and "black middle-class," they not only live in close proximity to other residents with markedly different socioeconomic realities, they also have social interactions that cut across many class lines. In Paul's case, he recognizes and negotiates class-inflected differences within his familial and friendship networks by carving kith and kin into two discrete social groupings for his birthday celebration. He has one party for his professional friends, "the black movers and shakers . . . my peers," and another for his "peops,"[5] the people who know him from when he hung out in the street "like a wild man." Paul thus sets the parameters for an important distinction between "peers" and "peops" that meshes with and foregrounds class-based concerns. Peers and peops stand in as proxies for different members of his multiclassed world:

> **Paul:** I mean, I don't know how different they are. Just makes me feel more comfortable. Because people have very, very different kinds of lives. So they won't like the same things, talk about the same kind of things, even talk the same way, and it just, I don't know, we'll see. But people like different things. Some have Masters degrees and these kinds of things. Big deal jobs. My mom hasn't been to college. Most of my family hasn't been. This is the truth.

Of course, Paul's dualistic approach to class differences among the people he knows is hardly the only way to go about dealing with disparities in education, occupation, interests and lifestyle, tastes, speech patterns, behavior, and social experiences. These are all areas that Paul slices in half and connects to the "very, very different" attendees of his two parties. These people are almost all African American; race doesn't distinguish the groups, but class-inflected differences most certainly do. Paul invokes these class-marked differences to justify the need for two separate social gatherings in celebration of his one birthday.[6]

Chapter 2 offered up slices of the actual life histories and socio-economic trajectories of several African Americans in Harlem—histories that, I argue, transcend crudely wrought class categories. These are folks who live, work, and play next to differently classed neighbors. These kinds of class-varied *intra*neighborhood demographics are often disregarded for a twofold geographical framework of underclass prisoners and middle-class expatriates. Recent social science research shows that differently classed African Americans are more likely than their white counterparts to share the same general areas.[7] However, as real as this spatial contiguity may be, it says little about the actual nature of the social exchanges people have across class lines. In this chapter, I examine a few of the actual relationships that several Harlem residents have with friends, family members, and acquaintances from different socioeconomic positions, residents forced to deal with various classes of African Americans every single day of their lives.

"The Peops" versus "the Peers"

Many of the folks who attended Paul's two get-togethers didn't even live in Harlem. The second party's attendees, "the peers," were from places like Greenwich Village, different parts of New Jersey and even California—a friend in town for the weekend. Most of the people in his first party, "the peops," lived in Brooklyn—where many of them have always lived. They grew up with Paul—a few (like his Uncle Ronny and Cousin Dee) in the same low-income housing complex that was his social world for a good portion of his life. The rest of the peops at the first party either knew Paul's family very well or were his extended family: Aunt Leslie from Brownsville, cousins from different parts of Brooklyn and the Bronx, and, especially, his sixty-two-year-old mother, sitting like a proud matriarch on her living room sofa. Some of Paul's "running buddies" from "back then" attended as well. Jimmy, thirty-three, is living in the same apartment he lived in when they were kids. Still with his mother, Jimmy's been unemployed for the past two years. Another old friend, Tim, also in his early thirties, talks longingly about wanting to be a firefighter, but he's currently selling "warm" electronics on the street and off the books. Devon, late thirties, was like a mentor to Paul and his other buddies when they were younger; now he's a bus driver for the city and doing "pretty damn well," in Paul's estimation, especially relative to what some of the people from their old neighborhood are doing for a living. Tim, Jimmy, Paul, and Devon don't get together often these days, at least not as much as they claim they'd like to, but whenever they do, as at his early birthday party, they still talk as if they "never missed a day," with a familiarity that belies their brief and infrequent encounters. During the peops party, the guys ended up in a kind of ad hoc rap session in the back bedroom over a foldout table and a game of cards:

> **Jimmy:** There ain't no way we could ever, I don't think, not be tight. That just ain't possible to me. It—
>
> **Paul [interrupting]:** We are brothers, we *are* brothers, we are family, you don't speak, you do speak, but you always thinking about family, and they know you thinking about them. You don't have to see each other every day or nothing like that to know that.
>
> **Jimmy:** That's what I'm trying to say.
>
> **Devon:** Man, but it ain't like old times. I mean, we used to run tight. All day and night like that.
>
> **Jimmy:** True. True. True.
>
> **Paul:** Brother's gotta work and get that paper together.
>
> **Jimmy:** Make it happen.
>
> **Devon:** You gotta grow up and do your thing, no doubt, I just know we used to roll hard.

Curlicues of smoke filled the room as the men enjoyed one another's company and memories. They all talked about how close they felt to one another, but with a slight tinge of loss since their friendship's childhood dynamics (which, they claim, were more "tight" than they are now) have changed, as if the bonds that once bound them together have loosened just a bit—in ways that can't easily or fully be restored.

Paul's mother lives by herself most of the time, even though relatives from out of town, or just crashing overnight from other boroughs, often stay in this second room, where Paul, Devon, Jimmy, and Tim played cards. The hallway and living room areas, where most of the attendees mingled, glittered with party decorations taped up to the ceiling, cursive "happy birthdays" accordioned across the walls. The lights were dim; the place was dark. A record player pumped out mostly old 1960s Motown tunes and 1980s soul music. The younger kids danced enthusiastically but eventually managed to get a tape from the rap group De La Soul into a cassette deck over quite a few adult objections. Paul surveyed his well-wishers and shouted to me over a hip-hop tune's extra-heavy bass line: "I could go broke tomorrow, and they would still be there for me. They would still love me. They would still say 'that is Paul.' All the other stuff is extra."

Although three people who were at the first party also attended the second one (Paul's girlfriend, his uncle, and me), most of his family only took part in the first. When Paul got himself ready to leave for his second engagement, everyone simply kissed him, congratulated him, and offered him their best wishes. Some didn't even know that he had another party brewing for later on. Paul's aunt Mary, an elementary school cook or custodian ("or both"—Paul's not sure), offered this response to my passing query about the other party: "Paul is a grown man. He don't have time to just be hanging with us all day. He got his own life and his own business. I'm just glad I get a chance to see him. I'm too proud." Paul's mother smilingly puts that second party in perspective: "This is where his family is. He'll tell you that. He'll tell you that himself. If you ask him, he'll tell you that."

Paul's girlfriend Laura, his uncle Rudy, and I prepared ourselves to leave with him, informal escorts to the next shindig. In fact, Paul almost didn't tell me about this early "peops" gathering and instead had me earmarked for only the "peers" event that evening. "I just didn't think to tell you about it," he explained about my early peer-placement. Paul assured me that he thought it was a good idea that I had come along to the peops party after all: "I guess I thought, I don't know what I thought, but then I said, this might be interesting for you to see my family since you have never really seen them that much. You don't really know that part of my life."

Paul conceptualizes some of the difference between the two parties in terms of business relationships versus nonbusiness relationships, a line that is not easily crossed. He thinks Laura makes the move better than most:

> **Paul:** The second one [party] we were gonna talk business, talking about making money, getting things done. It was more business. I knew we would have a good time, don't get me wrong, but we are going to be making moves as well. Wil[son] had made sure some really interesting people were gonna come. That is why Laura is so bad. That is what is so cool about her. She can roll anywhere. We can be at a hip-hop concert, at a, a play, at a business meeting, what have you, and she is perfect in all those places. That's the kind of woman you need. Someone who is just comfortable in all kinds of circles and arenas. She does that better than me.

Laura is able to bridge the peers-peops, business-nonbusiness divide rather skillfully, a talent Paul admittedly finds essential.

By the time we left the first party, the place looked well spent. It had started slowly that afternoon at about 3:00 and lasted until 9:00—at which point Paul, Laura, and I traveled to Paul's house so that he could change clothes before we took off for round two. Rudy caught up with us there. Wilson's place was larger and several folks milled about on both floors. A soft and mellow instrumental jazz tune massaged our eardrums. Wilson, the official host, had only invited the black professionals with whom he and Paul often hang out, imposing their own brand of self-selected, self-enforced two-worldliness on Paul's social universe, a two-worldliness analogous to many social scientists' understandings of black America as bifurcated into two estranged and mutually isolated halves. However, this bifurcation isn't a function of Paul's having no access to poorer, less successful blacks. It is contingent on the fact that he does have such contact, and unavoidably so. Despite his big-digit salary and his postbaccalaureate success, Paul still has relationships with differently classed African Americans that he must think about and negotiate. That summer, those interactions had the seemingly trivial effect of forcing him to throw two separate parties for at least two "very, very different" parts of his social network. Other Harlemites' social networks show some of the same socioeconomic variety that Paul's does. I want to look at a few of these class-varied relationships to see how people describe them. Where and when were they formed? Do they create particular problems for social navigation? What do they mean to and for the people involved?

No Friends

Some of the class-stratified relationships that I found in Harlem cut across friendships, others through family ties. Some people are able to negotiate class differences while maintaining the vibrancy of the relationships in question; other people recognize class differences as an insurmountable chasm across which meaningful and substantive relationships have difficulty thriving. Sometimes, when I tried to get at the issue of friendship networks head-on, specifically querying Harlemites about their friends, many adamantly maintained that they did not have any friendships with differently classed people at all. It seemed evident, however, that some of these folks did have powerfully class-stratified social relationships—even if they were not willing to call them friendships during formal, tape-recorded interviews. Zelda was one of the first people to exemplify this very split in conspicuous ways:

> **John:** Do you know any people who are really doing well?
>
> **Zelda:** You mean like money and stuff?
>
> **John:** Yeah, or whatever you think doing well means.
>
> **Zelda:** I know people that are happy. Not making a lot of money, maybe, but they happy. That are doing good. I think there is a lady down the hall who works for the Board of Ed. I don't really know her. We ain't really, like, close. We speak from time to time, but I don't really know her. I try to stay out of people's business. . . . I figure, I don't need that aggravation.

Several months later, I first met Kate, one of Zelda's co-workers. The two hang out and "go clubbing" periodically, about "once every couple weeks or so." Kate has both a B.A. and an M.A., and she works higher up the occupational food chain at the center where Zelda works. "She's up there with the bigwigs," Zelda offers. The two women get together fairly often outside of work and have very different socioeconomic realities, but Zelda didn't initially point to Kate as an example of a friend of with a markedly different socioeconomic reality—or even as a friend at all—in some of our conversations. Likewise, Janet doesn't seem to create space for class-varied friendships:

> **Janet:** I think that I have the same friends now I've had all my life. None of them live in Harlem because I don't know many people in Harlem. Not that I couldn't have friends, but now I have acquaintances. The guys who run the store on the corner. The people who I see around the block, most of the people. But most of the people here are not my friends. I'm pretty introverted. I keep to myself. I'm not a big, "hi, hi, let's hang out" person. Especially not with somebody who might not be positive or productive, that kind of thing. Just wants to act like they are fools and want you to prove you can be a fool too. Who needs that? I got my own drama, why would I need yours?

Janet's notion of "positive" people who are "about something" serves as a kind of substitute phrasing for notions of class-related success. She's quick to admit that she is "not from the street" and doesn't want to have to pretend that she is in order for people to like her or want to be around her. Janet also claims that she doesn't really know that many people in her neighborhood. Janet's real friendship network has not changed much since she moved uptown, at least not enough to include many members from her Harlem neighborhood.

Dexter prides himself on being able to talk to anybody, but even he can make a case for his substantial relationships being class homogenous:

> **Dexter:** It's hectic, son. We all just wanna make it, you know what I'm saying. Living. Just living. I know people who are living what I'm living. Trying to get that paper. Paying rent and trying to keep it moving. I don't run in million dollar circles like that. Not everybody is like you, bruh.

Dexter jokes, but he is also serious (as were Zelda and Janet) when he maintains that he doesn't really have friends of different class positions. Even Paul (a person whose varied social networks I know first-hand), who talked specifically about class stratification within his social networks during subsequent discussions around the time of his two birthday parties, made a case, during one of our more formal interview sessions early in my fieldwork, for the fact that he only had friendships with people in the same socioeconomic position he occupies:

> **John:** Tell me more about your friends. Who are they, and what do they do?
>
> **Paul:** I hang out with people at work. People at the gym where I work out. People who do what I do or go places where I go, and they are mostly pretty well-off, I guess. We can relate to each other.
>
> **John:** Why do you think that is? That you hang out with people from work?
>
> **Paul:** We relate. You share things with people that have experienced some of the same things. You know what I'm talking about? That is important. You won't agree on everything, but you have things in common.
>
> **John:** Things like what?
>
> **Paul:** The job for one. Things you like to do. They'll be people you went to school with. You have those things in common. Or you just happen to do the same work.

The first time I ever met Paul face to face, I conducted the interview from which the above is excerpted. I can almost remember him saying the words. They seemed clear, precise, measured, and sensible. However, half a year later, after the birthday parties, after going back through some of this material, it stood out as problematic. Paul did have friends that he called "friends" who were not colleagues from the job, who did not share the same occupation, and who weren't even working full-time. I was able to revisit these earlier responses after the birthday parties had come and gone, asking him again about the class stratification he did not mention earlier:

> **John:** What about your boys, the ones from the party? Jimmy and those guys.
>
> **Paul:** Dev and Jimmy and those guys. I guess that is true. It's definitely true. Yeah, but I don't see them that often. I'm usually busy working.
>
> **John:** How often do you see them?
>
> **Paul:** Maybe once a month, but they are definitely my boys. I can't forget them.

There was a kind of pattern with respect to class and friendship networks among many of the Harlem folks with whom I spoke. Like Paul and Zelda, several other Harlemites at different points in time tended to dismiss or "forget" their contacts with people from different rungs of the socioeconomic ladder. Many people found it easy to minimize all nonfamilial relationships, often going so far as to say that they have no close friendships whatsoever—not with anybody, regardless of class differences or similarities; that it is too "dangerous" and leads to "bullshit" or "drama." Many people claimed that they choose to keep to themselves instead:

> **Dexter:** I don't have no friends. I know people. But all motherfuckers is triflin'. I've seen it. It's real out here. You know what I'm saying. I mean I know heads. I know heads, no doubt. And they know me. And we may talk or give each other a pound or hang for a minute, but you can't be thinking that means it's all good. That ain't what it means. Not at all.

Brandi, too, doesn't have real friends. "I'm not interested in that," she offers. "People try to use you. They try to use you like that. Then you get thrown into bullshit for some 'friend,' for 'that's my friend.'"

Brandi, Dexter, and others reiterate time and again that they don't necessarily have friends or the time to actively cultivate friendships with anyone—let alone with people of different classes. This is an interesting theme that comes out of many of my interviews and discussions with Harlemites. Folks are sometimes quick to argue that they don't have any friends at all. They don't know people of different classes very intimately and don't really have any relationships outside of their familial circles that they would characterize as particularly close. But is that the end of the story? As in Paul's case, many of my informants do have nonfamilial interactions with individuals that look and sound like friendships even though they may be hesitant in applying the term. Zelda, for example, is quick to say that she, too, is a loner:

> **Zelda:** I have always been the one who stayed to herself. Always. That's what I did. I still do. I just don't feel like I got to be up under somebody to be happy. I don't need that. I can have fun home. If I go out, to the movies or something, I'll take myself. That is fine. I like that. It's less problems.

Zelda's statement that friendships lead to "problems" (reminiscent of Janet's earlier equation of friendships with "drama" and Brandi's argument that friendships throw one into "bullshit" situations) would imply that she too has no friends, that she even avoids friendships. Still, Zelda has an active social life, going out every few weekends with several women from her job. "We usually, when we go out, it's like party, have a few drinks, wink at some cuties and then go home." And a couple of ladies in her "regular posse" are doing really well in terms of most socioeconomic indicators; a few are even "bigwigs" like Kate, that fairly high-level supervisor at the center. Kate hangs with Zelda all the time at work and work-related recreational activities. "We are like just running around. She is mad cool, too. And she has juice, so people always want to be kissing her ass. I don't kiss her ass, though. She's cool, but I'm not trying to kiss her ass for it."

Even if he doesn't consider them his "friends," Dexter knows just about everybody he passes on the street. The kids, the cops, the local shop owners—many even call out to him by name. But they aren't friends, he says, they are just "people you know." According to Cynthia, thirty-two, a college graduate and office manager at a Harlem-based educational institution, a woman named Karen "used to be" a friend back when they were in high school but now is "not really" a friend. When I first met Karen, wiry and tall, she was hanging out on the corner of 133rd Street and Seventh Avenue. It was early in the afternoon, and she had on dark and dirty clothes. I had stopped there to meet Cynthia, who was connecting up with me for a visit to the Studio Museum of Harlem. Cynthia is a bit of a fledgling artist, and I figured it would be nice for her to see the exhibit, particularly since she didn't get a chance to get out to museums very much. Karen spotted Cynthia as soon as we passed by and immediately smiled.

The two women exchanged pleasantries: what was going on with families; who had seen whom; details about Cynthia's Aunt Rita moving to Atlanta with some doctor she recently married. After about three minutes, Cynthia and I took our leave of Karen and headed down the block toward 125th Street. As we walked, Cynthia and I discussed Karen a bit. Cynthia is particularly clean-cut, well-groomed, and professional-looking if one's standards are creased pant suits and beauty salon hair. And Cynthia's well-groomed look made Karen's disheveled appearance that much more noticeable. In spite of their obvious history (a history I, as yet, knew nothing about, but could sense even from their brief conversation in the street that day), Cynthia seemed a bit cold and aloof toward Karen—even a bit rude, which wasn't like her at all. I'm not sure if Karen recognized it, but I most certainly thought that I did. Cynthia was cordial and polite enough, I guess, but she kept Karen at something of a distance—possibly because she was a bit anxious about being fifteen minutes late already. Even with Cynthia's purposeful social distance vis-à-vis Karen, I wanted to think that I could still glimpse, hidden beneath all of that nonchalance and indifference, a closeness and affection that Cynthia held for this woman who looked old enough to be Cynthia's mother:

> **Cynthia:** She's my age. Drugs and stuff done that to her. Because she is not that old. I know she looks it though.
>
> **John:** That's awful.
>
> **Cynthia:** Oh yeah. She and I used to be girls. We still cool, but I mean we used to hang hard. We were always together. She got pregnant and got hooked on smoke. . . . She is still my girl, I guess, we do go back, but she's on some other tip now. Off the hook, you know. She's done some stupid shit too, and all that is, she needs to try to get help.
>
> **John:** Does she work?
>
> **Cynthia:** No. On the street. Selling her body for a smoke. And I am like, girl, are you crazy. Her apartment is in a shambles. She has a pretty baby, Shannon. I feel so bad for that baby sometimes. That's who I feel bad for. Sometimes I'll watch her [the baby] for a bit. . . . [S]ome people don't have money, but that is not the same thing as living in a pig pen. We never had money

when I was growing up, but we still had a nice home. Clean, you know. With nice stuff. Being broke ain't the same thing as being nasty and dirty.

Cynthia voices a popular perception about the difference between being a "deserving" poor person who still has American values and being one of those freeloading, lazy, shiftless, dirty, and pig-pen-dwelling poor people who are poor because they refuse to do anything positive with their lives. At the time, Cynthia had a full-time job and a well-kept apartment. Karen was on welfare and hadn't worked full-time in years. That was especially terrible, in Cynthia's opinion, because the two women started out on the same road. Karen just veered off track. Cynthia can begin to offer the beginnings of an argument about her difference from Karen as a function of the simple things her own mother did, such as keeping their apartment clean and neat when she was a child:

> **Cynthia:** Drugs will do that, I guess, but she was always not clean. And when you not clean and on drugs you just a different kind of nasty. She looked at least decent when me and you saw her. The last time I saw her before that, she was looking crazy. She just looked terrible. I mean, it makes me want to cry to think that I grew up with her. I know her family, her mom. We were all kinds of close. My mom wasn't very sociable, but she hung out with [Karen's mother]. Our parents did the same things. I can't believe it. I just thank God. I really thank God. A lot of people have fallen to the drugs and stuff. But God has been good. I just feel almost like it's my responsibility or something. I know she is like her own problem and all of that, but I just feel as though if I wasn't so busy, I would just be able to help her.

If Cynthia feels somewhat responsible for Karen because of their childhood history, Ms. Joseph feels just as responsible about Damien, her twenty-nine-year-old neighbor who is "like a nephew," someone she first got to know only a few years ago. "The first time I met Damien," she recounts, "he was the meanest looking thing. Always frowning. And one day I was just walking, and I just asked him 'what are you frowning for, you are so handsome, why you so mad and mean?' And he smiled the prettiest smile after that. And I told him that I don't ever want to see him frowning and looking mean with that smile. . . . And every time I see him, he's smiling now."

Ms. Joseph's relationship with Damien hasn't had the long history that Karen and Cynthia share, but she admits that it is still her biggest joy to take the little she has, some money, a little food ("I love to cook"), and share it with him. Ms. Joseph and Damien speak all the time. Sometimes, he'll carry her groceries or push her shopping cart the two blocks to her home. And they often use those times to talk:

> **Ms. Joseph:** He told me that he was in jail. . . . I know he's had it rough. That's how our black men get lost in the street. . . . You know, no father, not in school, all of those things. . . . He's never asked me for anything, but I know he is struggling. And I don't want him to start selling those drugs and whatnot, to start getting into all of that trouble. For all I know he could already be, but I just know that I want to help him out even with a little. Not a hand-out, but just a few dollars here and there. Just to say I hope you're doing okay. I guess I don't know what it's saying, but it makes me feel good to do it.
>
> **John:** Good in what way? Why do you feel good? [Pause] Like, what is so good?
>
> **Ms. Joseph:** I'm being helpful. That is important. I haven't met his mother. I don't know how close he is to his mother, but I do know he is kind. I could tell that from the beginning. You can look in his eyes and see he doesn't belong on the street like one of those hoodlums. . . . He went to church with me a couple of times, too. I liked that. It wasn't about what I had or what he didn't have. He just came with me to worship, and none of that other stuff ain't have nothing to do with it. That's a nice thing. . . .
>
> **John:** Do you know his family? Friends?
>
> **Ms. Joseph:** Mostly hoodlums, I'm sorry to say. I don't know his family. He's told me a little bit about them, but I don't think I want to say too much about that. He's had it tough. But he's a kind spirit. People see that as soon as they meet him.

Cynthia can see that she has a different lifestyle and class-based reality than Karen. And Ms. Joseph can see the same thing with respect to Damien, an ex-con who, though periodically unemployed and hanging out with "hoodlums," has still occasionally accepted Ms. Joseph's invitations to worship with her at her church. Both Cynthia and Ms. Joseph try to be helpful because, as Cynthia put it, she thinks that she should. It makes her feel good and allows her to thank God for her relative successes in life.

Zelda (who knows Ms. Joseph by sight) also doesn't have many friends that she'd label as such. She does see a guy named Jordan all the time around her block. He isn't a friend, but he's always making passes at her. Zelda is sure that he doesn't really want "anything to be serious even though he can say that." She has a baby, she isn't making a lot of money, and she is admittedly "not bringing all that much to the table" in terms of forming a long-term relationship. Jordan is a "big professional, a big-time social worker. You know, suit and tie. . . . He has a good job. He is that kind. Fly." Zelda feels that his flirting with her is either just being "nice" or "trying to get a piece," but it can't be anything more substantive because of the social distance (signified by dress and occupation) that she believes separates the two of them.

The first time I met Cynthia's high school friend Karen, Cynthia and I had just bumped into her on the street. The two women shared a very brief conversation—as if Cynthia was uncomfortable with the whole scenario, and as if Karen wanted to respect the fact that her high school "homegirl" was walking about town on a breezy morning with a black man she didn't know who was wearing a suit and tie. When I first asked Cynthia about her friend, she had very little to say, dismissing Karen as simply "off the hook" (someone who is crazy and beyond explanation), as someone she "used to know." We ran into Karen again on another day, this time on 125th Street. Cynthia seemed a bit more comfortable as they talked and laughed at length about that crazy boy who got their other high school friend, Liz, pregnant at fourteen—and about when and if Cynthia's Aunt Rita would ever move back to New York City. The conversation ended with Cynthia sliding Karen a few dollars and a hug. Once we are out of earshot, Cynthia, unsolicited, seemed to feel the need to justify her generosity.

"At first I wouldn't give her shit," she admitted, "'cause I knew what she was doing with it, but then I said you know what. I'm just gonna pray on it and ask God to step in and just do what I can."

When I accompanied Cynthia to Karen's apartment for the first time several weeks later, any reservations Cynthia held about their closeness seemed to dissolve in the warm heat of their laughter and stories. The two joked and reminisced with one another—and were even joined in their merriment later on by Liz, the woman who had grown up with them and gotten pregnant very young. I don't know what the three women talked about that night. I only walked Cynthia over to Karen's apartment, was introduced to Liz, chatted for a minute, and then left. In those few moments, I could see that these women shared a great deal and still, despite what I had interpreted as Cynthia's attempts at downplaying their relationship, gained tremendous amounts of pleasure and enjoyment from one another. A few days later, in another discussion I had with Cynthia about her relationship with Liz and Karen, the weight of the two other women's difficult lives almost brought her to tears:

> **Cynthia:** I don't know what happened. But it's fucked up. [Pause.] They used to be my girls. I mean that was it and a bag of chips. You don't know. I feel like now that is all fucked up. They are still cool, but they are so fucked up now with all of this shit. And not just the welfare. Shit happens like that sometimes, I guess. Fine. But they are like just not trying to get out of that, they are just like accepting it and getting deeper down the hole.

When Cynthia offers that Karen and Liz "used to be my girls," she's still placing the friendship in the distant past as opposed to the very real present of, say, that joy-filled get-together where the three of them were able to catch up with one another. Cynthia isn't sure where Liz is living these days, since Liz's mother threw her out about a year ago because of all "the stupid shit she pulled." Even given this ambivalence about her relationships with these women, Cynthia is just as quick to help them out as she is to downplay the importance of such assistance and to argue against the significance of the relationships in general:

> **John:** Are they good examples of the people you grew up with? I mean, are most of your friends in the same boat that those two are in?
>
> **Cynthia:** No. I don't have a lot of friends. They aren't really my friends, I mean, Liz used to be, and I'm not nasty to her, I feel sorry for her, but she isn't my friend. I can't do anything with her, unless I wanted to do something stupid.

One Sunday morning, I spied Cynthia and Karen through the window of a local eatery. Karen was finishing off a breakfast that Cynthia had paid for. It was only the fourth time Karen had seen me over a two-month period, but she treated me like an old friend. And I appreciated her warmth.

Weeks later, Cynthia again downplayed her relationship with Karen, describing buying Karen a meal on Sunday morning as "nothing really, I'm just like, I got some time, she is, she needs food in her belly, what? I can do that." However, Cynthia did admit that she wanted to try making their weekend breakfasts a more regular thing. She thinks that's the least she can do, especially since Karen "used to be" such a good friend.

Playing Basketball

Paul and Tim (one of Paul's "peops" from that first birthday party) are basketball buddies. They meet up at least every few weekends or so during the summer and fall months to play a little ball, usually back in the neighborhood where they grew up, and where Tim lives to this day. It's a very self-conscious thing for Paul. "I know I'm not rich," he said, swerving down Kings Highway toward the above-ground subway's rusting trestlework, "but I do see that Tim is, like, really getting his ass busted. I don't want to roll out on him just 'cause he doesn't have it all straight and narrow." Tim, about three inches taller and twenty pounds heavier than Paul, lives frugally with the mother of his third child. According to Paul, he's unemployed and "trying hard to be lazy."

Once we got to the concrete courts, it became as clear as that morning's bright sky how many steps I've lost since my days as one of the first seventh graders able to graze the metal rim on the lowest of eight basketball hoops in our neighborhood playground. On this day, Paul and Tim shared smiles and not-so-furtive chuckles at my expense as the recent years of basketball inactivity made me a decided nonfactor during our morning's basketball game. I very quickly figured out that I should step aside and stop embarrassing myself for no good reason. Leaning breathlessly against the wire-meshed backstop beneath the backboard, I watched the two men attack one another with drives and jump shots at the netless basket. Every shot was contested, every point celebrated. They played hard for two vigorous games of 21; both times Tim clawed out a hard-fought victory by only a couple of points. Eventually, two more players just beginning to hold on to their early twenties entered the basketball court and challenged Tim and Paul to a two-on-two match. They accepted, teaming up valiantly in what was ultimately a losing effort against younger and more agile foes.

After dropping Tim off at his home, Paul explained how the two men use basketball as a means of keeping their relationship viable. After a game, they'll usually get something to eat and just talk a bit. "I'm not trying to change the man," Paul insisted, his car idling anxiously in front of my West Harlem building, "just play some ball with my boy." Paul feels that Tim's main problem is simple: he needs a job. If he got one and stuck with it, Paul believes that Tim would be on the right track. Paul even once tried using his peer contacts to get both Tim and Jimmy a job about a year earlier. He called in a favor, and "they fucked it up." After that fiasco, Paul believes that his buddies aren't really ready for his help.

Paul: I tried to push it on them, you know, big brother style. Let me hook you up, that kind of thing. They were just not there. They came late, got into shit that was just awful. If they tell me they are ready, if they come to me like, put me on, that is one thing. But that is not the same thing as trying to force someone who isn't ready. . . . But we'll call and touch base for a second or two. Play some ball sometimes over here by my place, 'cause he has no beef down here with anybody, sometimes Brooklyn, just working up a sweat.

Jordan, Zelda's "fly" social worker acquaintance, the one she thinks might possibly be just "trying to get a piece," often deals with decidedly poorer African Americans as a function of his occupation. Thus he has clear opinions about the nature of the differences that separate him from the poorer blacks in need of his professional assistance:

Jordan: I see poor black people, poor people, all the time. I mean I could tell you stories. People who are barely holding on, and I respect that. But sometimes, I get so frustrated, they get on the white man, but really they just aren't doing what they need to do. Not the white man. Some people are just not taking care of what they have to take care of. It's as simple as that.

Jordan's been called a "house nigger" and an "Uncle Tom" many times on the job, usually when he fails to fulfill the expectations of black people sitting on the other side of his desk. In that context, he's pretty leery of dealing with blacks as a function of the work he does. Sometimes, he even claims he wants to leave social work altogether, because "it's like they hate you for having what they don't have. Not everyone, but enough." Until he finally does decide to actually leave, though, and until he finds that new job, Jordan often tries to avoid any extended contact across class lines with the black people coming in for help:

Jordan: People will take advantage of you. And if you don't give them what they want they are quick to call you out your name and all that kind of shit. I just want to stay away from folks who aren't about anything. And focus on what I need for me and not what other people think of me and put on me that is really about them and not me.

Jordan's is another argument about class-based avoidance, similar in some ways to the kind that Paul used to explain why he needed to keep his two sets of guests separated. And it's also akin to Dexter's thoughts about certain kinds of people he tries to avoid every now and then. For instance, the last time Dexter had an encounter with the police, he got harassed just because he was hanging with one of his boys, Dupree, a twenty-two-year-old whom he describes as "knee-deep in all kinds of shit." The police questioned Dexter because he was standing on the corner and just talking with Dupree. Dexter admits to feeling a little on edge even when he's just walking alongside Dupree, because "when people want to settle they score they do that irregardless of who is there in the way. I don't want to catch a stray or something, some stupid-ass way to go out." Therefore, Dexter watches his back when he walks down the street. He calls himself paranoid, but that's because he knows a few people who are living a more underground lifestyle, "living kind of foul." Dexter has a job and responsibilities on the home front, and he doesn't want to get pulled down into any street confrontations. Consequently, he tries to be careful about when and where he hangs out with Dupree. In a similar move, Ms. Joseph won't let Damien's other friends in her house, "only him," she says. She doesn't feel as comfortable with them and what they might be up to. Even Paul will play basketball with Tim only in some parks—and only on certain days:

> **Paul:** We almost never do the weekend unless it's real, real early. I'm usually working and too many people are out. It's good that he isn't working because he can go whenever. I'll just drive by his place and pick him up. We'll go to a good park and throw down for a few hours and then drop him back. No fuss, no muss.

Paul believes that weekdays or "real, real early" on weekends are the safest times for the two of them to play. As for Cynthia, she can pay for Karen's meals every once in a while and give her some change, but she doesn't bandy the term *friend* about in describing that relationship, at least not very easily, distrusting the term's application to a relationship that links her to a woman she grew up with who is now not doing very well. Cynthia is clear about not wanting to spend too much of her time with Karen, at least not every day. She feels that that could put her in compromising and dangerous social settings. Just as Ms. Joseph won't trust Damien's friends and Paul won't trust the "fuss" and "muss" of overcrowded basketball courts on weekend afternoons, Cynthia doesn't trust more than infrequent contact with Karen—even though she dreams of much more frequent exchanges.

Cynthia, Ms. Joseph, and Paul are not the only individuals with agency and intentionality in these social relationships. Karen, Damien, and Tim also have thoughts about these same interactions. And sometimes it means that they jostle over how to define the most common aspects of the lives they share. For instance, Karen seems to talk about Cynthia as a friend with much less hesitation:

> **Karen:** That is my girl. I swear to God that is my girl. What to say? She is my ace. That is my girl. . . . We used to dress the same. I was always over her house. Every day. You kidding. I know all her business. Especially from when we was kids.

Karen is quick to call Cynthia a friend, even her "ace," and she is much more likely to place that friendship in the present tense than Cynthia sometimes is (even though Karen also calls upon a shared history to ground that current friendship). The two jostle over what definition seems most applicable for describing their lives together. They use the labels they affix to their relationship as a way of tugging on the interpersonal boundaries between them, tugging in different appellative directions. These kinds of moves are more than semantic double-talk; they provide people with the tools they use to identify their social worlds in personally acceptable ways, to assign people to very particular places within cultural landscapes designed with recourse to equations about the length of common histories and current degrees of recognizable commonality. Paul's basketball partner, Tim, corroborates Paul's assessment that the two have a long history, but he thinks that he and Paul have different things to take care of now, his little girl cuddled in his muscular arms:

> **Tim:** He got his thing. I got my thing. Trying to make my shit happen, too. We both got shit we doing. And he got my back from day one. You know what I'm saying. From like this big. From when we was here. [Tim places his right hand two feet from the tiled floor, palms down.] Nobody could say we ain't been doing this thing from day one.

Tim obviously thinks that the two men's common history is vitally important. It is a history that no one can take away from them, that no one can say they don't share. It is a history that they hope can give them the means to at least partially cross the class lines that might divide them.[8]

Family Ties

If interclass "friendships" are often difficult to imagine and sustain, how much more so are familial ties? In many ways, this is where

class-isolationist models of black America are least helpful for understanding the ways in which race and class inform the lives of black folks
today. Paul set up two class-distinct parties, at least in part as a response
to the familial ties he negotiates with relatives who are obviously near
and dear to his heart, even if they are not among the "movers and shakers" invited to his second birthday gig. It is important to notice the class
differences that separate branches of family trees, affecting the qualities
and contours of familial relationships.[9]

One of the most obvious ways in which class carves up families is
intergenerationally, as is true in Paul's case. Welfare kids turned first-
generation college graduates and middle-class professionals bespeak the
quickly formed and often major social distances that can strain some of
the interactions between parents and their children. Paul grew up as a
member of the working poor. Most of his family still is. One cousin was
killed five years ago in an altercation not too far from Paul's old neighborhood. Another cousin hasn't held down a job in more than two years.
An uncle who never graduated from high school has been in prison for
the past six years. He tries to visit him but can't bring himself to do it
all that often. It's a lot different from a few mornings of pickup basketball games on half-empty concrete courts, games where one can leave
the class-inflected baggage of a demanding social milieu just out of
bounds beyond the metal mesh fence, slashing and driving to the
basketball hoop in momentary indifference to the many chasms that
separate his life trajectory and future from his family members'. Paul
takes note of the fact that even his own mother, whom he loves dearly,
has a markedly different set of class realities than he does, a difference
that often translates into Paul having to sacrifice some of his personal
needs whenever he's around her.

> **Paul:** I think I'm just sensitive. I don't think I was always like
> that, but now I'm just out of my mind trying to make other peo-
> ple feel comfortable. You have to make yourself happy first, and
> you can't be not happy thinking that you gotta do this and
> that. And then it's like, where are my needs, what I need. . . . I
> love my family. That isn't the thing. But sometimes I feel like
> we can only talk about the same two or three things. And I have
> to hold some of myself up. I don't want to sound selfish, but
> sometimes I just don't want to do that. I do it, but I don't want
> to have to do that all the time. I just wouldn't feel comfortable
> to have to do that all the time, all day and night. It isn't a good
> feeling.

In a sense, it was Paul's desire to "feel comfortable" that made him have two parties in the first place—and that also makes Laura (someone who can be equally comfortable with peops or peers) his ideal mate. When he can't get his interests met in some of these familial contexts, Paul feels limited and stifled. He often finds the family he loves a group with which he can't really talk at all:

> **Paul:** They don't understand me. They don't know what I like. Things get on my nerves that they don't even think about.
>
> **John:** Like what?
>
> **Paul:** Like, I don't know, stupid things, ghetto things, you know what I mean. Sometimes people want to act like they are niggers because that's all they're used to.

Cynthia loves her older brother Kenneth, and he loves her right back, unequivocally, but the two almost never have any time to speak or see one another these days. Kenneth is usually busy "running all over the place trying to make money in computers," she explains as we wait for her brother's cab to drive up to her orange brick building. As we wait, she jokes about not even remembering what he looks like because she hasn't seen him in so long. I assure her that two months probably wouldn't have aged him beyond recognition. Kenneth, during our one and only (and very brief) interview, admits that sometimes when he's only in the city for a few days, he'll not even call his baby sister, because she'll want to see him, and he'd be too rushed and probably have to disappoint her. If Cynthia felt "responsible" to Karen (someone she only equivocally calls a "friend"), Kenneth feels even more accountable to his little sister.

> **Kenneth:** That is my heart. I love her more than anything. I want to help her, that's what I'm supposed to be doing. And she's not hurting all that bad. She's working. And I kind of trust that she's gonna be all right, but I know she can be doing better, much better, and I always tell her that. She can be where I am financially, if she just applied herself and focused.

Daniel lives fifteen minutes from his mother and brother, but there are times when he purposefully avoids them for long stretches. Getting together with them can sometimes make him depressed and discouraged, he says, especially his older brother Jay, who argues forcefully with Daniel about the merits of going to school, contending that it is little more than a waste of time and money—especially, Jay argues, since

Daniel will probably just end up getting a job that isn't going to pay him much more than what he earns without a degree. Daniel refuses to let Jay dissuade him from his educational goals. Instead of fighting with his brother about the usefulness of continued schooling, Daniel tries to hang around with people who are also in school—an indication, he maintains, of the fact that they actually want to make something out of their lives. He tries to purposefully steer clear of Jay sometimes, not wanting his brother's cynicism to deter him from achieving his own dreams:

> **Daniel:** As much as I love him [Jay], he ain't worth a shit. He's supposed to be my flesh and blood, you know. He know what I been through and all of that and he still talks that stupidness.
>
> **John:** Stupidness like what?
>
> **Daniel:** Just being negative about everything, about what I do. Not positive. About school. About me writing. That ain't right. You don't do that to people, not family. You can't. That's why his ass is always begging for shit. You can't get nothing if you're doing what he's doing.

Tears appear to well up in the corners of Daniel's eyes as he voices his frustration over Jay's lack of encouragement. I stop the tape and give him a second in the bathroom. I figure that he must be more tired than anything, especially since I stopped by after one of his more arduous days—a double shift on the job along with a two-hour class session. Daniel emerges from the bathroom and decides to cut our sit-down short; he is tired and wants to get some sleep. When we speak again at the end of that week, Daniel tells me that he called his brother Jay to "curse him out" the night of the interview. Two weeks later still, the two brothers shared laughs on a train ride to visit family members in Pennsylvania. The trip reminded Daniel that his brother Jay has good moments, too. Daniel just wishes there were more of them, especially as far as offering encouragement and positive feedback is concerned.

Some people can obviously negotiate class differences within familial networks more easily than can others. Daniel's difficulty with Jay sometimes overtaxes the ties that bind them. But that is not always the case. Carl is often happy to see his less financially successful brother, Lee, a thirty-three-year-old husband and custodial engineer at a small office building in Harlem. Carl even goes out of his way to do so, driving to Lee's home or office on a whim sometimes just to check in on him. Carl gives Lee money to "help keep him together" as Lee struggles to sustain his family of four on a job that pays hardly more than minimum wage. Carl also tries to give his brother emotional support. That, he says, is most important:

> **Carl:** I love that man. He's *my* role model. He's beautiful. The most kind and beautiful man you'll ever meet. Whatever he wants, whatever he needs, I'm there. No questions asked. And he knows that. He knows. He could have all my money. It's not about the money.

Trains, Telephones, and Job Applications

Dexter used to try being as supportive of his two closest cousins as he could be, but now he's actually avoiding them a bit. The last time he saw them, he almost "wrung their necks" after he helped get them jobs at a store where they allegedly stole something from the back office. Or at least that is what the white man who hired them claimed. And this very same person "had the nerve to act like he thought I was in on it, that I took some shit. So I just told him 'fuck you' and said I was never going to do some shit like that again for somebody." After that, one cousin went to jail (but is now out) and the other was wounded in a fight. "That's the kind of shit they like," Dexter offers in disgust, almost throwing his hands up in defeat over the entire thing.

The ability to be soiled and tainted by another person's misdeeds or underachievement is another vital factor affecting relationships across socioeconomic distances in black people's social networks. Stories like Dexter's, about extending a hand, getting burned, and then being unfairly implicated by that burning, offer important insights into how differently the calculus of black class stratification might work from class stratification within all-white social networks. In fact, some Harlemites speak very directly to that difference, arguing that a broad-bristled brush can unfairly paint over more successful blacks with its clumsily applied strokes:

> **Dexter:** The managers tried to help me, they said, and they got messed up. Look what they got in return and shit. And I was like, fuck them, but I was kind of feeling the same way about [his cousins]. That's if they did it. I know they could have, but they always said they didn't. But the thing is, they wouldn't have treated me the same way if I was a white man. I don't think so. If I had been a white man, and I brought some people in, it wouldn't have been the same thing. Because what they

basically was saying was, you're black, they're black, they stole, you must be stealing, too.

Toney, twenty-seven, is an aspiring writer who lives in West Harlem. He has just landed an agent and may be close to a book deal for his first novel. He keeps his fingers crossed. Toney tries to stay in touch with his buddies, especially Lloyd, a chronically unemployed twenty-six-year-old man who lives with his mother and younger sister in a two-bedroom East Harlem apartment. They were on AFDC, but changes in the way the system is restructured under Temporary Assistance to Needy Families (TANF) have serious implications for what their household will look like in a few years—and for what they will need to do to keep themselves afloat. Toney tries to see Lloyd as often as he can. "I can't turn my back on him," he says. "Now he has to save his own self, you know, save himself, and get his life in order, but as rough as the brother is on the outside, he is all heart in here. He's just having a hard time." Toney doesn't go to Lloyd's house very much these days because he thinks it's "too depressing." He describes it as "dank" and "claustrophobic," and says he usually just tries to avoid all of that by calling Lloyd on the telephone instead of visiting.

Who speaks to whom on the phone (and about what) has important implications for how some individuals negotiate class differences in their social networks. Telephones may be a bit undertheorized in cultural anthropology as sites of moral suasion, value boosting and even class interaction.[10] Some of the people who don't like to visit use the telephone as a way to make contact without having to put tremendous amounts of time and energy into travel and face-to-face social niceties, especially when class differences also translate into a significant geographical distance:

> **Zelda:** I know this girl, Carmen, I haven't seen her in a while, like a year, but she is mad cool, and she's off in California and she calls like every couple of months. She's an actress. Not rich, but I seen her on commercials. Maybe she's rich. I don't know. Like a computer commercial or something she was on. She comes in New York and sometimes we hook up, but she's always busy doing her thing. So we don't see each other a lot.

As Zelda argues in the context of her relationship with this actress, sometimes the telephone can be an important conduit for keeping the lines of communication open between people who live very different lives and move in different socioeconomic circles. Paul called his mom during his second birthday party just to thank her again for the earlier one and to tell her how much he loved her and enjoyed seeing her that evening. Cynthia makes sure to call around asking for Karen whenever she hasn't seen her in a while. And she sometimes has to call quite a few different people, because Karen's phone is almost as often disconnected as not. When it is out of service, Cynthia will try to call Liz's mother, provided *her* phone is on, and ask her to walk across the street and tell Karen to call Cynthia back on a pay phone or something. Or she'll just ask if anyone's seen Karen recently, and if so, she'll inquire about how she seems to be doing. If none of that phone-calling works, Cynthia will head out looking for Karen herself.

Janet remembers her first four months in Harlem as a kind of culture shock. It was a far cry from Ohio. During that time, when Janet seriously considered leaving the city for good, she would use the telephone to call her slightly younger cousin, Shelly, in Cleveland. Shelly's life has been very different from Janet's on various levels. Although Janet has advanced degrees from top-tier institutions, Shelly doesn't have her GED and still she lives with her mother, Janet's aunt, in a small one-bedroom apartment in one of the rougher parts of town. Janet believes that those long-distance phone calls to Shelly (all on Janet's dime) were extremely important factors in helping her adjust to Harlem when she first moved to New York:

> **Janet:** We would spend hours on the phone. She kept me alive. And I never saw her that entire time. Not once. She always wanted to come, and hopefully, one day, I'll maybe send her a ticket or help her buy a ticket, or something. But she knows. I would call her, four nights a week.
>
> **John:** What would you talk about?
>
> **Janet:** Everything. What's going on in Cleveland. She's never been to New York so I would tell her New Yorker stories and about Harlem. Literally anything. But it helped me talk my fear and the newness out of my system I think. And it worked, mostly.

These telephone calls to family and friends beyond the boundaries of Harlem are another explanation of ways in which Harlem becomes Harlemworld—as Harlemites describe their exploits in this famous neighborhood to other people all over the world.

Carl has his own story about when his brother Lee got his phone disconnected, and it was off for so long that Carl eventually decided to pay the bill himself. Lee says that his daughter had run up the phone bill on the Internet, and he wasn't able to find extra cash in his checks to get it turned back on, at least not quickly enough for Carl. "If I didn't pay it," Carl laughs, "I thought I would never hear from his ass again, so I just paid it."

Sometimes, the telecommunications revolution also provides ready strategies for not communicating, and class differences are often the excuse for such evasive telephone tactics. Paul, for one, has phone number juggling down to a science:

> **Paul:** Someone will have my pager number and not my home number. So they can't just reach me whenever they want and talk about bullshit, that's like for the people at work. My mom has everything, of course, but she knows not to give my cell and pager numbers out to Jimmy and them. That way I can make sure they don't page me whenever they want to.

Access to cell phones, answering machines, pagers, and inexpensive prepaid calling cards become ways to keep in touch along class-inflected routes. People can touch base with one another quickly and easily. However, it can also be the mechanism for stalling potential interactions indefinitely and segregating one's calling circles along various demographic lines, even and especially if the individuals involved don't live in the same community or hang out in the same daily haunts. Dexter still talks to some of his old school friends from the Brooklyn of his youth, but he can't always take the time to travel back and forth to do it:

> **Dexter:** I don't make it down there much, it's mad far on the train, but I speak to some heads. I'll give them a buzz or they give me a buzz and we catch up. You gotta keep in touch and get fueled.

Even leaving a short and sweet message on an answering machine is often the easiest and least time-consuming way to touch base across class lines without "drama," "bullshit," or any of the other potential problems that come along with social interactions of all sorts. People care for one another's babies, pay one another's phone bills, encourage or discourage one another's dreams, play some physically grueling games of basketball, and call one another on the phone daily, often using these as techniques for navigating the choppy waters of class difference. The jury is still out on whether these relationships across class lines and phone lines can translate into better jobs, schooling, housing and other opportunities for the lower-classed members of the relationship.

"I can't save him," Toney laments about his friend Lloyd in Spanish Harlem. "He has to save himself. The worst thing I could do is give him a push for something, a job or something. . . . And I don't want to be preaching to him all the time. That wouldn't be fair, either. . . . I'm not going to judge him. I just want him to know that I am here if he wants to talk or something like that. He should just know that." This is almost exactly what Paul says about assisting Tim, his basketball buddy. Instead of plying him with job announcements and the like, Paul just tries to beat him in a quick basketball game every once in a while, using that as an informal way to make sure that the two of them keep up with one another.

Zelda's present job came from a recommendation she got from "this woman with some clout who put a word in" at the drug counseling clinic. Zelda was riding on the subway with one of the administrators at her drug treatment program, and the two struck up a brief conversation. Zelda thinks the woman must have liked what she heard, because the next week they called her into the main office and offered her a job there. Another Harlemite, Vanessa, actually landed a job with the help of her anthropology friend, me. My landlord trusted me as a reference and hired her almost on the spot to work as an administrative assistant for his real estate business. It worked out for a bit, but she quit after schedule conflicts with school and other responsibilities made the job's hours infeasible. When Dexter was looking to change jobs, I tried to be at the front line of his search, also. He appreciated my help but claimed that potential occupational benefits are not the only things he can take away from our relationship. "Just seeing you," he maintains, "is like an inspiration. I feel like I can be where you are." Here, Dexter voices a kind of role-model notion of what is most important to him about class-stratified social relationships. It's not just that they can help one parlay an interest into an occupation, but also that they can let one know where else one could be located on the social ladder—and an example of just what that position might look and feel like. Most important, these differently negotiated relationships exemplify the continued meaningfulness that social stratification has for the everyday lives of black Americans after civil rights reforms.

Fleeting Moments in the Public Sphere

Many Harlemites recognize the significance of class-stratified interactions not only within familial and friendship-based networks but also in less substantial, more utilitarian interpersonal relationships in quickly passing social instants. For example, just going to the welfare office is a seriously class-stratified moment that people often think about and specifically theorize. Karen, for one, has many long stories about why she prefers interacting with white social workers in social service agencies than black ones:

> **Karen:** I hate, hate, hate them over there in social services. They are nasty and make you feel that way, like pieces of garbage. Black people keeping black people down. They the worst, much worse than the whites. Much worse. Trying to mess people up with that, their own kind, their own people. It's a shame.

Liz also singles out black social service providers to level a cross-class critique that is both strong and pointed, speaking to the power issues implicit in those specific moments of interaction:

> **Liz:** You know, sometimes that is the worst thing of all. That is really the worst thing. Because your own people are the problem. Not the white ones; they aren't the ones. It's the blacks.

Bernice, thinking back to her pre-college days when she was still struggling on public assistance, would concur with the point that Liz and Karen both raise:

> **Bernice:** These black house niggers, I tell you. I've gone over there to the Department of Welfare on 125th. . . . I go in there and I deal with those people from one level to another and I hate to really say this, sometimes I get my needs handled by my own kind and they send me through the ringer. I deal with somebody that's Caucasian, that's part of the conspiracy, and I get what I need done. . . . I think some of them [black social service providers] be taking out stuff that happened at home or in their personal life out on the job, on the clients.

Brian, another black male social worker, a member of Jordan's network, has many African American clients around the city, and he offers the flipside to these arguments:

> **Brian:** They come at you as if to say, well, you are black, you can break the rules. Hook me up. We're like brothers. You can hook me up. And they are so disingenuous. They don't mean a word of that. They just think they can work on your sympathy strings. But I don't go for it. You build up a kind of immunity. . . . These are people who have been making excuses and getting

over all of their lives. And they are just trying it again. I don't
fall for it.

Social service providers often invest in their occupation as a kind of
calling. Jordan and Brian are no exceptions. But some of the luster of
their professional mission has faded with time. Cross-class frustrations
can make them question their job choice every now and then. Jordan
and Brian feel that their work does a lot of good for a lot of people in
the black community, and they offer that up as one of its benefits. However, they also feel that success sometimes occurs in spite of the attitudes
of many of their black clients.

Shopping is another area where issues concerning class can swirl and
simmer. Tim, Paul's basketball buddy, maintains that he hates it when
"a man in a suit and tie can come into a store and they [the people
behind the counter] try to act like my money ain't as good. He's black
just like me, no? And his money got the same picture mine got." The
local store is an oft-discussed locale for class-based intraracial conflicts.
The petite bourgeoisie are characterized as pushy elites whose merchandise is often considered overpriced. Some blacks also portray them as
decidedly disrespectful to black customers:

> **Zelda:** Some of these black business people are nasty. Like they
> doing you a favor. Or like you got nigga money and that ain't
> real money. I'll take my stuff to the Chinese just as fast. Not
> that they any better. At least it ain't your own doing it to you. I
> know we're supposed to keep it in the community, but some of
> them make you want to go outside.

Zelda invokes the inner city's proverbial outsider entrepreneur ("the
Chinese") to ground her response to black business owners' dismissal of
her purchasing power.[11] Dexter, playing the role of devil's advocate,
takes the opposite position, arguing that it is the black masses who abuse
black-owned businesses and business owners:

> **Dexter:** Some black people want to think they can do what they
> want when they walk into a black store. "Everything should be
> free, we all from Africa." They want to take advantage, like be-
> ing black means you want to be broke from not being a good
> businessman.

One black business owner in Harlem jokingly contends that she needs
to hire a white person to stand in front of her store just so black people
brainwashed from years and years of institutionalized racism will believe

that it really is a legitimate place of business. Without that, she claims, black shoppers would just continue to take their money to more recognizably Jewish and Asian establishments nearby.

Another area where people interact across what they consider to be important class-inflected intraracial lines is on the street itself, on city sidewalks.[12] Tim sees black people "with suits on" in the street, and "some days I just feel like I want to drop [punch] them." At other times, he says, "it's like I feel a little proud." Paul talks about walking past homeless people and feeling like they expect more from him just because he's black and wears expensive-looking business attire. Sometimes it makes him feel bad; sometimes it just makes him angry and frustrated. David, who used to be homeless himself, thinks that homeless people deserve to expect more from blacks than they do from whites. After all, he argues, "we know what it's like to be without."

Class-stratified relationships and interactions aren't reducible to the presence or absence of role models—or to the mere possibility of utilizing others' social networks and financial resources. The class differences that people see in their friendship circles, their family relationships, and even more ephemeral social settings (during a trip to the store or to a social service provider) craft complicated topographies of self that help define one's relation to the rest of the world. The people in Harlem are living and negotiating complicated, stratified worlds, and the choices they make in such contexts are contingent on complex rationales for interacting with or avoiding certain individuals based on what that sociality tells them about themselves and their place in the world.

The New York City Police Department is often invoked as a tentacle of a racialized governmental bureaucracy pitted against the black community time and time again—through the confrontational handling of things like the Million Youth March, through the remorseless shooting of unarmed black males, through the Mollen commission scandal, which exposed corrupt Brooklyn cops, and through the highly publicized racial profiling cases that Harlem's community leaders and black law enforcement agents have marched to publicize. Black officers themselves become a particularly interesting point of discussion in the context of cross-class concerns within the black community:

> **Dexter:** I always stay away from any police shit, because the last time I tried to even just exercise my rights, they were like they were gonna lock me up and all of this kind of stuff.
>
> **John:** Black cops?

Dexter: Both. The black cops will do things to you only because they know you can't really do nothing back. They wouldn't do it to white people. They wouldn't do it to blacks who have money to sue they asses. But they love to flex their muscles on us and try to get their rocks off by making us feel like shit because we struggling, and they know that nobody gives a damn about what happens anyway.

Dexter sees different classes of blacks (those "who have money to sue they asses" and those who don't) getting very differential treatment from their race-mates in uniform. Bernice offers a strikingly similar class argument:

Bernice: I've had interactions [with black police officers] because I have a son who got into a little incident with those police, and the guy that interviews me and my son at the same time, he has dreads in his head and he's full of locks and all that—

John [interrupting]: The police officer?

Bernice: Yeah. Yeah, the police officer. And I'm looking for some understanding. Some humility. You know, let's work on this incident. Oh no, he went there. He went to the other level "and this is the bottom line" and "this is what has to be done" and we ran back and forth for over a year. And I guess they gotta do what they gotta do because they have to eat too. But see, somewhere along the line what I see as the problem is that black folks forget where they came from. You know what I mean? They get these different positions, and then they run up against somebody that's under them in the lower class or the underclass and they step on that individual. You know? And it's sad because you gotta go home and sleep with yourself after doing this to folks.

Comparing Bernice and Dexter's position to Carl's, one finds a decided contrast:

Carl: I've never really had a bad run-in with a black police officer. I just speak to them, and they listen. They can see I'm not trying to get over. I am not just running around in the street. Most people aren't, but I can articulate that in a way that they understand. "Okay, leave this guy alone," you know. . . . Not that it couldn't happen tomorrow, but it hasn't yet.

Black police officers are sometimes considered the most pernicious class-based race traitors around. Like the elitist black business owner who is said to disrespect black customers, the black police officer is sometimes characterized as being extra willing to carry out the racist will of the state. The hip-hop artist KRS-One pleads with them to put down their guns and stop shooting other black folks in his underground hit "Black Cop." And the filmmaker John Singleton immortalized the trope of the self-hating black officer in *Boyz 'n the Hood,* in which he depicts a black policeman who has so internalized his denial of black humanity that he can't even understand why the lead character finds his indifference to black life so problematic. However, there is something about Carl's ability to talk his way out of confrontations with black officers that seems to hint at the relevance of class-inflected behavioral differences (in terms of speech patterns, mannerisms, and so on) to concerns about the interactions between black police officers and black civilians—an important link to the next chapter's examination of how people think about class and its connections to everyday behaviors.

Conclusion

Many of the Harlem residents I met argued that they didn't have serious social contacts across class lines. Even when people may initially say otherwise, they sometimes do have such interactions. Class differences within one's social circle can mean you celebrate with two separate parties for two "very, very different" and seemingly separable parts of your social network. Or it can mean that you designate your everyday interactions with poorer African Americans as other than clear friendships—even when they might seem to have all the trappings thereof.

Some Harlemites have people they work with, as in Zelda's case, whom they know pretty well—people they hang out with at nightclubs but who never, say, invite them over to their suburban home in New Jersey. Other Harlemites seem to know that they have friends who could use their help but approach that fact very carefully: either because they don't want to offend by appearing superior (not wanting to "preach") or because they can't justify risking such assistance when the person isn't ready to receive it. If friendships are difficult to hold onto amid class differences, familial ties can be just as hard. Some people live fairly close to relatives of different classes or status positions and purposefully avoid them. Maybe the person who has achieved a bit of socioeconomic success doesn't want to feel the guilt of that success juxtaposed against other people's failure. Or maybe they feel a potential danger in mingling too closely with the disillusionment and cynicism that sometimes burdens the lives of the poor. On the other hand, some people who have "made it" try to stay around specifically and self-consciously to model behaviors for the less successful.

Class-stratified interactions don't necessarily have to be substantive to be important and formative. Sometimes a fleeting moment or a brief encounter with a stranger or a series of short interactions with acquaintances can have tremendous significance in terms of how people think about class. Even small and seemingly minor contact across class lines can have benefits. Cynthia, for instance, traces some of her present successes back to her next-door neighbor's uncle, Montgomery, whom she knew when the girls were not even teenagers. He only came over a few times a year, as she remembers it, but he wore fancy suits, had lots of money for candy, and always told Cynthia and her friend Robin that they could do anything they put their minds to, anything in the world they wanted to do:

> **Cynthia:** He's still around, retired I think. But he really made an impression on me. He lived far away, but every time he came, it was cool. He loved Robin so much, and he was just a good role model. And he was just nice.

Role models may be important, but that is not the only way class differences affect people's lives. In Zelda's case, interactions up the class ladder landed her a job as a drug counselor. And people can sometimes take advantage of occupational opportunities that their networks provide—if, as Paul put it, they are ready to benefit from a friend's ability to help. Even when people see a dichotomously classed world, they are not necessarily invoking that dichotomy to talk about class homogeneity in their social networks as much as to think about the different types of people with whom they do have contact. As important as these interactions are, their mere existence is hardly the end of the story. I'm also interested in whether interactions across class lines have serious implications for how people behave, for their actions and activities, for how they perform belonging and social solidarity.

Many African Americans have family members, friends, former friends, acquaintances, colleagues, bosses, social workers, and case managers who occupy various class positions. Often, the significance of these interactions is downplayed (by both the people themselves and the social scientists who analyze them), but they exist nonetheless. Class isolation is not the only possible narrative model for discussing how blacks of various socioeconomic positions experience their social worlds. Surely, it is a convincing enough argument to make if one wants to offer that isolation as an explanation for transgenerational poverty and inequality. However, if you look at the relationships people actually have (social workers dealing with recipients on the dole, parents interacting with full-grown children, doctors treating patients, "friends" helping or not helping each other), these relationships often push and pull at the boundaries of belonging in several different directions at once. Class-stratified interactions don't always translate into occupational opportunities for the poorer partners (it might only mean a free meal on an occasional Sunday or a ride to church where class "ain't got nothing to do with it"), but these exchanges are important nonetheless—if for no other reason than the fact that they don't let social scientists off the hook with easy explanatory models for perpetual poverty.

Social scientists offer truncated social networks and inadequate social skills as an important part of the explanation for perpetual poverty. Surely, social networks can translate into gainful employment and other opportunities more easily for the rich than the poor.[13] And maybe some people who have interactions across class lines are unwilling (as Paul, Dexter, and Toney are) to extend an extra hand once they've been burned after offering such hospitality in the past. My argument is not that class-stratified interactions always or necessarily lead to socioeconomic advancement, but only that the lack of such advancement is not reducible to the idea that there are no such networks at all. People often do have relationships across class lines—even when they might hastily offer that they do not or question the term used (friend, acquaintance, former friend) to define such persons. They often have relationships that reach up and down the class ladder. Sometimes such relationships land people jobs. Other times, as in Paul's case, they can mean little more than semiregular pick-up basketball games where the class-stratified social world is left out of bounds and out of play, if only for a few sweat-filled hours. Or, it might mean a free breakfast for one person and the sense, for the other, that one is "just doing the right thing" for someone who "used to be" a friend. Whatever the case, Harlemites are constantly dealing with the socioeconomic stratification inherent in their social networks—even if that just means attempting to impose class isolation and trying, with different degrees of success, to keep purportedly "very, very different worlds" apart.

CHAPTER 4

CLASS(ED) ACTS, OR CLASS IS
AS CLASS DOES

Hidden Injuries and Visible Actions

"All that it takes is hard work," Todd says emphatically, "and anyone who doesn't make it is just lazy. They have no one to blame but themselves." We sit across from one another at an old oak desk inside a tiny office at the university; a sun-shower noisily spills raindrops through the cracked frame of a rickety windowpane. Todd and I try to wait it out before heading up to his place thirteen blocks north. He spends a good portion of that period retrieving the tiny shreds of information he can still remember about a guy named Jeffrey who went to junior high and high school with him. Jeffrey lived in a tenement building cattycorner to Todd's when they were kids. Todd recently heard that Jeffrey practices "law or something" in Baltimore these days, and Todd uses the present professional success of his childhood friend as an example of what he means by the benefits of hard work. Easy and confident pronouncements like Todd's take on Jeffrey's professional achievements, and their implications for questions of meritocracy, often convince many social scientists that black inner-city residents share roughly the same cultural belief system as the American "mainstream," which I would not dispute. Todd's words are said with feeling. He believes them, but he also believes something else that is not completely compatible: namely, that the United States government is allowing companies, such as the one producing the fruit beverage Tropical Fantasy, to place dangerous chemicals in their products, chemicals specifically intended to sterilize black men.

Todd offers this conspiracy theory rather matter-of-factly on a warm spring morning as we wait for a traffic light to change on the corner of his block. At our backs, his tenement building shoots straight up into the patchy white sky. The traffic light changes and we head west, Todd toting poster-board-sized advertisements for a New York–based hip-hop artist. I escort him down the street as he pauses periodically to fasten these posters to and around anything he can find: street signs, parking meters, garbage cans, chain-link fences. He even joked about stapling a couple together and placing them around me like a papery overcoat. I could advertise the artist to an entirely different demographic over there at Columbia, he joked. As we walked, Todd continued to explain his racial sterilization theory, a theory he offers with the same level of certainty and intensity that accompanied the more mainstream ideas I had recorded weeks earlier in that Columbia office space. And he clearly holds on to both of these seemingly oppositional and conflicting convictions at one and the same time: that anyone can make it in America; race can't hold you back. But there is also a government-sponsored conspiracy of the gravest proportions that ultimately seeks to commit genocide against blacks.[1]

The issue is further complicated by Todd's present social circumstances: he's a twenty-four-year-old unemployed high school dropout who lives on the kindness and largesse of his mother, a short and slender woman who herself fights to stay afloat and above the poverty line. One might wonder how Todd accounts for the setbacks and stumbling blocks in his own life. Whom does he blame for his less-than-prosperous situation? Based on the arguments that he proffers about the accessibility of upward social mobility to anyone willing to do "hard work," he should hold himself responsible. And he does. But this self-condemnation is tempered by some of his more conspiratorial views, and both of these opinions, both sides of this Janus-faced ideational coin, are vitally important in Todd's assessment of his past experiences and future possibilities.

Todd is by no means the only person I met in Harlem who expressed such conspiratorial beliefs. Similar rumors make their way around many black communities about Church's Chicken, Old English malt liquor, and other items allegedly being sold in black neighborhoods, and black neighborhoods exclusively, because of their treacherously sterilizing ingredients.[2] These claims seem to problematize any overly simplistic conflation of African Americans' ideas and beliefs with those expressed by the "mainstream." Todd offers both a fairly standard view of American meritocracy and a hyperparanoid stance against it at one and the same time.

Several related issues are highlighted by Todd's seemingly inconsistent views about his own chances of success. For one, there is the age-old question of structure versus agency. That is, how much of an individual's social plight is a function of some overarching (in this case, conspiratorial) social structure that generates ultimately impotent individuals, and how much is the sole responsibility of a fully culpable human subject? This question has often led to critiques of supposedly bourgeois notions of subjectivity and intentionality, notions criticized for privileging a certain middle-class sensibility characterized by an easy, confident self-control and autonomy not afforded the socially marginalized.[3] Some critics see these kinds of structural arguments as excuses that allow individuals off the hook for their own careless and irresponsible behavior, which society, in the end, is forced to pay for.[4] If everything is structural, they ask, where is personal accountability? The agential side of this same equation is criticized for downplaying the structural and institutional strictures that always surround individuals' personal choices and potential alternatives.[5]

One of the key issues in this debate pivots on a concern for how we should interpret actions and their outcomes. How do we define success? How do we explain it? Can an individual be fully lauded for his or her wealth and financial achievement? Can he or she be unequivocally blamed for the lack thereof? What does success even mean in a context where structural variables differently and unjustly predetermine the confines within which social actors operate? What does success indicate about the persons who have achieved it, and what kinds of relationships exist between achievers and nonachievers? Answers to some of these questions are crystallized in very particular ways within African American communities.

Todd's thoughts emphasize one of the important fault lines fissuring black psyches all along the class ladder. His twofold argument about blacks' life chances (you can work hard and achieve anything your heart desires, but you can also be trapped within the boundaries of a conspiratorial antiblack racism that unfairly stifles blacks' true potentialities) is a kind of internalized structure versus agency debate, one that makes it difficult to adequately and unequivocally explain others' (under)-achievements—or one's own. One of the many manifestations of the difficulty of distinguishing the structural from the agential with respect to the plight of African Americans is predicated on the sensitivity people often show to the ways in which their relative successes or failures are interpreted by others through recourse to behavioral proxies for social position. Class differences become a major node of distinction and judgment because class is often read as other than exclusively a function of one's birth—especially in an America that has built its patriotic and nationalistic rhetoric on the dreamiest of beliefs in the possibility of un-fettered social advancement.[6]

I want to continue to look at what class differences tend to mean in African American communities and the kinds of significances that people wring out of these differences. In everyday public spaces, where pedestrians and other passersby do not necessarily have access to specific economic details about the income, educational background, and wealth of every single person they meet or pass on city sidewalks (and even when they do), behavioral markers become jumbled up with notions of class achievement in ways that bolster citizens' understandings of socioeconomic success and failure. The important outlines of class in the African American community (and in society more generally) are inextricably connected to contentious notions of practice and performance, to explanations of how people behave in the social world. Folk theories of class are figured out by examination and interpretation of what people do—and not strictly in economic terms, not simply as determined by what kinds of jobs they have or bank accounts they can draw from. How people behave interpersonally is an important indicator to many of the Harlemites I interviewed of their particular class placement. In this chapter I discuss some of these actions, which often are implicated in people's generally accepted and often commonsensical wisdom about socioeconomic difference, examining how these behaviors are granny knotted into perceptions about class distinctions and their most meaningful consequences. I'm interested in what people do with these class-linked behavioral arguments, as individuals and as an interpretive community within which individuals share many basic premises underpinning discussions about social markers. Far from being blind to class variation within black America, many of the folks I met in Harlem not only recognize the hard and soft facts of class difference, they also see them everywhere and in almost everything people do—a corrective to some popularized images of contemporary black America as blinded to other trajectories of difference by the ubiquity of essentialist racial thinking.[7]

Class Differences, Class Similarities

The last chapter teased out some of what's at stake in Paul's take on the two "very, very different" types of people composing his variegated social network. The disparity between these halves of his social circle causes Paul to enforce his own kind of class-based segregation. These are different types of people that he claims can't necessarily communicate with one another. They have a hard time carrying on meaningful conversations across socioeconomic distances. They don't have the same interests. They share few concerns around which mutually interesting discussions can take root. Paul isn't alone in this assessment. Cynthia also talks at length and often about a kind of communication barrier linked to class difference. She claims that class differences lead to conversational arenas rife with frustrating and upsetting miscues. For instance, Cynthia's uncle David, owner of his own suburban home and small business, is an example of someone she considers very materially successful, living a life very different from the one she lives on a daily basis. She also thinks that that very success makes him difficult to talk to and deal with, at least sometimes:

> **Cynthia:** [W]e are cool, you know, but then he'll act so stank. So stupid. And not what he says, it's not what he says, the things he says, as it is the way he says them. Like just because he has, I don't know, money and all that, and I'm not there, he can make me feel like I'm stupid. Like I'm a dummy. I just feel like saying "whatever," and telling him to kiss my ass sometimes. . . . He tries to pull that shit with me all the time.

As Cynthia sees it, "money and all that" ("all that" being, among other things, a college education, a successful stock portfolio, and sole ownership of his own twenty-employee business) causes her uncle to speak to her disparagingly, in ways that often compel her to close off her end of the communication process. She'd rather opt out than be made to feel stupid. Ironically, Karen, Cynthia's "used to be . . . friend," has similar critiques of Cynthia: "Sometimes she talks to me like I'm a child and stuff," Karen complained to me as we waited for our order to come up at a local dive on Amsterdam Avenue. "I just don't like that. I have my own baby. I'm not a baby so don't talk to me like I'm one. She think she bossy; she's not the boss of me. She just can't talk to people."

I never actually witnessed any very "bossy" words from Cynthia to Karen during any of the times I saw them together. That obviously doesn't mean that Karen was wrong or just hypersensitive. Along with being hesitant about describing their relationship as a friendship, Cynthia often told me that she didn't think Karen was responsible enough to adequately take care of Shannon, her baby. She feared that Karen might one day accidentally hurt Shannon and that Karen may even need to be put away somewhere so that she didn't harm her baby or herself. It's not inconceivable that some of Cynthia's less-than-flattering assessments of Karen's parental abilities could have flavored their conversations as recognizably infantilizing comments.

Zelda has a "rich" female "acquaintance" who, she claims, simply "tolerates" her because she isn't as financially well off. "The husband is nice," she admits, "but the wife is a bitch, like her nose in the air, stuck up now, like for her to say something to you is a big thing that takes all her energy away. All stuck up. He's cool, but he ain't normal for them, you know. Most blacks with [money] want to act like they better than you."

In traditional Marxism, the working class consists of people with similar interests who perform similar actions, eventually becoming collectively conscious of that univocal fact.[8] The class of capitalists against which they rally can be said to share actions as well—or, some would argue, inaction, insofar as they exploit others' labor in lieu of laboring themselves. In either sense, it is the similarity of social practices (particularly labor practices) by members of a discrete working class that is said to unite and define them, a class in itself with potential to organize for itself. Social classes are social classes only insofar as members share actions and interests in direct opposition to the interests and actions of other classes. For most conventional readings of Marx's brand of historical materialism, these two main classes with diametrically opposed interests and actions wage war until the workers inevitably lead a revolutionary movement against an economic system of class-based exploitation and create a classless society wherein everyone's actions (their work in relation to the production process) and interests are aligned, not alienated. However, according to many, America is a different kind of "classless society" in that Marx's model of working-class consciousness and revolutionary potentiality has proven to be wholly unresponsive to its soil.[9] There is, instead, a focus on small differences along a socioeconomic continuum of indefinite microdistinctions.

In some ways, the main differences between these takes on class in the United States can be schematized in terms of the discrepancy between objective and subjective notions of class. By *objective class* I mean to invoke the measurable criteria (income, education, occupation, residency, social networks, wealth, and so on) used to place people into distinct social categories based on these quantifiable trajectories of social difference. *Subjective class,* on the other hand, refers more to the kinds of ideas people have and hold about their own social positions, ideas that may not be as systematically arrived at or as exclusively tied to hard and fast economic charts, ideas that can even give substantial weight to noneconomic criteria of social worth. There are interesting ways in which objective and subjective notions of class can be combined to create a multi-faceted composite of someone's complete socioeconomic portrait. For example, the sociologist David Halle paints what is by now a well-known description of some New Jersey chemical plant workers who think of themselves as working-class on the job (because of the hard and manly labor they perform) but middle-class at home (because of the kinds of suburban lifestyles they lead).[10] In some sense, they are correct on both scores, and it is this mutable and fluid property of class and class-consciousness that makes discussions of socioeconomic differences within a racialized space like Harlemworld so rich an endeavor. People see class both objectively and subjectively. And even those objective markers of class must be carved up in arguably subjective—even arbitrary—ways.[11] One can't talk about any of these "objective" notions of class without thinking about their connections to more subjective determinations. People are carving their social worlds into clear relational classes at some points in time and more gradational social stepladders (based on both status and class, on both objective and subjective assessments of socioeconomic difference) at others. Moreover, these class distinctions are steadfastly connected to observable behavioral matrices that are used to index these kinds of social differences.

The *Poor* Black Middle Class

Traditionally, the black middle class has been held responsible for rallying the racial troops in defense of the black masses, for "uplifting the race."[12] Class-related differences have not always or necessarily translated into the strictest class-based consciousness on the part of wealthier African Americans. It has not always been undeniably clear that wealthier blacks have a different set of socioeconomic needs, desires, and goals than their lower-classed race-mates. The more operative question has usually been how best to perform the much more pressing task of racial uplift: either by teaching the masses to be self-sufficient manual workers (Booker T. Washington's Tuskegee Machine strategy), or, as W. E. B. Du Bois preferred, shepherding blacks into a cultivated appreciation of the finer arts and sciences, a higher order of knowledge that could finally prove their separation from the beasts of the field.[13]

Many relatively well-off middle-class blacks today still follow a kind of racial uplift credo. Class differences are often seen as less important than the racial ties that are said to bind all blacks together within the continuing strictures of white racism. There have always been successful

African Americans who distance themselves from the black masses.[14] But the most common paradigm of black upper-middle-class responses to the black masses has tended to fall into the uplift camp manifested in organizations such as the Niagara Movement and its offshoot, the NAACP—and culminating in the mass mobilization of a 1960s civil rights movement substantially spearheaded by black leaders with decidedly middle-class backgrounds and credentials. As some middle-class blacks argue, in a racist society there are commonalities of oppression that join the wealthiest and poorest of African Americans together in racial solidarity. The argument is that racism and racial prejudice are leveled at all blacks regardless of class position, and so rallying for the black masses has always meant rallying for all black people.[15] Historically, many middle-class blacks felt obliged to use their resources to help the black poor.[16] Today, some Harlemites still seem to hold onto these racial uplift sentiments, using them to clasp blacks together across class lines:

> **Janet:** I feel like I want to do what I can. I'm only one person, I mean, I can't help every black person or get everybody off welfare and drugs or whatever else, but I can do something for the people I know in my community. I can do that.

Carl speaks about responsibility in the same kinds of terms that Janet uses:

> **Carl:** It's like this; you have a responsibility. It's like in the kid's cartoons: Spiderman with his super powers. You're supposed to help people you can help. If not, it will come back at you. It will. You have something other people don't have and you have to make them better, help them out.

Janet and Carl voice a common cross-class contention that racial identity presupposes a certain "responsibility" to poorer blacks, even if you "can't help every black person or get everybody off welfare and drugs." You can at least do something and so you should. Even less well-to-do members of the black community feel obligated to help others further down the ladder. Cynthia is less socioeconomically successful (in terms of income, occupation, and education) than either Janet or Carl, but she can still look a few rungs below her and emphasize the importance of racial uplift. In this case, she refers to Karen:

> **Cynthia:** It don't mean nothing to me to make sure I check up, give a couple dollars if I have it. That's what we got to do. If we

don't do it, you know they [white people] won't. We gotta stop being selfish and look out for one another. If you are okay, you should try to make other people that way, I think.

Cynthia, Janet, and Carl (with his superhero's caveat about what "comes back" to those who don't give back) all feel that they have to reach down and help out a decidedly racialized "we" in need. As Dexter put it, "if I ever got on, I won't forget where I came from. You can't." And like Dexter, many try not to forget their humbler beginnings and upbringings. Paul can't forget his life in the projects before going to college and achieving a middle-class lifestyle. David tries to convince his buddy Harold to help drug addicts in their community because even though they are both drug-free and working now, they were once unemployed and homeless themselves—so they should never forget that; they should always help as many other people as they can. Whether it's because of the historical ties that link successful blacks to their less successful race-mates or because of supposed "deeper impulses" of race as the faintest hint of essentialist familiality, racial thinking can unite blacks who are otherwise separated by socioeconomic status.[17] Moreover, Jim Crow segregation and overt white racism once meant that the poor masses were unequivocally the life-blood of the black elite, the patients and clients and customers that the black middle-class counted on to maintain their standard of living. Middle-class blacks owed their very livelihoods to the consumer needs of the black masses.[18] Segregation meant that black educators taught at black schools. Black doctors treated black patients. Black merchants set up shop in black enclaves. The black middle class needed the black masses, and that practical necessity, that symbiotic connection, gave the black elite a vested interest in the strivings of the black poor. Sure, there were those who fought for more altruistic reasons, for hallowed principles like justice, liberty, and equality, but pragmatic concerns and self-interest made the laudable tenets of antidiscrimination that much more palatable.

The post-1960s black middle class has integrated the mainstream such that it is no longer exclusively connected to black consumers and clients, taking some of the fire from their more utilitarian motivations for class-transcending concern about the plight of the black poor. Many folks even argue that the black poor today are engaged in a kind of newfangled class warfare with elite blacks as fierce and potentially damaging as their racial struggle against white privilege, that the real interests of the poorest and wealthiest African Americans have recently become irreconcilably opposed in the shadow of minority-led pleas for color-blindness and the elimination of affirmative action policies.[19] According to some, racial tokenism means a smaller portion of the American pie for African Americans to fight over, allowing, say, Cynthia to compare the countervailing desires of certain black people to the proverbial antics of barreled crabs:

> **Cynthia:** People don't even have to have a lot. But once they get a little something, they afraid you gonna take it from them if you don't have it. And black folks are the worst. We like crabs in the barrel. If I got money and you don't, you want to take mine. So I'm gonna keep you way down there. It's selfishness, really.

Cynthia fears that the racial parameters of a crab-filled barrel enveloping contemporary black society make it easier for momentary gains to be challenged and revoked along decidedly racial lines.[20] If there can only be one token black, because of white racism, then the present token will be leery of other black "crabs" who would seek a position at the top of that thin-ledged barrel. Racial discrimination is the context within which class-based differences are experienced and even re-energized. And according to Cynthia, these racial parameters are a reason for tension and anxiety regardless of any African American's individual success. Race, she says, is often a zero-sum game pitting the black middle class very directly against the black poor. In this light, controversies and conflicts between blacks—social workers and social service clients, cops and male teenagers, business owners and patrons—can all be read as class conflicts highlighting the extent to which the racialized interests of black Americans can be made to diverge along social tracks laid out through pathways of class-inflected difference.

People have social interactions across class lines every day in contemporary black America. Sometimes they forget, downplay, and deny their existence, but folks are still theorizing and utilizing substantive and ephemeral exchanges across class lines. But not only do people have such relationships, they also behave differently in various kinds of relationships, that is, when interacting with what they consider to be differently classed interlocutors. This was hinted at when I discussed the differences between how people explain their social relationships up and down the class ladder. A person whom one assists and eats with regularly may still not be considered a "friend" by one half of that dyad (Cynthia), while the other half (Karen) reciprocates with the much less equivocal designation "ace" (read: best friend). Two people may not be able to communicate effectively as equals (or agree on the definitional contours of that relationship) because of "money and all that" separating them. I want to take this point a step further by arguing that not only do people have relationships across class lines every day in a place like Harlem, they also use those contexts to perceive and perform class-inflected social behaviors, actions that are said to differ depending on the class or status of the people involved. Everyday behaviors become specifically indicative of class differences, and I want to delineate some of the behavioral criteria at play when African Americans recognize class differences within the black community.

Doing Class

Do rich people act differently than poorer ones? Several useful books have been written about those with old money and the kinds of cultural practices that distinguish their ranks, and these everyday practices become very important.[21] Many Harlemites of all stripes easily offer a take on behavioral differences deemed coterminous with class divisions:

> **John:** Do richer people act differently from poorer black folks?
>
> **Damon:** Yes.
>
> **John:** How so?
>
> **Damon:** Everything. If I had money I wouldn't be sitting here with you. I'd be on my yacht and things, eating with Donald Trump, Clinton, or stealing some more from somebody else. That's what you do. That's what I'd be doing. Straight up.

Damon is obviously talking in very broad terms, and he's also referring to a local scandal from just a few weeks earlier, when one of Harlem's leaders was accused of using his position in the community to increase his profit margins on a piece of Harlem property for which he served as both landlord and tenant, allegedly overcharging his tenant self at taxpayers' expense so that his landlord self could increase his personal coffers. Not many months later, community leaders involved with the Apollo Theater Foundation were publicly accused of financial back-room dealing at the expense of the government-funded nonprofit foundation that runs the Harlem landmark—and at the expense of poorer Harlemites. These kinds of accusations frame assessments of the black middleclass as self-serving and disingenuous—whether or not the specific accusations ultimately stick, whether or not other community leaders, as in the Apollo case, write editorials and hold press conferences in the community to dispel rumors of wrongdoing and to clear their names.

Damon's rich people are defined by their illicit activities. But that is hardly where wealthy black difference ends:

> **John:** Does money effect the way people act, especially black people, or no?
>
> **Robert:** First of all, it's just an attitude. Just a snotty, nasty attitude. Like stuffy. Can't just relax and hang. They stiff and tight. Snotty is what it is.

Robert's is a fairly standard argument. Stuffiness, snottiness, and nastiness become aligned with moneyed blacks in this argument about class-specific behavior. Class differences distinguish those who can "relax and hang" from others who are just "stiff and tight." Cynthia also makes attitudinal distinctions linked to class in contemporary black America:

> **Cynthia:** Why it got to be that when black people have money they gotta think they are better than you 'cause you don't have on rich clothes and stuff? For one thing, they don't know what nobody got. They just gonna assume. Fine. But then they walk like they shit don't stink. Like they sit on the toilet and kick out daisies and whatnot.

Cynthia wonders aloud why wealthier black people use their fancy clothes and assumptions about their own exceptionalism to justify some of the same kinds of snottiness, stuffiness, and nastiness that Robert's comments highlight. In fact, it isn't just class that explains the dismal ways in which some well-off blacks are thought to interact with others. Dexter argues that black elitism can feel even worse than white versions:

> **Dexter:** To be honest, a lot of black people with money act worse than white people with money, which is ridiculous. And stupid. They think they can do whatever. They brainwashed by the money.

The example of black store owners and managers is a good one here. As some complain about the rudeness they encounter in black-owned specialty stores and other business establishments, that rudeness is often understood through a class-chiseled template linked to discussions of self-hatred:

> **David:** That's niggas. They hate themselves. They don't even respect the people they trying to sell to. You know. White people wouldn't try the kind of shit that some of these niggas be trying

'cause they know we fuck them up and burn they shit down or something for some old stupid shit. But these motherfuckers, most of them don't even live here, they from Jersey or some shit, and they roll up in here talking about buying black. Fuck that!

This self-hatred and disrespectfulness aren't the only telling characteristics of class difference and black entrepreneurial zeal. Here, David offers some "buying black" slogans as little more than the disingenuous and manipulative tactics of outsiders who aren't exposed as interlopers quite as easily as are white store owners who wouldn't dare try some of the things black store owners get away with, because "they know we fuck them up and burn they shit down" if they step too far out of line in terms of the ways in which they treat their black customers. David's formal interview took place only a year after just such a scenario transpired at a clothing store on Harlem's main thoroughfare, where a Jewish business owner was targeted as an outsider. His store was burned in what was labeled a racially motivated murder-suicide.[22] However, it doesn't take only purposeful snobbery and elitism to define the contours of class-specific differences with the black community. According to Zelda, something as simple, natural, and seemingly neutral as walking down the street can also be a class-inflected activity:

> **Zelda:** Rich people walk around like they own the world, like get out of my way 'cause I have to get to the stock market. I have to make some money. I have to see a show or spend some money you ain't got. They always running. Like they walk-running. Poorer folks take their time more. They don't have the, like, the emergency. They aren't as in a hurry like. Not the same way.

Zelda's rich people run as much as they walk. They are on rigid business and recreational schedules that necessitate true power-walks in a different sense of that term, power-walks predicated on the socioeconomic power of the walker. Judith, thirty-one, a psychologist working with the elderly in Harlem and living a couple of blocks north of City College, also recognizes the classed nature of walking down the street:

> **Judith:** If it's my, I mean I feel like I might be sounding silly to say this, because I'm saying this, but I walk a certain way. And it is a way that separates me from the people in my community. It makes me stand out.
>
> **John:** How? In what way?

> **Judith:** First of all, without a baby carriage, which might sound a bit mean, but it is true. A young black woman, a woman of color, walking around without pushing a baby is kind of rare, sadly. But it's true. And I walk with a purpose. I walk fast and quick, maybe some of that is just me too, but I think it is also because I am a professional person. Walking is transportation. For some of the people around here, especially if you're not working, no job, walking is the activity. That is the thing. Like hanging out.

For Judith, walking is a mode of locomotion that gets her from one place to another. It is purposeful and streamlined for the straightest and quickest journey possible. She can peer down the class ladder (at baby-carriage-saddled young women "sadly" slowed down by such parental accoutrements) and spot lower-classed people of color who walk less forcefully, with less purpose, much less like a "professional person" than she thinks she does. For people in her social position, she contends, walking is a means to an end; for those below her, it is an end in and of itself.

Cynthia also sees social classes as connected to certain forms of walking, and she would even add sitting to the class-specific behavioral formula:

> **Cynthia:** When you don't have anything, like to do, you just sit around, shoot shit. These older black guys just chill downstairs, they must not work, 'cause they are always out there, always, and they just chill, and kind of slide in and out of the store with beers and maltas. . . . And they are good people, but you know, they obviously aren't doing all that well, and you can see that, you can just look at them get around, and you can see that, but they got their own thing, I guess.

Cynthia frequently goes downstairs or past the small grocery store around the corner from her home and spots these "older black guys." She likes stopping by there to briefly talk and listen as the men sit around. Moreover, when Cynthia finds herself out there among them, she recognizes particular classed actions that cause them to "kind of slide in and out" of that downstairs storefront. These men occupy class positions that she makes out simply by "look[ing] at them get around."

Jessica identifies the "storefront culture" of these same kinds of "streetcorner men" as an interesting and enjoyable way of being in the world:[23]

> **Jessica:** I just like the atmosphere. It's laid back and people just hang. Kind of just doing their thing and living. They are harmless and funny. Funny. And they love, I mean, love to talk. You wouldn't believe.

Jessica enjoys hanging out and laughing with these "harmless and funny" people, and she also enjoys the atmosphere and the conversations. Sometimes, when she's a part of that scene and interacting with some of those men, Jessica notices herself slightly modifying her own everyday behaviors:

> **Jessica:** I grew up speaking Standard English, and I go in there and I catch myself, just like a word or two. Because that is what I know. But I can speak ghetto or whatever, and so when I go in there I do, like, do that. And sometimes I don't even do it consciously. I don't know if it is, what, Ebonics or what, but I am speaking it. And then I catch myself.
>
> **John:** Why do you do it? I mean, you know what I mean? Why do you think you do that?
>
> **Jessica:** I don't know. I'm not sure. I don't know. Sometimes I don't even know I'm doing it. I just hear myself. And I guess I'm sounding like them. Or trying to. Not on purpose, I don't think.

There is, of course, a long and rich history of academic discourse on language use as a mechanism for making distinctions between people and groups. Jessica's "sounding like them" in this context is an instance of someone speaking in class-sensitive ways. Jessica, the Ivy Leaguer, doesn't "even do it consciously," but she still sometimes catches herself talking as she thinks she hears the people in the grocery store talking—in an Ebonics very different from the Standard English she grew up with, an Ebonics more subconsciously slipped into than purposefully invoked. Jessica slides into black English "not on purpose," but rather as a barely conscious attempt to reach across class-, gender-, and age-based differences between her life and the lives of the streetcorner men.

Language as an example of class(ed) behavior has a long history in African American communities and in linguistic studies about black American speakers.[24] As the Oakland, California, school board's 1997 Ebonics controversy made abundantly clear, the debates on black English are associated quite directly with notions of African Americans' opportunities for success in terms of educational achievement and that achievement's payoff in occupational choices and income. Some of the same scholars who argue over the necessity of "soft" personal skills and styles in negotiating job markets can offer Ebonics as a kind of confrontational and glaringly ignorant form of speech, at least as heard by potential white and black employers.[25] You can't get a job with Ebonics as your prime form of linguistic capital, the argument goes, so you need to know Standard English, or at least how to code-switch, moving from Standard English to Ebonics and back again in context-sensitive ways. Many Harlemites know the code-switching argument backward and forward, accepting its usefulness as a technique not only for putting employers at ease but also for indexing one's connections to other African Americans further down the class ladder:

> **Jessica:** I would never speak that way if I was with the head of the hospital or someone like that. I mean, I don't think I would fall into it accidentally. Unless I already have. [She laughs.] Maybe for other reasons.
>
> **John:** Like what?
>
> **Jessica:** Well, how can I say this, black people with a little money like to speak like they are "down" sometimes, they like to sprinkle it in conversations. Black professionals often want to act like they have a little touch of street in them, but it's usually fake. But it makes them feel good.

Language is one of the primary performative and behavioral sites where class differences are perceived, negotiated and contested, where being "down" is achieved through speaking down the class ladder—in this case, through self-consciously trying "to sprinkle [black English] in conversations" as a way of implying that one has "a little touch of street" in one's background despite otherwise middle-class credentials. Jessica is quick to tack on accusations that question the authenticity of some such tactics ("it's usually fake"), but she concedes that they make many black middle-class people "feel good" about themselves and about their commitment and connection to the lower-class blacks who might be able to use their uplifting hands.

As we all know, speaking skills and styles are often used as the first indications of a person's general social location. Poorer blacks are supposed to speak in distinctively different ways from members of a black middle class whose speech patterns are said to more closely approximate Standard English. Linguistic repertoires are commonsensical vehicles for first readings of other people's social class. We all use these linguistic differences in morphology and phonology to pin down others' class locations:[26]

Ms. Joseph: As soon as someone opens their mouth you can get the best autobiography of them like that. You get all you need. How much money they have. How much education. The job, occupation. Everything you need is right there if you want to listen for it. It's there. Even when you don't think about it.

Ms. Joseph talks about objective characteristics of class (occupation, income, education) as the very attributes identified by speech acts. Many people speak quite specifically about the connections between linguistic practices and the class positions they represent. Damon has a persuasive and oft-mentioned explanation for why language is even related to class in the first place:

Damon: When you're poor, you don't know the rules for how to speak. So you don't speak the way other people do who know the rules, and that goes back to schools and all of that. You speak the way you hear other people speaking in your community. You speak like the people in your community. If everybody in your community is poor, you will sound poor too. If everyone says "nuffin'," not "nothing," that's what you say.

Damon associates poor people's language skills with the hothouse of linguistic ignorance cultivated in poor schools and class-specific community interactions. The poor sound poor because "schools and all of that" (that is, other "equalizing institutions" where people obtain middle-class and marketable social skills) in poor communities do "nuffin'" but reinforce the language learned and shared with other poor folks. Even more particular about his language assessments, Carl would separate "regular" speaking from wealth-specific linguistic attributes:

Carl: Some people speak like they want to broadcast the news on television, you know. All proper. That's not the way regular people talk, white people or black people. . . . I think I speak more regular. You do, too. You don't have to sound like you have money, and all rich and educated. Not that you sound dumb, but you know what I mean.

Carl and Damon correlate language with relational socioeconomic differences, with a class-inflected continuum of rich to poor speakers: a typology that can be either binary, as in Damon's example, or tripartite, like Carl's, with rich speakers at the top, poor ones at the bottom, and "more regular" ones somewhere in between. Here, language usage isn't just an extra-economic status symbol. It also indicates economically specific distinctions. When people change the way they speak depending on who they are speaking to, whether purposefully or inadvertently, one of the most important characteristics of such exchanges is the class-implied social difference being marked off by such maneuvers:

> **Carl:** If I'm home, with my boys, I speak one way, when I'm trying to make some money and get my stuff done, I speak another. That's all, you just talking to different people.
>
> **John:** What's the difference?
>
> **Carl:** One, you're talking to people you know, you don't have anything to prove. The other, especially if you're black, you have to make sure that they don't write you off because you sound like a nigger, excuse me. You always have an uphill battle as a black man, you know that, and you want as few strikes against you as you can get. If you sound like a nigger, you are out. If you can speak as well as they can, they'll keep you around. They won't listen to you, but they'll keep you around.

Lisa, a thirty-four-year-old elementary school teacher born and raised in Central Harlem, has to watch the way she speaks in front of the class because, she argues, her students will take advantage of her based on what she sounds like. One can see a class dynamic at play in her analysis of students' reactions to her linguistic moves. In this particular pedagogical context, speaking styles indicate levels of learnedness:

> **Lisa:** I used to try to just be cool, you know, slick, and all of that, with the slang, Ebonics talk, but now I am usually just trying to sound kind of professional. You have to be careful, because they won't always respect you if you sound like them and you talk like them, and you use slang. They'll feel like, you can't be all that smart, you can't teach me anything. You sound like me. You sound like my brother and my mother. I don't know anything. They don't know nothing, so you don't know anything, and I won't listen to you.

Lisa maintains that sounding "like them" (a reference to underclass, working-class, and lower-middle-class black Harlem kids in her third-grade public school class) by using slang or Ebonics means that one will probably not get respect from the youngsters. Lisa has to invoke linguistic difference, authority, and even superiority to get the respect she needs to successfully teach her class. She implicates the black family in her assessment of these kids' presumptions about how linguistic repertoires connect to class-based foundations of authority and expected knowledge. However, Lisa's point is not the only argument for how class-inflected speech patterns affect individuals' social interactions. Some people argue the opposite—for example, Dexter, in his assessment of the linguistic requirements for an urban anthropologist, at least an anthropologist who wants to be able to get folks comfortable enough to open up. His is a related but differently directed argument about how one uses particular linguistic registers to connect to people across class lines:

> **Dexter:** You talk like you not from Columbia. You know. You are good about not sounding unreal, and I think that is what works. Even if you have money and an education and all of that stuff, a good job and stuff, you know, the whole nine, you should still be able to speak to people. Some people get all that status, all that weight, and they get caught up in not being here and can't talk to people who ain't making the kind of ends they making or what have you. That is why people would talk to you, because you still sound like me and talk right here to me. I can tell Columbia didn't take all of BK [Brooklyn] from you. It's still there.

Whereas Lisa consciously foregrounds a more authoritarian and standard variety of English because she feels that it more effectively encourages young people to respect her (fostering communication in a specifically pedagogical setting), Dexter offers an argument about linguistic practices and respect linked to the opposite choice—where the capacity to still "sound like me" is an asset that improves communication across class lines instead of undermining it. In both cases, language is a key variable in equations about the capacity for productive and beneficial conversations across class boundaries. And many people theorize it in just that way.

Besides walking and talking (two very foundational human behaviors, indeed), many other elements of people's everyday behavioral lives are also classed or perceived as such. The way someone looks, for instance, can reveal class differences as well. Some aspects of the way people look, such as skin color, are less amenable to tampering and change. Historically, light skin was the defining criterion for membership in many blue-blood societies of the black well-to-do.[27] In fact, it is often considered to be a kind of naturalized modality for the expression of class. "You never see pretty, light-skinned homeless people," Dexter offers in an *Entertainment Tonight*–induced conversation about Eddie Murphy's wife, implying that skin tone and facial features are class-inflected phenomena at least insofar as they are correlated with homelessness and marriageability. Once black men "get a little bit of money," Janet argues on a trip through the West Village, "they go out and get the lightest, almost whitest thing they can see. It's like a trophy. See what I got." Skin lightening creams (historically, big business in black communities) and other attempts to look lighter, in this context, become not aesthetic issues alone but decidedly class-implicated ones as well.

Certain seemingly individualistic aesthetic flairs and styles are also tied to class differences between social groups. Marilyn, twenty-four, an undergraduate at a college downtown, got her hair done one weekend with a specific experiment in mind, allowing her hairstylist to add a few blond streaks and runs through her otherwise black hair. She wasn't sure if she'd like it in the end, but she went for the change anyway. I was scheduled to conduct an interview with her on the day of her hair appointment, so we met up at her hair salon and traveled together to her home uptown afterward. I liked her hairstyle, and I told her so, but she was unsure of her own opinion. She would have to sit with it for a little while before handing down her final aesthetic verdict. Still, she did know one thing immediately, from the moment she first glanced at the finished product: her dad wasn't going to like it. Sure enough, when we got to her home and she showed the new look to her father, Roger, a retired electrical engineer, he was quick to point out the class-based implications of her new hairstyle:

> **Roger:** Let me get my car so I can drop you off in the projects with that.
>
> **Marilyn:** What are you talking about, crazy man?
>
> **Roger:** You know exactly what I'm talking about standing over there looking like you want to be a female Tupac [Shakur]. Why can't you just get your hair cut and washed and not get all ghetto?

Hairstyles are easily implicated in discussions about class-based differences and distinctions between people from the ghetto or the projects on one hand and the "cut and washed" (more middle-class or mainstream) world beyond their borders. Along with hairstyling and skin color, the clothes one wears can also be considered indications of class differences—and often in ways that read differently across the color line:[28]

> **Janet:** Sometimes I feel bad because if a black person is in baggy jeans, not well dressed, I always think of them differently than I think of white men, even if they have on the same kind of street clothes, the baggy jeans. Like if I'm in an elevator or something. I don't know. If a black guy isn't in a suit, if you're in an elevator you feel in danger, but a white person can wear anything and you don't think you might be in danger, and that they don't have a job and might be up to no good and all this other stuff. If it's a black guy, I know I feel threatened, I feel bad saying it, but you want me to say the truth, right?
>
> **John:** Why?
>
> **Janet:** Why do I feel threatened?
>
> **John:** Yeah.
>
> **Janet:** I just feel like you can't trust nobody. It's like you don't know what they have. If they have a knife or a gun or just want to get into some mischief. You know, the baggy jeans hanging down. That is just a warning sign. A red flag.

It's not just denim jeans themselves that are the red flag here. Janet specifies that it has more to do with the way those jeans are worn: "baggy" as opposed to well-fitting, beneath loose sweatshirts as opposed to well-tailored oxfords. Even the clothes one wears can indicate potential criminality—and, by extension, a kind of underclassness linked to unemployment. Janet maintains that she "can't trust nobody," but she is explicit about the racialized nature of her class-inflected and wardrobe-based mistrust. A white man in those same baggy jeans, she claims, would be less threatening. She hates admitting to that, but it is the "truth," exposing the peculiar ways in which race, class, and gender issues intersect in the lives of people caught up in the vexing racial logic of contemporary American society, a logic extending even to the politico-economic aesthetics of covering one's body.

Yet another class(ed) behavior is, simply enough, standing. One afternoon, I was hanging out with Robert on the corner of 125th and Lenox Avenue as we casually talked and scoped out passersby. Not fifteen minutes earlier we had been further west watching neighborhood activists marching in memory of Malcolm X and asking neighborhood stores on the busy strip to close for a small part of the business day as a part of that commemoration. We hadn't been out for fifteen minutes when Robert piqued my interest by making a big deal of his ability to look at people and tell if they were wealthy based on the way they were standing at the curb waiting for the light to change. For instance, where they put their hands (in front of them, fingers through one another; at their sides; behind them) indicated whether they were well-off. Their posture was also indicative of wealth status according to Robert's theory: "slouched over," "straight and stiff," "relaxed," "regular." Obviously, some of this standing-as-class argument is molded in the rhetoric of snobbishness discussed above. But what is interesting is that these distinctions can be carried to even the most innocent and seemingly mundane of social practices, not just those with obviously foregrounded sociopolitical implications. I received my own first-hand and unsolicited class(ed) standing performance the first time Robert escorted me to Columbia. We had bumped into a suit-and-tie clad black professor on campus, and I noticed that Robert had struck (and not to be funny, which he often does) some of the very same postures and positions he critiqued and laughed at as "stiff," "corny," and indicative of cash when we were on 125th Street. The gestures and postures Robert critiqued and assessed so nonchalantly also seemed to be actions he imitated and embodied when necessary. I asked Robert, after we had left the campus and began making our way through Morningside Park and back to his apartment in Central Harlem, about the changes I thought I had seen in his posture as we interacted with that black professor. Robert responded, a little defensively I thought, that he did what he did because he didn't want to "embarrass" me. When I assured him that I wouldn't feel embarrassed if he just acted naturally, he added that he didn't want to embarrass himself either. "Besides, you do the same thing," he retorted. "I'm looking at you talking to these crackers. And you do the same thing."

I initially scoffed at Robert's accusation, dismissing it as mere defensiveness and deflection. I mean, we weren't even talking to one of those "crackers" he so readily invoked. This was a black professor, not a white one. However, thinking about the incident later, I wondered how much of my own body language did, in fact, change between Columbia University and, say, "Africa Square" at 125th and Adam Clayton Powell, whether I was slipping into a different way of standing, walking, and talking almost without my even knowing it, kind of like Jessica's after-the-fact recognition that sometimes she eases into Ebonics without even realizing that she's done it. I notice this most clearly in myself when I self-consciously control my gait, facial gestures, and posture during treks home from interviews and "hanging-out" sessions on dark and starry nights, carefully making my way from East and Central Harlem to a five-story walkup in the Manhattanville section of northern Manhattan, sometimes purposefully swaggering my social belongingness and familiarity with the place in self-consciously amplified ways, deep and lopsided strides with interpretable local value.

From a slightly different angle, if Robert can claim to detect an artificial sense of middle-classness as embodied in particular ways of standing, then it is important to think of all such performances as equally artificial in the sense that they are all modified—however greatly or slightly—from one setting to another. All actions are contextual constructs. Even when we are standing or talking or walking by ourselves, we perform in a kind of internalized social context that calls for particular actions regardless of the fact that there are no observers to heed them except for our own interiorized social selves, Erving Goffman's internalized audience.[29] Rest assured, however, that Robert uses his body-based knowledge not only to assess people's class at a glance but also to perform a certain version of middle-classness in social spaces with more immediate financial benefits: job interviews. "Believe me," he says, "it works, kid."

Class-stratified relationships create interactive spaces where people conduct themselves in ways that take those class differences into account. How did Zelda, for instance, behave that day on the train when her supervisor was impressed enough with their conversation to later offer her a full-time job? Was it different from the way she would have acted had that supervisor not been present? And did her supervisor modify her behavior at all in class-sensitive ways? How about on that basketball court? Does Paul have a different way of behaving around Tim (and vice versa) that is distinct from the way he might behave, say, with Wilson, the colleague who helped organize that second birthday party? Does Paul act differently with peops than with peers? We already know that he feels the need to suppress a part of himself with his peops, especially his family, a suppression he believes is necessary even if it's not enjoyable. Karen and Cynthia's interactions are rife with class-loaded issues, not the least of which is the possibility that Cynthia may speak to Karen in infantilizing ways, in ways that she wouldn't necessarily speak to someone she considered her social equal. In all of these instances, class differences are embodied and performed in meaningful ways when people are interacting across class lines, when they jostle with one another about status and identity using class-marked behavioral criteria to shore up and vouchsafe their social identities.

Fooling People

Denise, thirty-eight, hates it when her friend Rick, forty-three, starts speaking "all proper" when I'm around. "He don't never speak that way," she complains, "so why he gonna perpetrate when you here. What he think he getting away with? He ain't fooling nobody." I laugh, and I think I'm supposed to, as Rick dismisses her criticism with a wave of his hand and ushers Denise and me into his bedroom for a look through some old photo albums. Classed actions, according to Denise, can be used to "fool people," but she isn't fooled because she sees her friend in other settings where he doesn't speak in the same way. Rick, of course, denies that he does anything of the kind, and he leaves Denise no option but to threaten him with exposure: she swears that she will secretly tape him one day and play the tape for me so I can hear his "nigger voice."[30]

I never received that tape, but it did seem that the more I got to know Rick, the more I saw and heard him, the less he was self-conscious about the way he spoke to me and the less standardized his English sounded— or maybe it was just the power of Denise's suggestion. *Code-switching* is the linguistic term for going back and forth between registers, dialects, and the like, from Standard English to African American Vernacular English. In one context, for example, a job interview, you speak Standard English (accompanied, à la Robert and Janet, by standing and walking in certain class-inflected ways), and in another context, say, when you are on a basketball court, you speak and stand differently: to belong, to fit in, to protect yourself, or even to let people know where you come from. In all of these cases, everyday language and behavior are connected and used to index socioeconomic histories and implicit arguments about social worth. "When I'm hanging with my boys," Dexter avers, "I speak like, 'yo, what's up, son?' When I'm on the job, it's like, 'hello, how you doing?'"

Code-switching and its physical form, *behavior-switching,* are not just used to land jobs. They put friends at ease, let down your guard, or raise those very same guards way up. They also anchor a person's sense of self to his or her model of sociality and class stratification. People read different social situations for class-based cues as to how they should behave—and look at others' behaviors for class-based cues about their social position. These actions are not reducible to speaking—even though most of the literature concerning class and behavior focuses almost exclusively on linguistic practices. It is also how one stands, sits, walks, and so on that, combined with other quotidian activities, indexes relevant class particularities.

One can find class-inflected readings throughout the everyday lives of black Americans. For instance, one theme that came up several times during my fieldwork had to do with the class implications of flirtation, of making a pass. Janet, for instance, links the way she is propositioned on the streets of Harlem directly and self-consciously to class:

> **Janet:** These little hoodlums think they can just talk to women any old way. That's because they don't have no home training, and they are out here on the street with nothing but time. It's just disgusting.
>
> **John:** What's disgusting, exactly, about the way they talk to women?
>
> **Janet:** I see it myself, when I'm walking to the train or something, and they are, like, "psst, hey sexy, psst." First of all, what the hell is "psst"? That's so disrespectful. Like I'm gonna stop to that and talk to somebody. That's just so frustrating. Mostly Latino men, you know, doing nothing but drinking and smoking marijuana.

Jessica makes a similar point about sexual advances, one also bound up with both ethnicity and gender. It is frustrating, she says, when individuals who "should know better" do the same thing as Janet's "mostly Latino men." Moreover, Jessica would add that television viewing affects the actions of the likes of these "psst" men (or males who want to mimic them):

> **Jessica:** And now with the music videos and all of that stuff you have everybody trying to act hard and poor and like they are from the street. Like it's cool to be from the street. So then everybody is acting stupid. People who should know better are acting like they are killers and gangsters and that kind of thing.

In chapter 6, I try to speak more directly to the intersections between racial and class-based assumptions offered up by the mass media. For now, suffice it to say that Jessica claims many of these "hard" and "poor" behaviors are little more than disingenuous imitations of how class and race are depicted by the recording and cinematic industries. Of course, people in varied class contexts enact these class-based behaviors quite differently:

> **Carl:** When I'm rolling around here, I might add a little limp to my strut, you know, especially if I have a suit on, so folk know I don't feel intimidated and that I don't feel scared. And so they

don't get fooled by the suit into thinking I don't know where
I'm at. Or that I must not be a brother who will stomp-stomp
that ass if I got to. That is important.

Carl can be wearing a suit, the mark of middle-class professionalism,
but tacks on a limp to his strut to indicate that he is, in a sense, from
the street, that he can "stomp-stomp that ass" if he has to, an example
of the sociologist Elijah Anderson's arguments about black middle-class
public posturing as social self-defense.[31] But the reason why this can be
thought to work at all, or why Carl would use this tactic in the first
place, is predicated on an elaborate analysis of the linkages between class
positions and almost all other conceivable social practices. The way
one wears one's hair, walks, talks, stands, makes passes, or wears one's
clothes can be articulated with class and used to index important socioeconomic differences within black America. This performative picture
can be further complicated by offering similar behaviors as differentially
classed depending on the context and the rhetoric of the interpreter. The
behavioral facts of the matter are not transparent; they require rhetorical
scaffolding. Deborah is twenty-four years old and waiting for a callback
from the local branch of a video chain where she applied for a sales
position. Like Judith, she notices walking as a class-related activity, but
Deborah's take on that connection is very different:

> **Deborah:** Black people who got money got all the time in the
> world. People with money. You got time to just be like, la, la, la,
> la, la. Nobody don't got to tell you nothing. You don't got to
> rush. Nothing. When you poor, when you don't got nothing.
> You trying to get someplace. You on a mission.

Walking fast and with a purpose ("a mission") or walking slowly and
leisurely can both, it seems, be examples of wealth or poverty.[32] There
is a binary class model at work here, but the class actions discussed posit
people who can occupy, manipulate, and perform both sides of that class
divide. The ways in which behaviors and social practices are class(ed)
is not reducible to any easy one-to-one correspondence with wealth or
poverty. In fact, class differences and their articulation with practices
and particular actions can be thought of in any number of divergent
ways—especially if there aren't necessarily any "natural" ways of acting
to begin with, no prediscursive linkages between specific social classes
and everyday behaviors. The act of walking quickly and purposively can
be an example of middle-classness (says Judith) or underclassness (says
Deborah), depending on how walking is defined. It is the arbitrariness

of this entire picture of classed behaviors that allows for disputes about class's expression in everyday social performances. Maybe some of the divergences between Deborah's and Judith's versions of class walking can be eliminated by invoking the specific contexts of this middle-class pedestrianism. If they are late for a meeting, they walk quickly. If they are enjoying an expensive vacation that their high salary has financed, they can take the time to saunter. Even with this clarification of context, however, we still have the interesting phenomenon of people arguing for artificial linkages between striding gaits and class positions. Poor people can walk just as quickly or slowly as wealthier people do. The issue isn't whether these characterizations are right, but rather that people provide systematic attempts to reference class differences with behavioral factors that in and of themselves hold no intrinsic class valuations—only the values we retroactively apply as observational correlates for the socioeconomic differences that would exist in the world with or without our behavioral theories about them.

Class is not just a matter of where one works; it also takes hard work—both to recognize it and to represent it in everyday social life. People perform their notions of upper- and lowerclassness all the time. Sometimes these performances are attempts to fit in and not feel like you embarrass yourself or other people. Paul's two birthday parties seem to resonate well with this rendition of class actions linked to the potential for embarrassing and awkward encounters—meaning, in Paul's case, that you keep different classes of people in your social network separated from one another. Sometimes class differences are not just embarrassing but threatening. The class differences embodied by specific performances have life-and-death implications, such as when you wonder about the young black male with baggy jeans standing ominously over your shoulder in an otherwise empty elevator. Often these class performances are enacted purposefully (a teacher quite self-consciously speaking to her students like she isn't "from the street") in order to gain respect and authority. But sometimes these class(ed) behaviors can be less self-consciously slipped into, as when people talk about "catch[ing]" themselves speaking down the social ladder without trying to do so.

Class(ed) behaviors and practices can be invoked to gain authority, to save face, or to blend in. For an urban anthropologist, some of these same issues of authority and conformity dictate the actions that one uses to connect with informants in the field. In some ways, this is the linchpin of the participant-observation method; the anthropologist's performances, practices, and behaviors are contingent on these very considerations. The "fly on the wall" of traditional anthropological lore is nonobtrusive partially because he or she slowly learns to perform "the native" in ways that allow him or her to blend in slowly, if not perfectly. Even the so-called native anthropologist doesn't necessarily forge a perfect fit. As an anthropologist working on race and class in Harlem, I found that these concerns about fitting and blending in often entail distinct sets of behaviors for particular kinds of settings, especially when one is interacting with residents from varied social spheres: soup kitchens, college classrooms, state agencies, fraternity events, block parties, storefronts, nightclubs, and early morning Sunday worship services. Often, I found myself making quick assessments about the class positions of the Harlemites I met, assessments that I subsequently translated (mostly unconsciously) into specific behavioral responses aimed at putting these strangers at ease about me and my project. This is particularly difficult because the same folks can act differently in different contexts (standing at Columbia University speaking to a professor versus hanging out, say, in Mart 125). These context-contingent actions (where people with money can, according to Jessica, "act poor" based on television images of blackness—and where other people can change their behaviors in attempts at performing up the social ladder) make any attempts at reading class a difficult practice—but one that people undertake constantly nonetheless.

Sore Thumbs and Ripped Suits

On some occasions, performances of class are about sticking out, not blending in, separating oneself from the others. Once Carl nearly got into a fistfight with another man inside a Harlem diner because the man believed Carl was trying to act like he was "better than other people." Carl, in a dark blue two-piece suit, was making a comment about crime in Harlem, and the sweatsuit-wearing man evidently felt as though Carl was trying (in being "loud about it and sounding like he think he better than other people; you think you better than me?") to make some kind of underhanded comment directed at him. The unidentified man went so far as a push or two before a worker at the diner calmed him down, all the while Carl reiterating, "I ain't no nigga off the street," to which the man replied that he was "two seconds" from ripping Carl's suit off his back right there.

Frazzled and embarrassed by the commotion (and feeling guilty about the fact that my questions had prompted this entire exchange), I showed the man my tape recorder and emphasized that Carl was only answering questions because I was asking them, and not because the man was present to overhear. When the man, far from convinced, was finally escorted from the store, Carl talked about how important it is for him not to back down in situations like that:

> **Carl:** I'm not gonna punk out to these assholes. I can be just as hard and street as these assholes if I have to be. That is what they need to learn. Just because I'm not walking around with a sign that says "I'm ghetto" doesn't mean I won't whip a Negro's ass if he tests me. . . . You see, that's all psychological. He knows he's a failure, and he's angry at me because I'm not like him. And because I know I'm not like him. It's psychological.

Because of something about the way Carl sounded and the comments he made in that little rundown diner, the other man interpreted Carl's performance in class-inflected ways—as a hostile elitism challenging his own less-than-equivalent successes. Carl knew nothing about this stranger: what the man did for a living, how much he had in the bank, how far he had traveled along formal educational tracks. And that man was just as ignorant about Carl's personal biography. But what Carl was wearing and how he was speaking all implied a sense of social superiority that the unidentified man didn't appreciate. I would argue that the arbitrary calculus for class distinctions based on everyday performances spirals out infinitely and indefinitely—to the way Carl, say, held his knife and fork, how he sat in his chair, how he shook his head, as well as what he actually said about class and achievement in contemporary black America. Connected to any one person's assertion of class superiority is often a complementary accusation of "failure" for another—especially in *intra*racial, class-stratified contexts where people who seem to be succeeding and others who seem to be failing use the same restaurants and sidewalks, churches and grocery stores. In a sense, this is a version of the structure versus agency debate rewired to actual social interactions in the real world. How is Carl explaining his two-piece suit and occupational success? What does that explanation imply about his understanding of other people (such as that unidentified man) and their relative success? Moreover, just as people can see the same actions with divergent class implications, people can perform up and down the social ladder improperly. Class performances don't always work. People can be laughed at, beaten up, and disparaged as often and as easily as they can have their performances validated. Zelda is very critical of some of the social workers who try to talk as if they are "down" with her when it's all really just "phony" and "fake." Denise critiques Rick's attempts at sounding "smarter and stuff" around me not just because it's phony but also because, as she tells us both, it is poorly done. "He sounds stupid, anyway," she declares. "You don't even do it right." Even an anthropologist complimented by Dexter for being able to blend in can be teased in other contexts for standing out like a sore thumb.[33]

Some people might question whether the people in this chapter are performing class or status. Surely, individuals are using status-type markers (how you dress, talk, walk, stand, and so on), but they are using them, I argue, to create a kind of behavioral shorthand for class-specific designations. The same behaviors might be read differently in different contexts, but the differences are all still organized in terms of rich versus poor ways of being in the world. In these contexts, being and acting poor (acting out what is supposedly a quotidian behavioral assemblage of relative poverty) can be just as status-boosting as being and acting rich:

> **Robert:** I get my clothes at the Salvation Army. I don't have the cash like you Columbia people to go out and go to, where do you go?
>
> **John:** Man, I'm struggling too.
>
> **Robert:** Please.
>
> **John:** I go to Domsey's [a second-hand store in Williamsburg, Brooklyn]. You been there?
>
> **Robert:** Where's that? In Beverly Hills? We poor people can't get all that together. Go out to Beverly Hills for the weekend. Don't laugh just because you up there, and I'm way, way down here.

Indeed, class does separate Robert and me in important ways, but Robert exaggerates the specificity of that separation, however jokingly, to increase his status. There is something almost honorable about poverty in this context. Still, Robert can perform up the class ladder in other contexts (say, on a trip with me up to Columbia) in ways that belie any simplistic and static conception of poverty as the apotheosis of honorific social status in black America. Moreover, Robert is also using the exaggerated distinctions between our relative wealth to humorously create a bridge across which we can possibly meet on common ground. Even so, poverty is sometimes prime property, at least in ribbing. Steve, who does custodial work in Harlem on a part-time basis, not more than six blocks from where he and his girlfriend live, also jokingly uses money and wealth as a way to discuss the differences between anthropologist and informant:

Steve: I know that a brother like you got cash, Mr. Rich Man.

John: Where? Where, bruh? Where? In my ears?

Steve: In your bank account. Let me borrow that jet. I'll bring it back.

John: You the one with the money [pointing to the cell phone attached to his belt buckle]. Nice phones, pagers, all that. You don't see me with none of that. That's all you.

Steve: Stop denying, brother, and help a brother out.

John: You the one with jewelry and all the expensive gadgets.

Steve: See that's 'cause you rich folks don't show your money. You dress down, I see how you all do it. You got so much you act like you don't.

The jet that Steven posits me as flying must be the same vehicle I use for the excursions I take to Beverly Hills, according to Robert. Wardrobe, education, terms of address, and the way one speaks are all summoned to the fore as Steve makes his claims about my being rich. As a function of being at Columbia and finishing my Ph.D., I do occupy a different position in the social order than he does, but he too seems to exaggerate the extent of that difference (I obviously do not own a jet for him to borrow). Steve seems to give me the opportunity to deny the outlandish items I don't possess as a means of connecting with him on grounds of socioeconomic commonality and not just clear-cut class difference. However, he is also talking about divergent social trajectories and possibilities. I may not own a jet now, he might argue, but I am on a particular socioeconomic track that might lead to larger economic payoffs than he might be assumed to expect in his present low-wage job. He might also be making a genuine request for funds, a request cloaked in lightheartedness so as to allow him to ask without admitting that he may be in need—and without too much public embarrassment.

Harlemworld on the River

When Todd finally ran out of the hip-hop posters he'd been paid to plaster uptown for a few extra dollars (and finally finished schooling me on the Trilateral Commission's involvement in the sterilization of black men), he and I ended up across the street from the Cotton Club building at 125th and St. Clair Place, the exact spot where a rushing Apollo Theater stagehand's car rear-ended mine three years later on the way to a picket line beneath the Apollo marquee. Approximately thirty striking part-time stagehands had asked the International Alliance of Theatrical Stage Employees to bargain with the Apollo Theater Foundation on their behalf.[34] They joined Local 1 of the union in hopes of getting real retirement packages, more health benefits, and an increase in pay. Apollo stagehands made about $10 to $17 per hour less than most of the already unionized stagehands in the rest of the city. Several of Harlem's local leaders grumbled about the timing of the boycott, especially since New York Attorney General Dennis Vacco was concurrently probing activities of the nonprofit foundation's relationship with the Inner City Broadcasting Company (ICBC), a firm licensed to tape a television program using the Apollo's facilities and name.[35] Many local leaders argued that the Vacco probe was the latest attack in Governor George Pataki's ongoing attempt to orchestrate a coup in Harlem, destroying and discrediting its leaders and pitting them against the black masses—portraying local black politicians as privileging their interests over those of community residents.

Harlem congressman Charles Rangel linked the allegations of a "sweetheart deal" between him and Percy Sutton, head of the ICBC, to similar accusations leveled at the Harlem Urban Development Corporation, formed in the 1960s as a conduit for the transfer of state money to the Harlem community. In 1995, Pataki (implying that the HUDC was little more than an unaccountable coffer for Harlem's African American leadership) reorganized the HUDC as the Harlem Community Development Corporation (HCDC) under the Empire State Development Corporation. The very same area where Todd posted his last advertisement had been a major source of contention about the HUDC and its questioned priorities. Just a few intersections further west, strips such as Marginal Way state the obvious about this once-vibrant stretch of land on the west side of Harlem—home to Fairway supermarket and its parking lot, Manhattanville's MTA Bus Depot, the Riverside Drive viaduct's beautiful latticework, the Henry Hudson Parkway, a few meat packing businesses, other small retail operations, Amtrak train tracks, a gas station, body shops and auto garages (including the one that eventually smoothed out the dented fender from my collision with the Apollo stagehand), self-storage facilities, fast food restaurants, a smattering of nightclubs and social clubs, and a few large housing developments (including a towering Columbia-owned faculty apartment complex), as well as the Cotton Club, namesake of the original nightclub run by reputed mobster Owney Madden on 142nd and Lenox.

The Harlem pier area is about 30,000 square feet of space, the same stretch of land where, in the 1920s and 1930s, ferries shuttled riders back and forth to Bear Mountain and Fort Lee, New Jersey. During the 1940s and 1950s, its piers and esplanades were destroyed and left to rot. The HUDC's 1992 project Harlem on the Hudson was intended to rebuild this area with a new park, research facilities for area universities, a majestic marina, a 5,700-seat performance space, glitzier nightclubs, a luxurious hotel, and high-end housing units. The HUDC project was questioned by the local community board for being environmentally unsound and for ignoring the actual everyday needs of local residents.[36] Part of this complaint outlines a larger class-based argument about the divergent uses of social space by the black middle class as opposed to other segments of the black community in Harlem, an argument about how different classes of people need different kinds of things. Harlem on the Hudson's plans for high-rise apartments and indoor-outdoor malls with jazz clubs and seemingly high-brow restaurants beneath the Riverside Drive aqueduct were read as class-specific renovations of place that suited black middle-class desires for fancy recreational possibilities but neglected residents without the disposable income and free time to spend on such jaunts. Many residents considered this proposal little more than the creation of a new Harlem tourist destination and middle-class respite. Plans for, say, a new Hotel Theresa on the river, several blocks from that landmark's actual location as an office building on Adam Clayton Powell Boulevard, were part of a continuing effort to capitalize on Harlem's racialized history as a promotional tool to attract out-of-state tourist dollars. Some local residents and activist groups saw this as a scheme for the creation of a class-isolated social world on the westernmost tip of Harlem—indeed, as a kind of Harlemworld where assumptions that people make about the place, its history, and its local residents are rewired to marketing gimmicks that provide self-consciously racialized and historicized fare for middle-class tourists (and nothing more than dead-end service sector jobs for local residents). How space gets carved up and used along class-specific lines is always an important issue for communities with any degree of social stratification.[37]

In January 1996, George Pataki, Charles Rangel, Mayor Giuliani, and Assistant Secretary for Housing and Urban Development Andrew Cuomo took part in a ceremonial event organized around the signing of New York City's Empowerment Zone Agreement. New York City was to be one of a handful of places to receive block grants for community development and job creation. The federal, state, and local governments promised $100,000,000 each toward those goals. New York's empowerment zone was to be anchored in northern Manhattan (most especially Harlem) and the South Bronx. Local churches also joined the

picture, developing partnerships with banks as a mechanism for attract-
ing investment dollars to the neighborhood—and for providing vital
services to the community's decidedly underserved residents. Many
working-class and poorer Harlem residents see the empowerment zone
and its funding offshoots as a precursor to gentrification and their own
subsequent displacement:

> **Steven:** It's like, I don't like [that] sometimes in Harlem it looks
> like they're [black middle-class leaders] just like giving us up. I
> mean, like, they have the empowerment zone, but I don't look
> at the empowerment zone as being like a black thing. It's like
> the investment of a lot of white people to like really put some-
> thing in Harlem that they're going to benefit from. I don't
> know, you know. I want to wait and see what we're going to get
> out of it. So it looks, like, real attractive, but that doesn't mean
> that the benefits are going to be attractive to the people who
> live here.

Salimah, Bernice's daughter, has a similar argument about the potential
dangers of empowerment zone funding:

> **Salimah:** I'd love to open up a business, you know, like little
> candy stores, but like, you know, like the penny stores. You used
> to go there with pennies you could get like five candies or what-
> ever. I would like to have a store like that . . . something good.
> Like a mom and pop shop or something like that. Like a pizza
> shop or something. . . . . Like Michael Jackson, he forgot about
> us, you know. I mean, I can't really say Jordan 'cause I heard he
> opened up a couple of malls, but I mean, how many times can
> you go to a mall if you don't have a job to pay for the stuff in
> there, you know? Just like, what's that man, the one that has
> HIV? Magic Johnson. He opened up a movie theater in Brook-
> lyn. The lady [a television pundit talking about the theater] was
> like, how many times can you go to a movie theater? I mean,
> you can give kids a job there, but I mean, how many times can
> people actually go? And it's right across the street from the proj-
> ects, you know. How many times can they go to the movies? I
> don't know. I mean, I mean, there's a lot [of middle-class blacks]
> that forgot about us and then there's some that come back and
> help the community, you know?

Salimah tried to get a job at the recently opened Pathmark supermarket in Harlem only three months before she made these comments, but

the manager on duty informed her that they were only hiring people from particular zip codes further east and closer to the store. Still, she thinks that Pathmark at least provides a service to the community, a community that needs quality foodstuffs; residents need to eat. Some small businesses are also getting a boost from empowerment zone loans, but many Harlemites fear that the initiative's emphasis on tourism and entertainment puts outsider and corporate interests above those of local residents trying to make ends meet. This empowerment zone has become yet another source of concern in Harlem about the use of urban space—and that use's connection to class-inflected and racial concerns. Paul, Carl, Ms. Joseph, and many of the more relatively well-off Harlem residents I spoke to often voiced fewer reservations about the neighborhood changes catalyzed by empowerment zone funding. If anything, they are happy to have the same top-quality establishments uptown that are usually located far away from black communities. Harlem should have what every other neighborhood has, they argue, the exact same kinds of goods and services that other Manhattan communities take for granted.[38]

Classes of Actions

This class-inflected fault line between suspicion and support for the empowerment zone and its implications parallels the kinds of aforementioned folk arguments used to link everyday behaviors to class-specific social differences. Folk definitions of class describe it as a composite of performances, as combinations of behaviors that are all implicated simultaneously in the designation of socioeconomic position. Sometimes these combinations are easy to read; at other times they are not so easy. In community critiques of Harlem on the Hudson, local residents linked proposed recreational activities and venues to class-specific negotiations of entertainment and public space. In the next chapter, I want to look more closely at these combinations of behaviors as they are linked to notions of *racial* identity and authenticity. For now, let me just say that if walking, talking, standing, dressing, and other quotidian activities can be read as indicative of class (the same actions sometimes being indicative of diametrically opposed class positions), then when individuals look at others' performances in class(ed) ways all of these various behavioral characteristics are operative at one and the same time. This makes for a complicated tabulation of class-based success and failure, a tabulation that can easily change over time and space, that allows a person to succeed in one environment and fail miserably in another. Even when there isn't a transparent and substantial class difference separating people, classed behaviors (actions that are read in class-inflected ways) can be used to insert, create, or emphasize such a difference anyway—or to justify more substantial class differences by rigging everyday behaviors to bolster them.

This chapter extends a question about social interactions across class lines to another one about social behaviors read as class(ed) actions. People have particular ideas about what class difference means for the way individuals behave in a class-stratified social world. With these ideas and perceptual frameworks, people perform class—that is, they behave in ways that are cognizant of class as an embodied identity. This is a preliminary look at how a few residents perform class in Harlem—at the ways in which they recognize, perceive, and define those class(ed) performances. Moreover, these performances, actions, practices, and behaviors (and people's recognition of them) are as often about performing poverty, performing down the social ladder (acting "street" or "ghetto,") as they are about performing a decidedly highbrow middle-classness. In either case, class(ed) actions serve as interactive sites wherein people make distinctions within the black community. We may not be able to see into people's savings accounts and educational files as they walk past us on the street, but we can see the many ways in which their everyday behaviors differ along lines that link up with our notions of class specificity. People play with and manipulate these class-inflected actions in order to get as much social mileage out of them as possible—and to make sense of a hierarchical socioeconomic order by binding it to controllable social behaviors.

WHITE HARLEM: TOWARD THE PERFORMATIVE
LIMITS OF BLACKNESS

White Cultures

Brian was a little drunk, but he was still completely cognizant of what he said. I could tell by the way his eyes steadied on mine, with a single-minded focus, waiting patiently for his comments to register on my face. Brian is a twenty-eight-year-old black man who has lived his entire life in three apartments in Harlem. His parents moved here from the Carolinas before he was born. When he got into a little trouble as a teenager, they threatened him with exile to the South "to live with family." He even spent a few summers in North Carolina, but Harlem is the only home he claims. We were in the living room of the one-bedroom apartment he currently shares with his girlfriend, Keisha, and their one-year-old son, Darren, both of whom were away visiting Keisha's mother in Flat-bush. Earlier, he and I had spent a good portion of the afternoon at Harlem's annual African American Day street festival, eating what was billed as "ethnic food" from many cultures and nations, listening to hip-hop tunes imperfectly belted out by marching bands, reading pamphlets and brochures from historically black colleges at an open-air college fair, and enjoying gospel, R&B, and spoken-word performances on a mobile stage.

That evening, Brian and I talked about everything from the day's activities to gentrification, the empowerment zone, hip-hop musicianship, black movies' marketability, racism, and class conflicts in contemporary American society. One of the most pressing issues of the night, as far as Brian was concerned, had to do with the lack of real occupational opportunities for black people today. And he used a personal anecdote to flesh out his mostly macrostructural critique, a critique organized as much by "white supremacy" (his term) as by color-blind economic forces. Brian knew this topic first-hand and from very personal experience. He'd been trying to find a job for several weeks and hadn't come close to landing anything "even half-way decent like." He was fired from his last one, in the proverbial mailroom of a downtown office building, after only a week because he got into a verbal altercation with one of his bosses "over some old foolish type shit." As Brian described that termination, his boss "wanted to get his rocks off" by making Brian feel stupid and inadequate "all the time." Brian "wasn't having that," and so one Friday he was asked to leave and never come back. And that, quite simply, was that. "It just didn't work out," he remembers being told. As he relays this story, a heightened and theatrical inflection in his own voice indexes both his former employer's indifference and his own present disgust. He'd been pounding the pavement ever since then (I knew he had, since I'd tagged along once or twice for support), but he wasn't having much success.

Brian was on his second forty-ounce bottle of malt liquor as I nursed my first, sipping on it slowly as he waited for my reply to an earlier comment he had made about whiteness, white culture, and racial difference. We were talking about what I do, about cultural anthropology and my fieldwork in Harlem, when he decided to use that discussion as an opening to provide evidence for an argument about the connections between culture and race:

> **Brian:** White people don't have culture. They don't have it. We created all kinds of things, and everything they have they just stole from us. They ain't creative like us. They just ain't. You know what I'm saying? Not at all. Not at all. I don't care what the hell it is, we did it. No matter what. All they can do, all they do, is they good at faking so it's like they done it. That's it.

This argument, a racialized assessment of cultural productivity (comparative racial achievements as measured in creativity and the amount of cultural genius to which a group can lay claim) is almost exactly the same argument about race's linkage to cultural practices that I had overheard two months earlier, in an entirely different context. A young African American political activist at an academic conference in Washington, D.C., was challenging anyone within earshot to give him one example, just one, of what he called "white cultural practices." Earlier that day, he had talked about his work with at-risk boys in local public schools. He described these children as geniuses and as "uncontrollably brilliant." While eating lunch with some of his friends at the conference, he wanted someone to provide him with one distinctive item that could be claimed by "white culture." I listened attentively and inconspicuously as his main interlocutor, a nice-enough twenty-something white woman, appeared stumped and even flustered by this forceful challenge. With that tiny space of silence the young man claimed victory, professing to have proved his irrefutable point: that whites could claim not a single, solitary specifically white cultural practice, that only blacks have a distinctive cultural history—and a specific way of acting in the world rooted in that fact. I have actually heard this very same argument rehearsed many times in conversations with several of the folks that I met in Harlem, an often elaborate and self-conscious understanding of "whiteness" as cultural lack, as behavioral emptiness, as the absence of cultural creativity, or even as social and cultural thievery—a whiteness that is anything but an unmarked social category.[1]

In the previous chapter I attempted to look at how certain Harlemites discuss and practice class differences, how they use behavioral cues to mark socioeconomic diversity in quotidian social activities. Folk notions of class difference posit its expression in the extra-occupational actions that make up people's everyday lives. Class significances are gleaned from more than just one's location in the economic sphere vis-à-vis production.[2] Rather, class analyses continue to be fastened to careful interpretations of everyday behaviors. And these behaviors are used for reframing class-based differences as glimpsed through particular on-the-ground practices in the everyday (and not just workaday) world. The operative social actions are not relegated to those performed on the factory floor. These actions are reflective of wealth-based differences, however, and these same behavioral definitions of class allow individuals to manipulate and massage otherwise hard-and-fast socioeconomic criteria and their links to representations of self.

I want to continue this discussion about how people explain social stratification by examining various everyday actions (especially those associated with class in the previous chapter) for their racialized interpretations. Race, like class, makes sense in people's daily lives in terms of performances, practices, and perceptions. Moreover, these practices and performances show the inextricable connections between race and class as theorized in contemporary black America. I want to start this discussion off with a very brief survey of the major fault lines along which racial theories in the social sciences diverge, connecting those arguments to the explanations and definitions of race that I found during my fieldwork in Harlem.

Studying Race

There are many competing schools of thought on the continuing significance of racial identities and racial differences. Scholars dispute the very meaning of race, debating how it is best understood and defined.[3] Even though race and culture are not always treated as coterminous spheres, they are often conflated in interesting ways. For Brian, as an example, racial differences are indicative of cultural differences, of major racial disparities in the magnitude of cultural production. Moving across economies of scale, from global cultural measuring sticks to individual public behaviors, race is made meaningful for many of the people I spoke with in Harlem not just in terms of easy essences at the core of beings, but also through action-oriented sociopolitical appraisals of how people navigate their social settings. If, for Brian, different races have different legacies of achievement and histories of collective action, individual members of separate racial groups (particularly blacks and whites, in his example) have drastically different kinds of everyday actions, of cultural practices. Furthermore, class-inflected or -coded actions are often the same behaviors that become racialized in discussions about black racial particularity. I'll briefly outline some theoretical arguments about race and racial identity that have helped frame current academic debates, after which I want to unpack what a certain kind of folk notion of performative racial identity might offer to discussions of race and class in black America today.

The earliest academic arguments about race and racial differences were steeped in biological determinism.[4] Anthropology as a legitimate social science earned its own stripes by delineating the natural, biological, and physiological truth of race as a human taxonomic level below that of species. Carleton Coon was only the most famous of many scientists who attempted to classify the entire world's population into distinct racial groups. For Coon, Caucasoids, Mongoloids, Australoids, Congoids, and Capoids each evolved independently and from separate *Homo erectus* populations, with the darker races, the Congoids and Capoids, assumed to be the least civilized by virtue of their having arrived at the *Homo sapiens* stage most recently.[5] Traditionally, the dominant paradigm in anthropological understandings of race never questioned these kinds of biologized notions. Race was seen as a natural division of humankind found wholesale within the natural order, indeed created by that natural order. This biological conception of racial categories was coupled with an argument about relative racial development (in terms of important characteristics like intelligence) as a function of these natural(ized) differences. The natural inferiority of certain races was accepted as an obvious starting point for assessments of racial categorization.

It was a change in the collective political and social temperament of the West, especially after the excesses of racial chauvinism and genocide in Nazi Germany, that began to allow for certain biologized notions of race (and the eugenics movements they underpinned) to fall into disfavor among many mainstream social thinkers.[6] Moreover, as technological developments increased science's capacity to see the world in all its miniature specificity, nineteenth-century attempts to use physical characteristics (phenotypes) to define races and to delineate the measurable characteristics that most definitively separate them (Camper's measurements of facial angles, Retzius's cephalic index, von Török's five thousand measurements of the skull) all gave way to genetic measures of race (genotypes) that eventually led to more nuanced notions of human variation. Although genetics has been used to further racist arguments about racial inferiority and superiority, geneticists have also been the scholars most convincingly ringing the scientific death knell for popular assumptions about racial groupings as insurmountably biological realities.

In place of geneticized notions of race, various scholars have argued for an understanding of racial categories as less biology than naturalized sociality. Omi and Winant are two of the key social science proponents of this argument, canonizing the mantra that "race is a social construct," that society has created such a persuasive, powerful, and all-encompassing cultural significance for the physical differences we call race that it assumes a kind of natural and precultural solidity.[7] These social constructs only work because they can be passed off as less constructed than merely *found*, even stumbled upon, left out there to be discovered in the natural world. This is a naturalized cultural creation that feels so much like second nature to the people who have been taught to see it (and to see with it) that it passes for biological reality and covers up its own constructedness. By way of historicizing this argument, scholars argue that sixteenth- and seventeenth-century peoples undoubtedly noticed physical and phenotypic specificities, but they did not try to systematize and codify those differences into a racially hierarchical social taxonomy until race-based transatlantic slavery called out for ideological justification.[8]

Of course, viewing race as a social construction doesn't mean that its impact on people is somehow not real or important. It makes an indelibly real impression on people's everyday lives and potential life chances. It may be a biological fiction, social constructionists argue, but it is, with all due Durkheimian implications, a true "social fact."[9] As many race theorists argue, we must think of race not in essentialist terms (not as an absolute biological difference separating discrete and pure genetic populations) but as a malleable political and social designation that affects people's daily interactions and deep-seated beliefs about the world and their place in it.

Others argue that if "race" is in fact a cultural invention, then social constructionists and self-proclaimed antiessentialists are just as essentialist as anyone else if they continue holding on to notions of race in any way.[10] If race is not real in any natural or biological sense, they argue, then social constructionists should not be trying to cling to the concept. Why, they wonder aloud, is there even a need for an antiessentialist notion of race? Race is a folk concept that has always been about essences, they declare, and any attempt to maintain the notion of race without its essentialist underpinnings is misplaced from the start. In 1997, the Harvard University law professor Randall Kennedy published a controversial article condemning any and all forms of racial solidarity among black people—in a sense, extending this theoretical argument to its most obvious practical endpoint. "Neither racial pride nor racial kinship," he argued, "offers guidance that is intellectually, morally, or politically satisfactory."[11] If race is false, he proclaimed, then it is a mistake to think in terms of race. Period.

The literary critic Walter Benn Michaels takes on contemporary anthropological notions of "culture" (considered to be fluid, changing, and mobile instead of static, self-contained, and stationary) as part of a similar critique about race, culture, and essentialism. Michaels argues that present-day anthropologists utilize just as essentialist an idea of culture as the forebears they are quick to critique for assuming hermetically sealed-off and easily bounded cultural groupings. Michaels claims that those who hold contemporary anthropological notions of culture as fluid and nonfixed are guilty of invoking culture as a ruse for arguments that at heart are still biological. "The modern concept of culture," he writes, "is not a critique of racism; it is a form of racism."[12] He takes on James Clifford quite specifically here. According to Michaels, Clifford rejects certain traditional anthropological understandings of culture because of their "bias toward wholeness, continuity and growth."[13] Clifford denounces any essentialist uses of culture as the mark of fixed identities because such conceptions of culture tolerate few discontinuities over time and space, not allowing for the fact that "an identity can die and come back to life."[14] Michaels argues that for cultures and cultural identities to be considered lost, saved, reclaimed, reinvented, or resurrected, one must first posit an essential identity already predetermining whatever cultural practices and identities are in question. He uses Clifford's discussion of repatriation and the official recognition of contemporary Mashpee Indians as his primary example. For Clifford, the Mashpee need not behave the same way in the present as they did hundreds of years ago to be justified in their claims about cultural memory and legitimacy. Cultures can change, and the people who invoke them should not be judged by litmus tests of cultural practices from generations ago. For Michaels, Clifford's talk of cultural memory is not about culture but biology:

> If, then, the criteria of Mashpee identity are drumming, dressing in "regalia," and so on, it should be the case that anyone who meets [these] criteria should be a Mashpee. But if these criteria aren't sufficient, then some other criterion must be invoked. Clifford rejects culture as a mark of identity because culture tolerates no discontinuities. But he himself can tolerate discontinuity only if it is grounded in a continuity that runs much deeper than culture: drumming will make you Mashpee not because anyone who drums gets to be Mashpee but because, insofar as your drumming represents a lost tradition, it shows that you are already a Mashpee.[15]

According to Michaels, if culture is anything more than what one happens to do at the time, if it is what one should do, what one ought to do, if it is something that one "lost" and now has "found" or "reinvented," then there is a presupposition at work that says cultural identities prefigure cultural actions, that identities ground behaviors (no matter how fluid we think those identities may be). This, he asserts, is cut from the very same cloth of essentialism that Clifford attempts to combat. Michaels instead offers a notion of culture as simply and singularly what people do (what their behaviors happen to be). If they no longer do something, he argues, then it is no longer a part of their cultural repertoire—end of story.[16]

He also takes issue with Omi and Winant's notion of "racial projects" linked to a particular "political/programmatic agenda," arguing that race is first considered a "project" within class-stratified, intraracial contexts.[17] That is, race is only feasible as a project in spaces where class differences bend the limits of racial commonality. It can only become a project once it is no longer defined exclusively by biology or phenotype, but rather positioned somewhere at the slippage between the biological and the social. Class differences provide rich ground for the discussion of racial identity as other than ultimately and absolutely tied to

skin color, a kind of racial identity accessible through folk interpretations of everyday activity.

Race, Biology, and Culture in Harlem

The Michaels-Clifford debate is about how scholars and social theorists
determine the correlation between identities and cultural practices. I'm
more interested in how Harlem residents themselves theorize that linkage. Many Harlemites talk about race in ways that highlight this very
fissure between identity as being and identity as doing, between what
one is (ontologically and phenotypically speaking) and what one does
(behaviorally) in the social world. Race can be a difficult thing to define,
but many of the people I spoke with in Harlem took interesting pathways toward working out such definitions. For Dexter, race is linked, unavoidably and undeniably, to a clear-cut sense of biological difference:

> **Dexter:** What we have, we have melanin in us, and that, it is a
> chemical, that makes us different from white peoples. That mela-
> nin gives us certain, like, biological and, certain genes, certain bi-
> ological looks. We are black because of melanin mostly, black
> genes.

Dexter speaks easily and surely about "black genes," and he often cites
the work of Dr. Frances Cress Welsing, a psychiatrist who writes about
race, racism, and genetics, arguing that whites have a subconscious fear
of their own "genetic annihilation" as a function of intermarriage with
black people and their (dominant) black genes.[18] This fear, she says,
causes the suprapsychological reaction formation known as "white
supremacy." Her book, *The Isis Papers: The Keys to the Colors,* outlines
her "Color Confrontation Theory," an epic-like genetic battle in which
whites' repressed racial-genetic inferiority and inadequacy are expressed
as antiblack hatred. *The Isis Papers* was one of the first gifts I received
in the field—Dexter purchased it for me on a whim, as a belated birthday present from one of the book vending tables that still do business
on 125th Street sidewalks after Giuliani's vendor relocation.[19] Dexter's
notion of race is partially based on his reading of this very text and
others like it—many of which he could not have purchased at any
Barnes and Noble in the land. He is part of an alternative discursive community of readers who organize formal and informal reading groups
around texts written for blacks and sold almost exclusively through the
circuit of black bookstores and vending outlets that stock them for

Vending books (photo by Scheherazade Tillet)

their intended audience. Cynthia, too, has a notion of race that is biological, but she talks more in terms of blood and ancestry than genes and melanin:

> **Cynthia:** We [black people] come from the same place. We have the same blood; that is the family part. We all got the same stuff. It's like a family. We all the same on the inside. That's why Harlem was nicer when I was just growing up instead of now, there was more of a sense of community and unity, pride.

Whereas Dexter discusses melanin, Cynthia sees blood ties as defining elements of racial community and commonality—both invoking physiological notions of racial identity, one predicated on the seen (melanin as expressed in skin pigmentation), the other on the unseen (the red blood coursing through the veins just beneath that pigmented skin). These are fairly standard notions of race as biological truism, and many folks I spoke to in Harlem are quick to offer them. Still, this biological notion of racial difference is only one essentialist gesture—and not even the most hegemonic one. Along with these biologized and geneticized definitions of race, many Harlemites would proffer understandings of racial identity that are decidedly nonbiological. Sociality becomes a second cog in the wheel of racial difference. For example, Paul talks about race as a specific function of discrimination:

> **John:** When you think of racial identity, what do you think about?
>
> **Paul:** Race is what keeps the black man down.
>
> **John:** What do you mean?
>
> **Paul:** You know exactly what I mean, so don't even front.

"You know exactly what I mean" is Paul's concise effort to speak plainly about the seemingly transparent kinds of discriminatory practices keeping "the black man down"—practices that he assumes I should know as a function of my own black masculinity. He posits discriminatory practices that define race as a socially important phenomenon, practices so self-evident and obvious that Paul demands I admit my knowledge of exactly what he means. Robert offers a definition of race that tries, in a sense, to split this difference between the biological and the sociological:

> **Robert:** It is our skin color, our history, all of that. All of that. We walk down the street and we get arrested for bullshit, brothers is incarcerated left and right, that is what it is. When we go for jobs we discriminated against. That is the messed up thing about it. . . . It's the skin we in.

The "skin we in" is a biological—or at least epidermal—rendition of race. Here, too, race is linked specifically to gender. It is brothers who get incarcerated and "arrested for bullshit."[20] His logic of racial biology only makes sense, as he discusses it, by linking skin color immediately to social discrimination along gendered lines, to the criminalization and incarceration of male persons in particularly hued skin.

Resting in her office after a quick lunch, Janet finishes a heated discussion with some female colleagues about the city's attempts to lay off more city hospital workers. The Health and Hospital Corporation had already laid off more than eight hundred workers by that time, state senator David Paterson had recently received enough funds to just barely avoid more layoffs at Harlem Hospital, and the women were all happy about averting more job loss in their community. The other issue jockeying for airtime in their conversation was the recent City University of New York decision to end remediation. Every single woman was outraged. A CUNY student had found hidden cameras on campus, one woman exclaimed. Another thought that the students should sue. Still another said that they already had. When the women left Janet and me alone in her office, she immediately started in on the mayor and his insensitivity to the black community as evidenced in the Harlem Hospital and CUNY issues. When our interview finally got going, Janet talked about race in social terms—in the decidedly institutional sense that it is "big business":

> **Janet:** Race is the way they try to split people up.
>
> **John:** They who?
>
> **Janet:** Big business, the government, they want to keep people fighting one another and killing one another for nothing, so nobody's thinking that we all really just hurting, messing our own selves up. That's all it is.
>
> **John:** . . . Does that mean that race isn't real, if it is something, like, that is used to split people up?
>
> **Janet:** I mean I'm black, don't get me wrong, but that don't mean cheering and ra-ra and I hate white people and all of that. I'm black, but that's not all. I'm a woman, for one. I'm middle-class, for another. . . . I'm all of that.

Janet is critical of an exclusionary and overly celebratory notion of racial identity predicated on antiwhite racism—especially the kind that might elide questions of gender, class, and regionality. She doesn't want to invoke race like a cheerleader rallying her team against some identifiably "white" opponent, even though she also feels that Giuliani is a racist who hates Harlemites and baits black folks into hostile reactions. Janet is careful about her thoughts on race, but she also has no qualms about invoking racism as an explanation for contemporary community issues.

Zelda, for one, seems almost able to talk herself in and out of the notion of race within a couple of sentences:

> **Zelda:** What I think is bad, is when people try to say other people ain't black. If you black you black.
>
> **John:** Does that happen a lot? Does that happen to you? People trying to say that?
>
> **Zelda:** I am black like everybody else up here so I don't even think about that stuff.

John: And what does that mean?

Zelda: What do you mean?

John: When you say you're black, what do you mean, or what do you think about?

Zelda: I think that means that I am brown skinned, and I don't know. It means that I am part of the black community and things like that. That we came over here on slave ships. I don't know. Maybe it don't mean nothing. If it got to mean something else, maybe it ain't nothing.

Zelda's somewhat equivocal comments about race, voiced in her living room between sprints back and forth to a pie baking in the oven, are specifically solicited by my questions. Maybe she would never have had this exchange otherwise (in, say, more informal social interactions without a specific research agenda underpinning them); nonetheless, it still seems important to note that she is able to move from a clear and definitive statement about the certainty of her racial identity ("If you black you black. . . . I am black. . . . we came over here in slave ships") to a more ambiguous stance on race's fidelity and usefulness as a social concept ("Maybe it ain't nothing") in a matter of seconds. This is the slipperiness of race in the real world, its ability to appear so undeniably real and unreal at one and the same time. It is this space between race as real (either biologically or sociologically speaking—"Black is black," "You know what I mean") and race as unreal (as a myth that may "mean nothing" at all) that illuminates the connections linking race and class to the kinds of sociocultural practices that Michaels and Clifford dispute.

Karen maintains that "we [blacks] just act differently. We do things differently." For her, race is aligned with clear differences in actions and behaviors. Damon also stresses that "it is our whole operations, just completely different from white people all the way around," that makes black people distinct. Brandi also sees race in terms of cultural differences and uses white people as a foil for a discussion about black cultural difference:

> **Brandi:** Black people listen to a kind of music, we go to certain, we eat foods, we just do things the way we do them. I don't have any problem with white people, but they have a different style.
>
> **John:** Different like what?
>
> **Brandi:** It's like I said, they listen to that heavy metal and stuff.

They don't listen to, most of them don't listen to, R. Kelly; they like Anthrax. They don't do the things we like to do. They don't eat what we eat. Their food is bland. They just got a different way of acting. Like if a white person goes to a movie, they all quiet and proper, but we like, "all right now, entertain me up in here for my money," okay? And we get into it and all of that. They are just more quiet.

Michaels's arguments begin to offer a glimpse into how a cultural template for racial identity might relate to issues of class stratification and heterogeneity in the African American community. One interesting reading of my discussions with various Harlemites about their under-standings of race is that blacks from all across the socioeconomic spec-trum seem to hold on to race and racial identity as important and real, regardless of class position. They may differ on exact definitions, but they all offered at least a kind of lip service to the significance of race in their social lives. Indeed, how many of those responses were a func-tion of being "studied" by a black male anthropology student interested in race is probably open to debate. Nevertheless, many other scholars and researchers have weighed in on whether different classes of African Americans see race differently. Some argue that the black middle class may be more Afrocentric and pro-black because they have greater access to the white world and direct experiences with racial prejudice than do the ghetto-segregated poor.[21] Other scholars argue that African Ameri-cans higher up the social ladder are forced to rubber-stamp black mass cultural practices and productions (listening to misogynistic rap lyrics, wearing Dashikis and Kente cloth) as an effort to prove to themselves and to the black community more generally that they really are black despite their mainstream social positions.[22] Part of what I tried to un-pack in chapter 4 was the idea that black America may not be class-blind as much as willing and able to see class implications everywhere, hyperaware of the class-related differences that distinguish people and groups. This fact gets even more complicated as one looks to what class differences imply for a racial identity fashioned in the crucible of behav-ior. For many African Americans in Harlem, race is biological, but not just biological. It is also sociological (in terms of discrimination), but it is not just that, either. It is also performative, predicated on actions, on the things one does in the world, on how one behaves. It is this perform-ative mandate of race, I argue, that helps allow for race's linkages to class—that both reinforces and taxes essentialist explanations of racial hierarchies.

This performative understanding of race differs slightly from "culture" proper (that is, arguments about diasporic cultural traits) in that it encompasses them but includes many more actions in the equation. For example, this performative raciality need not invoke the weight of history to make its case. The rhetorical scaffolding can be much more contemporary, providing space for debates about racial difference that have the potential to be decidedly democratic owing to their unabashedly empirical nature. This is normally read as the slippery sand of stereotype. But it is not exclusively that. It is also the flexible organizing principle for a kind of "racial habitus" that mobilizes far too many trajectories of difference for any one person or institution to fully control.

Doing Whiteness

To advance this discussion a little further, I want to look not only at how black Harlemites theorize themselves through the frame of blackness, but also how they make sense of whiteness and white people as the performative alternative against which blackness is defined. Many of my informants have no problem talking at length about whiteness and white identity. Even individuals who may not have had much extended contact with whites on a daily basis often spoke at length about what whiteness means to them—a definition sometimes garnered as much from the mass media as from everyday experiences. The important baseline in many of these discussions of whiteness, as exemplified in Brian's earlier comments about the lack of white cultural output, is that it is often contingent on assessments of what white people supposedly do or don't do. Brian maintained that white people do nothing creative or constructive, and that argument allows him a sense of racial difference (even superiority) tied to black cultural productivity. Brandi used her notion of whiteness to signify a "quiet" and "proper" people, a distinction organized around minor differences separating black actions from white actions in a darkened movie theater. Carl also offers a strict racialization of everyday behavior:

> **Carl:** White folks just don't have that flavor. Period. It ain't about money or any of that stuff, but then again you have some white people who act pretty cool, but I would still say that most white people don't have that flavor, and that is what makes us different.
>
> **John:** Flavor?
>
> **Carl:** Hell yes!

White flavorlessness is an assessment of supposedly white-specific behaviors that are lacking a certain conspicuous flair. Carl can see that
some whites "act cool," an unmistakable concession to the fact that a
few whites can occasionally behave like they have some "flavor." But
Carl is confident that a race-based pattern of flavorless actions defines
and confines the white other. In fact, Carl's emphatic "Hell yes!" acts
as a kind of instantiation of the very black "flavor" and flair that he
wouldn't expect to hear within the world of whiteness.

Just as easily as Carl admits that some white people can act flavorful,
black people can be posited without flavor. When black people lack flavor, they are dangerously close to a pejorative behavioral territory often
termed "acting white."[23]

> **John:** Have you heard of acting white? If so, what does that
> mean?
>
> **Dexter:** A person is acting white, a black person is acting white,
> when they forget where they come from and try to pretend that
> they ain't got some nigga in they family. It's like just losing all
> of the things that make you black.
>
> **John:** What kind of things?
>
> **Dexter:** I knew you would say that. Things like, shit, what's a
> good example. Like our style. You know.

For Dexter, acting white is couched in terms of the ability to forget one's
racialized past and family tree. However, where Dexter was a bit stumped
in an attempt at elaboration and relied on a racial commonsense he assumed that I shared ("you know"), Cynthia might offer him some definitional help. For her, acting white is linked to some very clear and specific sets of behaviors:

> **Cynthia:** White people talk different. They move their bodies dif-
> ferent. They laugh different. Everything we do we do different
> from white people. And mostly they want to do what we do,
> you know, like us. Be like us.

Cynthia would see racial differences even and especially in rather everyday activities like talking, moving, and laughing. Her invocation of
laughter as a racial indicator seems reminiscent of Du Bois's "delicious
chuckle" as the description of black-specific laughter in the midst of pain
and tribulations.[24] Again, for Cynthia, the distinction between blackness and whiteness, black people and white people, is predicated on the
observable contrasts between their actions. Many other Harlemites

offer an understanding of racial difference highlighted by such discussions of everyday activities. Robert, for one, quite clearly sees race in the everyday:

> **Robert:** The way white people walk down the street. Eddie Murphy clowned them on that. Like they got something up their ass, all tight and just tight. Did you see that? It was mad funny. It's old, but when I saw that shit for the first time, I was like crying.
>
> **John:** I remember that. It was *Saturday Night Live,* I think.
>
> **Robert:** Yeah, and I was like on the floor with that.
>
> **John:** And then when he was alone with white people he would get treated differently by other whites, I remember it. It was pretty funny.
>
> **Robert:** That was wild.
>
> **John:** Do all white people walk that way? The way Eddie Murphy did in that *Saturday Night Live*?
>
> **Robert:** Ninety-five percent. Maybe ninety. Yeah. If they have some money and shit then definitely, yes. Then the tight-butt is in effect. Definitely true.

Robert may be unsure about the precise frequency with which white people meet the criteria for race-specific striding gaits, but his point is only that there is such a definitive pattern to it. He claims that most whites walk differently from blacks; race and class are mobilized here as areas of cross-fertilization. Not only can actions be seen as linked to notions of class and class-based differences, but also the very same actions are often and equally racialized. Walking was posited as a specifically class-related activity in the previous chapter, but it can also be linked to racial difference—with class categories looming ominously in the background all the while.

The same racialization can affect talk of talk as well. Janet identifies specific speech patterns within certain linguistic communities and uses that correlation to critique her own behaviors as she hangs out with some of the black female workers from her job, such as the ones she talks with about Giuliani and the CUNY remediation issue:

> **Janet:** I always feel like I am being phony when I'm around them. Like trying to speak black English, which is not me.
>
> **John:** What do you mean, black English?

Janet: The street, like trying to sound black. I am black, and I shouldn't have to sound like that to be accepted. I feel like if people don't accept me for who I am, then they don't deserve to even know who I am, then.

For Janet, speaking black English is concomitantly talking "street," a combination that bespeaks the racial and class-related nature of the linguistic repertoire she has admitted, now and at other times, makes her feel phony. For Janet, speaking black English is a misleading attempt not to be herself. When I asked her if she thought she acted white, she answered in a qualified affirmative: "All I know," she offered, "is that if I do, it's not bad. It doesn't mean I'm not black. I'm definitely black." This is a blackness that sometimes must be reaffirmed and confirmed in a world where blackness is propped up by specific behavioral corner-stones.

White Harlem

Now, these ideas of whiteness and acting white form an important arena in which racial identity and racial solidarity are made manifest. One can do many things in white ways, and the class implications Janet fore-grounds in her previously cited metalinguistic discussion are not always apparent:

Dexter: Sometimes white people can just be goofy. They just act flighty, silly. I think it's 'cause they won it all so they must be like, fuck it, I can do whatever the hell I want. Black people don't have that. We just trying to make it, you know. We act crazy they'll shoot our asses and that type of thing. So we gotta keep it cool.

For Dexter, white people have a luxury and security in their white-ness, a luxury that allows them to behave in certain ways denied black people for fear of death. It is this specter of white aggression and reaction that serves as another major theme in some Harlemites' discussions of whiteness. This is a notion of whiteness as oppression, of a race that "just stole from us" and tries "to keep the black man down" as Brian and Paul, respectively, put it. Whiteness can be a lot more pernicious than "tight-butt" striding gaits and stoic indifference inside crowded movie theaters. Zelda guaranteed, for example, that "white people teach their kids in schools how to run the world," a notion of white pedagogi-cal practices that has nefarious implications for the rest of the nonwhite world. According to Cynthia, that dastardly potential of whiteness links the materiality of race to racial discourse in inextricable ways. It also bespeaks other moments when purportedly white actions become decoupled from phenotypically white actors:

> **Cynthia:** They bring drugs up in Harlem. They bring crime up in Harlem. They bring all kinds of hell and mess up in Harlem, and that is how they trying to kill us. Physically and through what they say, what they believe. That is they stuff. Hope you not writing some kind of white Harlem. Ain't nothing real about that. So I know I wouldn't trust it, not that. Especially when they not gonna come correct 'cause they can't handle the blizity black that really don't need them and don't want to see them.

The idea of a black Harlem seems simple enough to imagine. The almost teleological story of Harlem's progression from a white to a black world serves as the discursive scaffolding for any and all invocations of black Harlem. But Cynthia's invocation of a white Harlem in the present (one that implicated my own ethnographic actions) scared and even disturbed me. Would I write (and construct as my field site) a white Harlem? And what would a white Harlem look like, anyway? Moreover, what on earth would be white about it? And just because it was white, would it be any more or less accurate than its black counterpart? I pressed Cynthia to extrapolate:

> **Cynthia:** When white people see Harlem, they see garbage on the street and poor people. They see evil. Um, they see murder, crime. And they see that and they think that they can make all kinds of, they can say things about Harlem. That it is a bad place. . . . But none of that is true. No matter what they say. They are the ones who are dirty trying to tell us we dirty. . . . These blacks, yayaya, they dirty and all that.

Is the "white Harlem" one of unexamined condemnations, of unfounded and unverified assumptions that link, as Mary Douglas might argue, a certain kind of impurity to danger?[25] How does a white Harlem change the cultural geography of Harlemworld? Against the presuppositional negativity of a white Harlem, it is easy to lapse into the same kind of romanticized "blizity black" Harlem nostalgia that I tried to touch on a bit in chapter 1: Langston Hughes lived here and Miles Davis played here and Fidel Castro slept here, a string of memories highlighting a "great day" frozen in the not-so-distant and ever-approaching past.

For many people, Harlem presupposes a certain degree of blackness. The *black* in front of the *Harlem* (in the term *black Harlem*) is used as more than mere redundancy. And it is evoked all over, even and especially by the cultural historians and journalists who have cornered the market on representations of Harlem's supposed blackness. That is also where one can find many invocations of the term *white Harlem*. There are many more white Harlems besides the one Cynthia used to problematize my own potential ethnographic rendition of her home. The whiteness that Cynthia refers to has a past, a present, and a future. For example, one kind of white Harlem is the preindustrial enclave of Dutch settlers turned English nation-builders turned Irish and Italian subway system construction workers, a historically white suburb transformed into a black ghetto, a transformation evident to many who reside there now.

"White folks used to live here," proclaims Dexter, "and they didn't want to have black people here, either. I know all about that. They wanted to keep black people out. But you know, that don't work. They try to do all kinds of shit, but we keep on coming."

"They rode buggies and horses," Asia offers succinctly, "and they had big houses and stuff and all of that. Something like that. Then we got here and they jetted."

Another brand of white Harlem uncovers a hot spot of the roaring twenties, a patronizing, philanthropic, and philandering white Harlem. After the speculation boom and the demand bust of the late nineteenth and early twentieth centuries, after Tenderloin and San Juan Hill moved uptown to fill the residential void, there was a Cotton Clubbed white Harlem of the dark night life.

"White people used to love to come up here," Ms. Joseph says. "To the clubs and the bright lights. Harlem was full of black folks entertaining white people. Singing and dancing. You couldn't be black and come in to some of these white clubs. And you had to be light-skinned if you did. But most blacks only washed dishes."

Here, whiteness in Harlem meant the exclusion of blacks from certain parts of the community, especially in class-inflected ways that meant these white-only hot spots were sites not of play but of hard work for blacks.[26] Yet another white Harlem would speak to the recommercialized Harlem, an undoing of Harlem, an almost postapocalyptic result of continuing gentrification, a threat not yet realized but fully recognized.[27]

"They wanna come and get rid of us," Damon asserts. "Whites have the money and they can raise the rents and stuff, and then where we gonna go? They wanna take over our neighborhood. They got everything downtown and now they want Harlem too. They do." White

Harlem here is characterized by a contemporary encroachment, a potential displacement. One of the most popular issues in the press today about the area pivots on the threat of gentrification, a theme that concerns many black Harlemites.

"Whites don't belong here," Dexter says. "And they know that shit. They know it. So you see them up here and they just try walking past you. They try to think if they pretend not to see you, you won't check them, you know."

Part of the point, then, is that this whiteness, an encroaching and invading whiteness, this boundary-challenging whiteness, can often make its way inside the fortress walls. There is a white Harlem not just of the perennial past or the gentrified future but also of the present, a white Harlem exemplified by tourist desire. Dexter puts it this way:

> **Dexter:** Whites in they little see-through buses. Just taking photos. Like, that is some shit. At the Apollo or something. And they can't even, like, see us. We look at them and get they whole life story like that [he snaps fingers]. But they come up here to take pictures and with video camera and they look right past us. We look at them and learning more about them than they ever learn about us from us, you know, from looking at us. They come up here and they the ones on display. We just doing our thing, living our life, and they snapping pictures. But we taking mental pictures in our head that last longer. And we check them out big time.

This tourism-based white Harlem, one that sets up a very specific dialectic of watching and being watched, exposes how it is that the eye that purports to see is often already seen as well by a suspicious reverse gaze.[28] But the counterhegemonic buck might not stop there. Chris, twenty, born in Harlem, is a self-published author of two small chapbooks (both "selling pretty well on the 125 [Street]," he brags lightly):

> **Chris:** These churches up here are getting a piece of that loot, too. Believe me. Don't be fooled. I know. My father was big in the church, and they would charge the tours to let folks come into the church and stuff. Like a couple dollars a head. I don't know how much, but it wasn't nothing to look down at. We was getting over and paid with these dumb folks who wanted to sit in a black church. And my uncle and dad and them was like, "Okay, just give us some cash." The churches knew what was up. They trying to get paid, too.

In some ways, this last white Harlem undergirds the central premise of the literature on black racial double vision, a literature indebted to the metaphors of Du Bois: the need for blacks to see both whiteness and blackness better than chauvinistic and socially secure whites who supposedly look but do not see behind the racial "veil."[29] This version of white Harlem marks time between whiteness as tourism and "whiteness as terrorism," a terroristic tourism that impinges on human beings in museological ways, forcing the living exhibits to see their very objectification and to return that horrific gaze in kind.[30]

"We gotta watch them like hawks," Damon admonishes over a slice with extra cheese, " 'cause they always got tricks up their sleeves. They always up to something. So I watch the news and see what's up. See what they doing now. Go to the library. Read up. 'Cause anything is possible with they asses. . . . But I ain't racist because I know some white people aren't as racist as other ones, you know. There are white folks who own this pizza store, and I even think, like, they live somewhere down the street from here, and I ain't never, never had no problem with them. But they ain't up in here trying to examine me and kill me and all of that bullshit."

A decidedly white Harlem of the present doesn't end with first-wave gentrifiers or Italian pizza shop owners who have never left. There is another catchall cultural invocation of whiteness that is specifically about a different dimension of white Harlem, an embodied if not epidermalized whiteness that stands as yet another articulation of purportedly racialized actions. Working on what "whiteness" means for white residents of Detroit, the anthropologist John Hartigan Jr. offers an amendment to Omi and Winant's notion of racial formations, the processes "by which social, economic and political forces determine the content and importance of racial categories, and by which they are in turn shaped by racial meanings."[31]

Hartigan takes issue with some of the ways in which Omi and Winant utilize notions of social constructionism. He argues that Omi and Winant's articulation of race's social constructedness (as changing form over time) shows that "racial meanings are never static or absolute."[32] But Hartigan maintains that they move too quickly and flat-footedly from abstraction to specificity in the way they work out these racial formations. His ethnographic work with whites in Detroit shows that white people in that particular area have regionally specific relationships to their whiteness, relationships that diverge from (and are not necessarily generalizable to) other communities of whites in other parts of the area. Whiteness, Hartigan asserts, changes not just through time (including and excluding, at various points in history, now Irish, now southern Italians, and now Asian Americans partial access to some portion of its hegemonic power) but with place.[33] That is, racial discourse's relation to location is just as important as its modifications through time.[34] As seminal as Omi and Winant's racial formation theory is as a starting point for theorizing the social construction of race, he maintains, it mostly glosses over the vast differences within the racial category "white" from region to region. Their formulation lacks an explication of race's spatial specificity, Hartigan opines, and ignores the differences in what scale, size, and space mean to and for white racial identity.

The whites who live in a forsaken urban Detroit operate from a different kind of whiteness than the white suburbanites who park near them to go to Detroit Tigers games, and he uses this argument to open up a space between whiteness and white bodies—between the abstract and the specific, the big and the small, the generalities and the particularities of whiteness in post–civil rights America. In that very gap he finds slippage between what whiteness means to and for specific white populations and what it means to and for white communities in general. The gap separating white particularities from one another (or from some abstract "whiteness") allows for the insertion, I argue, not only of white regional specificity, as he insists, but also of markedly darker hued persons into the cleft between whiteness and white bodies. Black bodies can be read as white bodies once behavioral specificities are added to the discussion. It is this slippage between identity and action that allows black bodies (and their actions) to be theorized along symbolically white lines. And that possibility provides yet another route into contemporary discussions about the importance of racialized behaviors in potentially white Harlems.[35]

As exemplified in the comments by Brandi, Dexter, Carl, and Janet, black racial identity is often and also contingent on what people do, and not just what black people do. This means that whiteness plays a central role even (and especially) in seemingly black-only interactions—where and when "white people," "acting white," "white folks," and so on are frequently used explanatory devices offered by a self-consciously "blizity black" Harlem to talk not just across racial tracks (in an effort to fortify its boundaries against the white threat from without) but also to look back into the kernels of its own posited black self. "Whiteness" is often used (as it was by Zelda, Carla, Cynthia, Dexter, and others) to make sense of the ideas espoused and actions performed by not only white tourists or clubbers but also, and especially, those of phenotypically "black" Harlemites whose actions belie any easy access to racial certainty.

White Actions and Black Bodies

Zelda is still working in the position she landed after a subway ride with the black woman, Anne, who is now her boss. However, Zelda is a bit unhappy about her life on the job because of the way Anne interacts with her. Zelda is not being treated rudely, not being overworked or exploited in any obvious way—common employee gripes. Instead, she is complaining about the very opposite:

> **Zelda:** She just can be so crazy. Like I don't like the way she acts. You know, it's like white people do. When they want to be friends and all of this stuff. I might, I don't know her and I don't want to know her. Not to be nasty, but I'm there to do a job. I'm not gonna be nasty about it, but I don't want to be all touchy touchy. I don't want to hear about your boyfriend and the dinner you had and all that. And that just trips me out, because then she makes it like because I'm not all nice-nice and all that. I don't want to grin in her face and all that kind of stuff. But I do my job and that is why she hired me.

Anne's desire to be "touchy touchy" is, according to Zelda, "like white people do." Here, she equates a certain way of interacting, a seemingly personable and informal way, with white people's actions. When asked to clarify the whiteness of her boss's informality and attempted niceties, Zelda maintains that "white people do that shit because, and it's completely bullshit, they'll talk behind your back and all of that stuff, but they will smile in your face and act all buddy buddy. Just two-faced." She leans back snugly into the pockets of her living room sofa as she makes her point. There is a pause. I prompt her to go on:

> **John:** Have you had that happen to you before?
>
> **Zelda:** Of course, you can't work with white people and not have that. I don't want it to, either. I'd just rather come in, I'll say "good morning" but then tell me what you need me to do that way and then leave me alone so I can do the damn thing. That is why I am getting paid, you know? She's my boss—not to be somebody's friend. I got my own friends.

Zelda doesn't exactly equate informality itself with white people, just a false and premature brand of it. When Zelda says that her boss barely knows her, she is offering a notion of whiteness as a kind of forced and insincere familiarity. For Zelda, her black boss is just "like white people" because she tries to impose disingenuous informality on an employee-employer relationship. In a sense, when viewed from Anne's position, one could quite easily read that informal demeanor as an attempt to downplay the occupational hierarchy, an arguably positive initiative to level the interpersonal playing field. For Zelda, however, this is not a genuinely democratizing move (after all, "she's my boss") but a manipulative attempt to mask power differentials and to misrepresent the true nature of their relationship.

Janet, who has admitted to being unwilling to speak black English since it makes her feel "phony," has been at the tail end of accusations of "acting white" many times before. She defines these jeers as a response to her strongly held position against code-switching and defends her linguistic practices:

> **Janet:** I don't care if you are black, white, green, rich, poor, on welfare, whatever, I talk to people the way I talk. I have a way I talk, and you might call it just regular English, no slang, and that is the way I talk, and I don't try to be what people stereotype black people to be, and that makes some people uncomfortable. That makes some black people feel uncomfortable.
>
> **John:** Why do you think that is?
>
> **Janet:** That is just what people are used to.
>
> **John:** All black people are used to this?
>
> **Janet:** I guess not, but when you deal with poorer people, at least when I deal with just the black people around here, and where I work, on the street and that kind of thing, they don't take the chance to get to know you. That is a big part of the problem right there. People don't take the time to get to know people, so they use stereotypes. If you fit the stereotype of a black person, you sound this way and act this way and things like that, then you are okay. If you don't, then you must want to be white. . . . I'm not trying to be white. I'm just being Janet, who I am. And if people can't deal with it, that is their problem. I'll be okay.

Janet unflinchingly asserts her right to keep doing and "being Janet" and not another person's black stereotypes. She is sure that notions of acting white are other people's failings, not her own.

Alice, thirty-seven, an administrator at a junior high school, offers another example of how phenotypically black bodies can occupy a place like "white Harlem." In describing her boss, Dr. Stevens, a forty-five-year-old black female with an Ed.D., and their relationship on the job, Alice offers an important insight into this world of white black bodies:

Alice: I can't stand her [Dr. Stevens]. She is worse than all of them. She's the worst one. Because she walks around like she think she's better than everybody else because she got some kind of degree and all. But she's not. She be trying to get up in here and get white on you. Like real bad, too. It just ain't fair.

John: What is white about how she's acting?

Alice: Like she is always looking down on people. She don't even see you, nose all up in the air. She all proper and will try to call you out like you a child. Like you just a little girl. I'm a grown woman. . . . I'm grown. And I don't want people talking to me like I'm a child.

If it is Dr. Stevens's actions (her on-the-job performances) that determine and predetermine Alice's assessment of her as someone prone to acting or "get[ting] white on folks," it is a whiteness that is finally and ultimately unresponsive to many other ostensibly "black" performances to the contrary:

Alice: She think just 'cause she got dreadlocks and Kente cloth and whatnot that she can talk to folks anyway she want. I am not the one. And she is gonna find out. One of these days she is gonna find out. You can't talk to people like that, you know. And you know, she think she slick. She be in here, and she know some slang words, not Ebonics now, slang she heard some teenagers say, or on TV, or something, and she think that she down. That don't make her black. She better take that, and her little African jewelry and her African hats and stuff and go somewhere else with it. 'Cause ain't nobody fooled but a fool.

Alice's boss's dreadlocked hair and Kente-cloth garments don't allow her an easy release from the clutches of performative whiteness. Even her slang (not "Ebonics," Alice specifies, but "slang"—an important distinction separating legitimate access to black speech practices from a kind of pseudo-black English) is not a performative escape hatch from the whiteness that Alice despises. Alice goes on, "I really do think she think she white. . . . And it ain't just 'cause she got some education, either. You got an education. I'm working on my B.A. and when I finish I'm gonna try, God willing, to get a better job or something, you know, more money, but I ain't never gonna be like her."

Alice explicitly distinguishes between class ("a better job . . . more money") and race. For Alice, acting white is a racial performance that is not reducible to class issues. In fact, Alice has middle-class aspirations of her own with respect to getting her B.A., but that is different, she maintains, from the actions that allow black people to seem white, to think of themselves as white. For her, moving up the class ladder is no excuse for Dr. Stevens's performative whiteness. Alice's critique of a black-bodied "whiteness" is not mitigated by Afrocentric garb or caused in any simplistic way by a disdain for educational achievement—the broad-brushed arguments that some scholars use about black culture's alleged anti-intellectualism notwithstanding.

Looking for a comparative opinion on "whiteness"-"blackness" and Dr. Stevens, I asked one of Alice's co-workers, Richard, twenty-seven, an administrator who had just recently started working there, to give me his take on their boss:

> **Richard:** Oh, she's OK, every once in a while she'll show her butt, you know. That's when you know she done been gone too long.
>
> **John:** How does she show her butt?
>
> **Richard:** Just like, just a little, like, I don't know, like she thinks she's better than somebody. But see, you trying to finish up at Columbia, right, and you don't get all stank and nasty. You can still be cool. You can still talk like a human being. I can. Most people can. She can't. It's like her knowing stuff makes her more stupid when it comes to just common sense and talking to people.

Richard talks of a "stank" and "stupid" difference distinguishing Dr. Stevens from "most people," a difference that exposes her lack of "common sense." As an anthropologist, one of the earliest and best lessons I learned was that if I wanted access to a behind-the-veil understanding of my most famous field site (through a few of the people who live there), I would have to perform a decidedly black Harlem in clearly nonstank and nonstupid ways—a repertoire that consisted of carefully chosen actions and gestures that would be received as acceptable forms of being in Harlem. Moreover, this would be a diverse array of code- and behavior-switching performances that are not the same in every ethnographic situation and don't always work completely:[36]

> **Dexter:** You're from there, you know, Columbia, and you don't come off corny. Well, maybe sometimes. But you know, you ain't all that whitewashed. It ain't that bad with you. [He laughs.] And that is the way we have to do it. Get the education but don't let it get you. Don't be fooled by those white folks over there, all around here. They don't care nothing about you,

and if you think they do, and forget about yourself, that is the
last thing you gonna do 'cause they will eat you up and won't
even believe, sometimes, that they doing it.

Dexter's idea of whiteness, one hovering around as a silent backdrop
to any and all black Harlems, elides ethnic differences and leaves little
space for redemptive white identities. Nonetheless, it is instructive in
that it does not define whiteness in exclusively sensationalized terms; it
does not leave whiteness to languish in the land of bald, tattooed white-
supremacist skinheads and Ku Klux Klan rallies. It is an everyday notion
of whiteness no less pernicious for its lack of hard-rock, slam-dancing
accompaniment and bullhorned racial epithets. Dexter's is a whiteness
that hints at just how race can become implicated with space and actions, decoupling itself in important ways from an easy reducibility to
specific skin colors.

I should stress that "acting white" is not a function of one singular
activity or form of behavior. It is, rather, about many large and small
actions that are bound up together in a complicated racial constellation
of behaviors. Social climbing alone, for example, isn't the only and deciding factor. Moreover, the mixture of variables is so complex that specifically black actions (linguistic registers, clothing, and other markers
of symbolically black identity) are often useless against accusations of
whiteness. Acting white (the connections between behaviors and racial
identity) is more intricate and entangled than that. This is why Afrocen-
trists don't control definitions of blackness in contemporary America
(and why Dr. Stevens's donning of Kente can be racially problematized).
No behavioral gesture is going to allow unproblematized access to black
authenticity. These gestures are always up for grabs because the behavioral facts of the matter are never wholly self-evident. It is the discursive
scaffolding constructed around these open-ended behaviors that imbues
activities with racial and class significances.

In discussions of black intellectual achievement, many scholars argue
that intelligence has become equated with whiteness for young black
children and their "oppositional" countercultures. Therefore, black children do not perform well in school for fear of sabotaging their racial
selves in the eyes of their peers.[37] This position, however persuasive, isn't
the entire story of how race and performance intersect in discussions of
black educational achievements. Take Zelda's nephew Timothy: seventeen, intelligent, and a straight-A student for as long as he can remember. Timothy has no problem juggling his racial identity and with above-
average school grades and achievement. He is able to do "blackness"

along with intelligence and strong school performance, and he clearly recognizes this fact. I heard him put that all in perspective as I spent several days sitting in his family's small living room, listening to his dreams about the future and his strategies for achieving them.

One of the potential problems with contemporary notions of acting white in the social science literature is that they often downplay the multiple performances and practices that constitute the category "white." Being called "white" or being accused of "acting white" is not simply anti-intellectualism. It is more about the microbehaviors in the school building (how one walks down the hall, sits at the desk, stands on line, talks to one's classmate) that spark the invocation of whiteness as a potential critique of racial identity. One's score on a multiple-choice math test in third period doesn't signify whiteness. It is not performing intellectualism that is the problem, but rather the other performances of self that are often seen as correlated with (but not identical to) intellect. Tim, for one, knows this quite well. Walking beside him up Lenox Avenue, I see that his clothes are obviously new and stylish; his walk is sure and confident. In his everyday behavior, he doesn't stand out from his classmates in any major way. This means that he is mostly safe from accusations of acting white, regardless of his extremely high grades in school:

> **Timothy:** I love to learn, that is it. I get off on that. My moms had me into books from jump. And I just never stopped. I hang out, get into trouble and that too, but I get my work done for me. And to be honest, the females love it.
>
> **John:** Love what?
>
> **Timothy:** If you are about something, and got a head, they love that.
>
> **John:** Has anyone ever said you were acting white?
>
> **Timothy:** Not to my face. They'd have had a problem. I can show somebody black if they want to see it, but they better want to see it.

Timothy adeptly juggles intellectualism and blackness—and even gets more racial cachet in the black community because of his intellectual accomplishments, especially from "the females [who] love it."[38] His jeans are just as baggy as the next kid's jeans. His baseball cap is tilted to the side at a respectable angle. His sentences are sprinkled with the phonological, morphological, and syntactical patterns of his peers. These are the performances that shore up his racial self. He is able to

maintain his blackness amid intellectual proficiency, because other behaviors are taken into account in assessments of "acting white." In full
bravado, Timothy maintains that he is safe from any accusation of "acting white" because the very accusation would be met by a decidedly
"black" behavioral response.

There are arguments about black racial identity and intelligence that
are not only safe from accusations of whiteness but also specifically
couched in terms that validate black identity through intellectual
achievement:

> **Carl:** I make my money, wear my suit, but I haven't forgotten
> what struggle is. I know how to talk to black people and encour-
> age them and not rub people the wrong way. I'm like this: black
> people need to be getting all the education and the experience
> we can get. If you not doing that, you might as well just be part
> of the plot.

Many blacks in Harlem manipulate the idea of intelligence in ways
that make ignorance and the lack of intelligence decidedly antiblack.
This too adds weight to the argument that "acting white" is not about
anti-intellectualism per se but rather a failure to negotiate the connections between class and race on various behavioral fronts at once. Carl
argues that knowledge acquisition should be considered the blackest of
things, because to be ignorant is to "be part of the plot" against black
success and achievement in the United States. The trick is that often
the trajectories of race's discursive and symbolic connections to specific
behaviors are impossible for an actor to completely and unproblemati-
cally control. Race as performance is about jostling for certainty over
which particular behaviors are labeled black or white—a certainty that is
never fully finalized outside of particular social contexts. The behaviors
themselves only have racial value once they are placed within explicit
frameworks organized to make claims about the connection between
behavior and racial authenticity. These claims constitute racial identity
(through a linkage with perceptions of behavior) and subject those
practice-based identities to constant scrutiny and challenge.

Making Race and Class in Harlem

Notions of racial performativity are about using practices to shore up
social identity. Specific actions are used to constitute racial identities and
to maintain them over time. However, there are guidelines within which
the performativity of race is forced to operate. Far from being indexes

of a racial essence that precedes them, everyday behaviors associated with race are what give the racial order its meaning, power, and symbolic significance. Often these performances are inextricably tied to ideas of class and to particularly class(ed) behaviors (ways of walking, talking, and so on) that are articulated with these racial logics.

On a recent trip to California, where I visited one of my best friends from college, we started talking about race, class, and performance—or should I say, I eventually began to monopolize the conversation with a long-winded and unsolicited monologue on my dissertation, a monologue that spoke more to my own preoccupations than to any more than cursory interest on his part. He nodded, asked questions for clarification, and then went to his stereo and put in a CD from the Atlanta-based hip-hop group Goodie Mob. I waited for the line he wanted me to hear. One of Goodie Mob's lead rappers spit it out succinctly: "You not a nigga because you black. You a nigga 'cause of how you act." There it was, I thought. Goodie Mob had the colloquial version of my argument, or its closest equivalent: that racial and class distinctions in black America are a function of behavioral criteria in folk ideologies about identity. Actions are not necessarily explanations for black poverty but rather the raw material for the rhetorical scaffolding we erect to define our black social selves—and one could undoubtedly make the same case for any and all social identities.[39] You are not black because you are (in essence) black; you are black (in the folk logic of racial difference) because of how you act—and not just in terms of one sphere of behavior (say, intellectual achievement in school) but because of how you juggle and combine many differently racialized and class(ed) actions (walking, talking, laughing, watching a movie, standing, emoting, partying) in an everyday matrix of performative possibilities.

Academic achievement and intellectualism can, at times, be likened to acting white. But it is not a simple one-to-one relationship. It is an assessment of multiple practices and their negotiation. A self-proclaimed "brainiac," Timothy is not criticized for his intellectual achievements because he can manipulate other symbolically important behavioral scales. His closest friends aren't necessarily good students, but they know that he is—and even envy it in some ways. People can likewise perfect certain aspects of their racial performances (say Dr. Stevens's black English and Dashikis) but not properly perform other behaviors deemed racially important. Furthermore, the discourse concerning class and behavior directly connects to this discussion of race and behavior. That is, people can make use of class differences to challenge racial identity or to make that identity appear beyond reproach.

Notions of "acting white" are often attempts at jousting and jock-eying for a nonambiguous social identity. In the social security office, not getting what one wants can be frustrating. There, race and class intersect in several ways, especially when all the parties involved are "black." In that instance, the black person with the social service job is the manifestation and personification of a kind of success that the other half of the dyad, by sheer fact of their presence there, does not have. Class becomes foregrounded in such a space, but in ways that link class stratification to racial authenticity. The welfare agent could be accused of acting white because his or her actions are holding a black person back from a desired goal—or at least operating as a potential roadblock, flesh-and-blood red tape. Likewise, the welfare recipient can be accused of (if not acting white) complicity with whiteness in the welfare agent's eyes because, as Carl argues, it is mandatory for a black person to act smart and industrious in a world of racist stereotypes, or else be considered a "part of the plot."

I should stress that when discussing these performative understandings of racial difference, we are always talking about articulated categories. That is, there are no folk notions of racialized actions that are not simultaneously classed, gendered, or ethnically or sexually inflected. For instance, one store owner in Harlem, a black woman who has lived and worked in the community for approximately thirty years, argues forcefully for a notion of blackness linked to gender-specific activities. She has been having a hard time procuring empowerment zone funding, and she complains that blacks will patronize white- or Asian-owned stores rather than a black-owned establishment like hers. She believes that she is not being taken seriously (by certain empowerment zone czars or certain local residents) because she is a black woman and not a black man. "A black woman ain't supposed, they say, to be doing what I'm doing here with a business and that kind of thing." She argues that many people would try to define black women as outside of the realm of entrepreneurial possibility or as not having the skill to run a successful business. If she were a man, she claims, the empowerment zone money might more readily flow—and fewer local residents would question her business acumen. The battle to win customers away from competitors (and to win funding for future renovations) is also an attempt to redefine the behavioral limits of black femininity. But even here, whiteness is an important foil. This is the person who jokingly claims that the next time I visit her store there will be a white man outside whom she has hired to beckon blacks inside. "That might be what I have to do," she sighs softly. "It's sad, but it's true. Then I'd be in business."

Behavior that is linked to class or gender is the linchpin of culture of poverty arguments that posit behavioral deficiencies as the ultimate explanation for poor people's problems. Instead of starting there, I argue that actions do not only dictate how whites view blacks or determine black life chances vis-à-vis the outside white world; they are also used to make sense of racial affinities, politics, and interests within the black community.

The black poor can use class-inflected behaviors to manipulate and critique the black middle class; blacks higher up the class ladder use class(ed) and racialized actions to critique lower-class race-mates and to make sense of race in their own lives. Racial performances can be read through gender to create divergent black male and black female behavioral mandates. But even these mandates can be questioned when people go against the grain. One can challenge other blacks for their lack of achievement by linking race to high performance in a battle against institutionalized and internalized racism. In such a context, academic achievement can be a testament to black racial identity and not a compromising of it. Here, just as the same type of striding gait, for instance, can be taken as lower- or middle-class, the same intellectual achievement can be racialized as "white" or "black" depending on the context and the purposes of the label. In this sense, it is important to stress that race(d) and class(ed) behaviors are mutable, allowing people to dispute the racial and class-based implications of their social actions all the time.

"Black people with money," Robert states most assuredly, "act like white people." The real point seems to be that there are interracial and intraracial differences that are discursively constructed and perpetuated in numerous ways. Acting white isn't about performing well in school, talking a particular way, or dressing in a certain style in some kind of social vacuum. Instead, acting white is about positioning oneself for the explication of one's social identity. In that sense, acting white is a notion that can be used up or down the class ladder and across gender divides in a kind of everyday social warfare where the ultimate prize is an unproblematic ontological existence and a valid place in the racial order. In the next chapter, I look at mass media images (particularly those of film and television) as spaces wherein the battle over what actions mean in terms of race, class, gender, and their interconnections are constantly questioned, negotiated, and reformulated. These images highlight the productive force of social actions on popular understandings of racial identities.

CHAPTER 6

CINEMATICUS ETHNOGRAPHICUS:
RACE AND CLASS IN AN ETHNOGRAPHIC LAND
OF MAKE-BELIEVE

Cynthia called and left a message for me after her first trip to the newly opened Magic Johnson Movie Theater on 125th Street, part of the $65 million, 275,000-square-foot strip mall, Harlem USA, located between Frederick Douglass Boulevard and St. Nicholas Avenue. Financed with capital from both public and private sources, Harlem USA was celebrated by many of Harlem's top brass for the approximately seven hundred jobs it is supposed to provide for the community.[1] This project had been a long time in the making. It was 1995 when Harlemites first began hearing the buzz about a possible Sony Theater slated for uptown. Many people knew how well a local Blockbuster Video store was doing once it finally opened alongside the state office building. Before then, Harlem's movie-watching community had been sorely underserved. In 1999, Harlem USA brought a Disney Store, an Old Navy, HMV Records, Modell's sporting goods, Harlem USA's "Walk of Fame," and that Magic Johnson Theater up to 125th Street all in one fell swoop.[2]

One recurring subtext for much of the ethnographic material collected here has to be the mass media and telecommunications. I've talked just a little about other modern technological and information-age variables that affect how people live their everyday lives: phone calls placed across countries, continents, or counties to keep in touch; cell phones sold cheap and managed to control others' access, sometimes along emphatically classed lines; television programs silently droning on in the background during formal interview sessions, filling in silent spaces with the fidgety light of multicolored pixels. I can't

Magic Johnson Theater
(photo by Scheherazade
Tillet)

begin to count the number of televisions that were left on in the background during sit-down interviews—or that I watched people watching as we just hung out together. It was so common a backdrop that a television being conspicuously turned off often begged for an unsolicited explanation—that it was broken, or maybe the cable was out.[3]

I escorted people many times to the makeshift cardboard palettes of first-run bootlegged feature films sold illegally by street vendors around the city. But could watching movies with people in their homes really be considered fieldwork? These television screenings are important, I think, because many of the people I met in Harlem theorize with recourse to mass media examples, with the assistance of public personalities only existent to them through the worlds of film and television. In this chapter I do some filmic theorizing of my own, arguing that contemporary Hollywood fare can be mined for performative theories of race and class similar to the ones that I've been trying to highlight through my ethnographic research.

The most obvious starting point in any ethnographic engagement with how race and class are represented and understood in everyday life would probably turn most logically on an analysis of television news programs as a main site for the creation and dissemination of powerful social representations. News is the most obvious point of entry into discussions about how race and class get represented as "real." Talk shows (from *Oprah* to *Jerry Springer*), court TV shows (from *The People's Court* to *Divorce Court*), and recent network attempts at voyeuristic game shows (from *Survivor* to *Big Brother*) show how readily so-called real-life televisual programming is reduced to mere entertainment, blurring the line between fiction and nonfiction. Instead of starting with nonfiction news programs, however, I want to take a slightly different track, entering self-consciously fictional cinematic worlds to engage their purposefully unreal representations.

It was a trip to the movies that sparked my own imagination on this matter in the first place, actually, a pre-film McDonald's advertisement. The commercial displayed black patrons of a movie theater watching a make-believe film in a make-believe movie theater as part of the diegesis. That McDonald's ad showed the power of its food to cajole the black actors on the screen within the screen, actors in that fictitious all-black action movie, to stop the film's plot for a McDonald's food break. The advertisers playfully posited a kind of "creative geography" that reminded me of another McDonald's fast food moment, Dexter's cartographic maneuvering of Harlem away from the confines of Manhattan. The fact that I was with Robert, not Dexter, inside a mid-Manhattan movie theater (since this was still well before the Harlem USA project was completed) didn't mean that I couldn't feel the pull of Harlemworld. Of course, the commercial's joke is about the power of McDonald's food to short-circuit the clear-cut boundaries between fiction and nonfiction, literality and metaphor, the very same line equally blurred in idealized representations of Harlem as drug-dealerless or poverty-free—and the same line to be blurred further still in the pages that follow.

I want to exit one section of Harlemworld for another, for many others, for a different kind of fieldwork entirely. Thus far, I have tried to look at the words and deeds of African Americans from across class lines within the actual geographical community of Harlem as a way of thinking about how black people theorize race and class on a microsocial level, about the types of attributes and characteristics that inform those thoughts, about how those ideas affect the interactions African Americans have across class lines. Far from being blind to class, many of the Harlemites I met not only recognize class differences but also see such differences everywhere, especially in people's everyday actions. As I've said before, race and class take work, hard work, both to see and to perform. This work creates an articulated racial identity that is viewed through a practice-based, action-oriented, and performative lens.

This chapter will examine fictional race- and class-based representations on the big screen and the small screen to argue that performative connections between race and class also organize the social logics of these mass media worlds. I'll use a few recent motion pictures (several that I watched on bootlegged videotapes in Harlem homes) to show (1) that essentialist notions of blackness can be completely decoupled from Africa and the African diaspora as ontological grounding (another spoke in the wheel of performative definitions of race), (2) that the performativity of race and class are wired together in contemporary Hollywood fare, and (3) that cinematic depictions of Harlem's history are interesting sites for analyzing how race and class intersect in representations of blackness and black America. I end this chapter with an analysis of the hip-hop community's "Harlemworld," a symbolic space that deploys race, class, and their imbrications in powerfully newfangled ways. The same folk theories of race and class discussed throughout this book are reworked here in fictional mass media offerings that call on race and class to fuel their narrative momentum.

Dying Hard in Harlem

The action film *Die Hard 3: Die Hard with a Vengeance* (1995) is the third installment in a financially successful 20th-Century Fox motion picture series starring Bruce Willis as NYPD Detective John McClane. In the first two versions, McClane is chasing down planes on airport runways, punching sky-jackers in the face, capturing political terrorists, and generally foiling an assorted lot of criminal minds hell-bent on death, destruction, and all manner of mayhem. For *Die Hard 3*, McClane is running around frantically all over the island of Manhattan because some unidentified, German-accented terrorist (Simon) threatens to blow up different parts of the borough unless McClane does exactly what "Simon says."

The film opens with a command from Simon that places this blockbuster's initial plot point squarely within the thematic and geographic reach of Harlemworld: "Simon says, McClane is to go to the corner of 138th Street and Amsterdam, which is in Harlem, if I'm not mistaken." That is all we know at first, as the filmmakers cash in on the world (in)famous symbolic currency of the place to set up the protagonist's opening obstacle. As McClane is driven up to Harlem in a police truck to be dropped off at the designated location, the police chief assures him that the truck will be stationed only a few blocks away, ready and waiting to retrieve him in fifteen minutes. In response to the chief's unsolicited guarantee, a plain-clothed, unkempt, and hung-over McClane responds, "I expect to be dead in four." But why this fear of 138th and Amsterdam? Why this fear of Harlem? The filmmakers have given us no further explanation for Simon's request or for McClane's fatalistic attitude about his prospects of surviving even five minutes on Harlem's streets. As the police truck makes its way to Harlem, McClane, the police chief, and a few other officers sit in a holding area at the rear of the truck, discussing the logistics of an event that we (the audience) do not fully understand. The viewer is asked to believe that the only thing amiss in this situation is the fact that McClane is a white man being forced to visit the proverbial black part of town. When the police truck arrives in Harlem, its rear doors open onto a sunny Harlem morn, hip-hop music filling the air. As McClane's feet hit the pavement, this music blares all over Harlem's streets—and from no particular acoustic device, just hovering in mid-air as McClane (whom we see exclusively in close-up) is bombarded with staccato beats and partially indecipherable rap lyrics.

Inside a pawn/repair shop just up the street, we find a bespectacled Zeus Carver, played by Samuel L. Jackson, a man who, like the social science literature's "Old Heads" of the ghetto's glory days, is admonishing a pair of young black kids to stay in school. Zeus is very self-consciously playing the function of role model, passing on words of wisdom to these prepubescent Harlemites. The two boys listen to his advice (which they've committed to memory and recite on cue) and then call him to the storefront window to take a look at a "crazy white man" in the street, which would be McClane. Zeus spots what we have yet to see and tells the kids to call 911. In a rush, Zeus exits the store, and the director cuts to a shot revealing what had been kept from us all this time: McClane is wearing a huge placard around his neck that reads "I Hate Niggers" as he stands in the middle of a Harlem thoroughfare. There, we see, lies the danger of Simon's command.[4]

This is an important moment in American cinema for several related reasons. The "I Hate Niggers" scene is the foundational plot point in a summer blockbuster action movie that is explicitly charged and wired throughout by a discourse concerning race and racism. This is a relatively new move for Hollywood. Traditionally, big-budget Hollywood fare has integrated blacks into the cinematic landscape with either stereotypical representations of black poverty or interracial camaraderie.

Neither of those options speaks directly to white racism, and instead they both provide black images that elide discussions of racism by supplying a colorblind context of racial equality and even black male moral superiority. When depicting African Americans, racial differences are accented or downplayed depending on the genre of film. However, explicit discussions of racism and racial discrimination are ignored in Hollywood action films and relegated to dramatic or comedic genres often organized specifically around issues of race and racism as either a historical fact or as a regional peculiarity of the South. What makes *Die Hard 3* such an important anomaly, then, is the fact that it is an action movie made for a mass audience that is written to begin with a racialized bang. Action movies are the cash cows of Tinseltown. The movie budgets are huge, and so the films are supposed to appeal to a mass audience, a demographic that includes as many potential viewers as possible. Given that mandate, issues such as racism are often bracketed out of their narratives to avoid controversial themes that might hinder the bottom line: profits at the box office.[5] Instead, race is usually incorporated into the action film without the obvious and messy taint of racism. One of the most successful attempts at this kind of racialized "visual integration" onscreen is the *Lethal Weapon* series (four in all), in which Danny Glover and Mel Gibson play two very different types of police officers. When racial integration is at the center of action movies such as *Lethal Weapon*, stereotypical racial differences are either repressed (no mention is ever made of race as difference) or reversed (behavioral stereotypes about blacks are grafted onto white characters instead). Both options are conventional techniques for Hollywood action films (usually going hand-in-hand), but only one was used in *Die Hard 3*. McClane and Zeus switch places in terms of racialized behavior (Zeus is the more seemingly mainstream figure), but race, racism, and reverse racism are talked about excessively and even obsessively throughout the film's narrative. The differences and similarities between *Die Hard 3* and its precursors in the genre crystallize a few important points about race, class, and performativity.

Harlem Anatomies

Robyn Wiegman argues convincingly about the complicit relationship between racism and sexism in a contemporary American society saturated by "the end of visual segregation" in the mass media.[6] Even though blacks are still not proportionally represented on film or on television, a recent increase in the number of black characters is beyond debate.[7]

Some critics complain that these black characters are just as stereotypical as Hollywood's traditional representations of mammies, coons, and bucks of yore.[8] Indeed, many maintain that these characters simply do not capture the complicated reality of black life today.[9] Blacks have been incorporated into the cinematic landscape in unprecedented ways, but at the expense of serious and sustained engagements with the concerns they might have about contemporary racial politics and its impact on their life chances. This particular kind of racial inclusion is "contingent on detaching from the historical context of race."[10]

In many of these mass media representations, a certain kind of middle-classness is used to signify racial indifference and commonality. Contrary to the facts of most recent social science research, the black bourgeoisie is often drawn as much more bourgeois than its white counterpart in the "narrative economy" of these films.[11] Race is depicted as a "settled site" in many of these movies' narratives.[12] If anything, it is the white male characters who are socially marginalized and in need of assistance. This is usually how race, class, and their interconnection are reconstructed in contemporary public discourse as crystallized in Hollywood storytelling. Murtaugh, the African American police officer in the *Lethal Weapon* series, is a middle-class family man with a loving wife, a suburban home, a conservative personal politics, a Standard-English linguistic repertoire, and a stable job that he is scheduled to retire from within two weeks of the film's opening scenes. His white partner, Riggs, is a psychotic social misfit who has lost a wife, lacks responsibility and maturity, chronically abuses himself with alcohol, and nihilistically attempts suicide. These men make no mention of race and racial difference in the narrative, and why should they? The only social distance between them is a function of Murtaugh's stability, normalcy, and mainstream familial life. In that case, structurally determined racial differences in the real world (or at least in the racial stereotypes made to index such differences) are irrelevant to the racial economy and symbolism of this police story.

Wiegman reads *Lethal Weapon*'s entire plot line as a fantastical erasure of racial differences; racially distinct bodies are coded along lines that obscure social context and downplay the present consequences of multiracial communities forged in histories of oppression.[13] In buddy films such as *Lethal Weapon*, black middle-classness (that is, moral, behavioral, ethical conservatism) and white male marginality combine to depict race without engaging the entrenched discourses of racial difference found in the real world beyond the reel world. Moreover, Wiegman claims that this black male centrality vis-à-vis white male marginality is accompanied by a simultaneous policing of masculinity. This gender policing allows the black male partial access to high social status and class privilege while wiring the white male character to a privileged form of masculinity—reinforcing the ultimate supremacy of the white male in the face of the black masculine threat. Whereas the conventional discourse on black masculinity formulates an oversexed black subject diametrically opposed to the Victorian self-control and temperance of the white world, Murtaugh is unable to access true masculinity or sexuality (he can't run as fast, isn't as overtly sexual, and can't fight as well as his nihilistic partner).

The consequence of this complicated rhetorical move with blackness, whiteness, class, and gender is an equation wherein representations of equality onscreen stand in place of real inequalities in our social world. This proliferation of black imagery in the public sphere bespeaks a complicated context for discussions about how race and class work in the mass media today. Wiegman's analysis is a helpful and informative way of looking at these interracial buddy movies as sites of cultural contestation, but it does not fully explain what makes *Die Hard 3,* a movie that is adamant about reintegrating contemporary racial discourse into its big-budget Hollywood story line, different from its predecessors. It is this fact that I want to think about and connect to my previous chapters about folk theories of race and class.

African Americans' Africa

In chapter 1, Ms. Joseph describes Harlem as "African Americans' Africa." That comment speaks directly to another consequential moment in America cinema that relates to the issues discussed here. To uncover this linkage, I'm going to move to another key cinematic exchange—this one in a canonical black film text. This move will take us even further from the Harlem of my field site only to place us more squarely back down within the Harlemworld that encompasses it.

In the 1990 film *Boyz 'n the Hood,* writer-director John Singleton captures an element of contemporary racial discourse that directly connects with Ms. Joseph's description of Harlem as a kind of Africa for African Americans. The *Boyz* scene in question is fundamentally important for its recognition of race's potential disconnection from certain places, for its rehearsal of a blackness that does not need Africa to symbolically supply it with an ontological and essentialized certainty. Early in the movie, we are in an elementary school social studies classroom full of black children. The teacher, a fairly young white woman, presents a lecture on the origins of Thanksgiving as a social ritual linked to the eating habits of America's first European settlers.[14] A young Tre Styles, the film's protagonist (later portrayed as an adult by Academy Award–winning actor Cuba Gooding Jr.), jokingly renames the hallowed pilgrims "penguins," which is met by an uproar of laughter from his classmates. The instructor, upset at Tre's outburst, asks him, sarcastically, if he would like to teach the class. Tre quickly accepts and walks confidently to the front of the classroom.

With a long wooden pointer, he directs the class's attention to a large pink picture of the continent of Africa on a world map hung in front of the chalkboard.[15] He asks the class if they know what he is pointing at. A young woman responds, "I know that; that's Africa." With her answer, Tre launches into a discussion about his "daddy" telling him that "the first man was found in Africa," which means that "everybody is from Africa. All y'all." Instantaneously, Tre moves the discussion from the European founding of America to the symbolic founding of black America, repositioning that foundational moment across the Atlantic. However confident Tre is about his lecture's veracity, it is met with immediate resistance. A young black boy in the front row is quick to assert, "I ain't from Africa, I'm from Crenshaw Mafia." The boy is clear about the fact that he identifies more with the immediate neighborhood (Crenshaw, Los Angeles) than with some bright pink drawing of Africa unfurled in front of the blackboard. Tre, frustrated with this boy's ignorance, reiterates that all of the children in the class are from Africa, to which the boy responds, "I ain't from Africa. You from Africa. You African booty scratcher." With that joke, the class erupts with even greater laughter than before, and Tre is not only losing his argument about identity but losing face in front of his peers as this naysayer gets the rhetorical best of him. The exchange quickly degenerates into the two boys calling each other "a bitch," threatening to get relatives to kill one another, and then finally coming to blows right there in the front of the class.

This scene in *Boyz* dramatizes an important debate that animates contemporary discussions about black America—the same debate hinted at and reconfigured in Ms. Joseph's invocation of Harlem as "African Americans' Africa." Indeed, if Harlem is African Americans' Africa, what is Africa to African Americans? That is, isn't Africa supposed to be African Americans' Africa? In Ms. Joseph's assertion, Africa is important as a symbol that grounds another symbol poised to take its place in contemporary discourse on black identity in the United States. She would posit a Harlem so important that it replaces Africa, even while invoking Africa at one and the same time. This same move is foregrounded in the scene where Tre's classmate identifies his subjectivity with a very different place from Africa—and a different people from those "African booty scratchers." This is a disavowal of Africa that some would label a form of internalized racism, the lack of a certain self-respect and pride, but it is not a lack of pride that characterizes either Ms. Joseph's or Tre's classmate's comments. If anything, it is pride itself that makes them assert their sense of identity as tied to a clearly determined site in the first place. Tre and his interlocutor come to blows not because Tre is the only one with a sense of self-pride and self-worth but rather because they conceptualize that pride differently.

It is not to be forgotten that this altercation arises in the context of a classroom, and Singleton is using that location as an important symbolic space for his own pedagogical discussion about what blackness is and is not. The classroom is a space for the learning of race, a race that is proud of its sense of blackness even when disavowing any connections across the Atlantic. This is a key notion of blackness, one that justifies the trek from the Harlem of my field site (that place in the world) to the Harlemworld of the cinematic landscape that extends all the way across that celluloid space to a sunny Los Angeles classroom. I want to argue that in all three of these spaces one is encountering a kind post-African black moment. This is not a cosmopolitan identity that jet-sets from here to there and thus has no roots that would ground identity.[16] Rather, it is a kind of blackness that defines its essential difference as other than predicated on some mythical African origin. Instead, this is a blackness that can shore up its identity only within the contours of experiences and actions exclusively linked to the so-called New World.

This is important because notions of black people's links to Africa (let alone questions of cultural survivals and retentions) underscore a contemporary and historical debate about black America that is still fought over today.[17] The self-conscious pull toward Afrocentrism is challenged by an equally strong push away from it, away from any discursive recourse to Africa at all. A blackness that doesn't need Africa as grounding for its racial distinctiveness uses other means to create that unyielding black difference. For example, Tre's classmate doesn't only identify with Crenshaw, his community, but with a particular subset of its members: the "gang-bangers" who comprise the "Mafia" of his neighborhood. He doesn't say, "I'm from Crenshaw"; he says, "I'm from Crenshaw *Mafia*." Here, what the young boy has learned outside of the classroom ties his sense of self to the illegal actions and activities that characterize the exploits of these neighborhood hoods. Indeed, even Singleton's title takes on a double meaning linked to this racial identification with specific actions. These are young boys who identify not only with their community (their neighbor*Hood*) over and against some far-away Africa, but also with a series of behaviors that have social meaning in that place, the behaviors of the hood(lum)s who run the streets— behaviors very different from the scratching of one's "booty." Moreover, when Tre and his classmate call one another "bitches," threaten one another with death, and eventually fight, Tre has actually lost the battle over black identity's linkages to some faraway pink Africa on a classroom map. Instead, Tre too does blackness as he has learned to do it and validates his classmate's disavowal of Africa for an affirmation of a racial self that is tied to the actions of the hoods in the Crenshaw community that they both call home. In this particular instance, the two boys are doing blackness, a blackness that is a performance-based identity as opposed to (contrary to Tre's assertions) an ancestral one.

Post-Tarantino

I want to argue for what I would call a pre- and post-Tarantino Hollywood engagement with race as exemplified by the racialized discourse I have already started unpacking in *Die Hard 3,* a big-budget movie whose entire narrative (against the Hollywood grain) is powered by racial difference and animus between the film's white and black leads. Zeus constantly foregrounds McClane's whiteness and white difference, using it as an important reason for why he does not want to help him catch Simon. "This is a white man, with white problems," he says, "so I'm gonna take my black ass home." In one scene, McClane has had enough of Zeus's race-talk and screams back in disgust, "Have I oppressed you? Have I oppressed your people?" McClane's point, of course, is that the two men have never met before; therefore, Zeus is unfairly injecting race into their otherwise equal relationship. Conservative discourses regarding affirmative action resonate loudly here.

Another important symbolic point is linked to the black character's name: Zeus (which McClane mistakenly pronounces Jésus [Hay-soos]). But Zeus is adamant about correcting him, exclaiming that his name is "like the Greek god." This too foregrounds the fact that a black character can be pro-black and antiwhite while still held within the discursive and historical field of whiteness and its nomenclature. Zeus does not need, say, an African name to ground his racial self. He can hate whiteness even while inhabiting the mythological seat of Western (Greek and

Roman) culture. Just as Tre's classmate doesn't need Africa to talk about black racial difference, Zeus doesn't need an African name to hate white people and to emphasize black-white racial differences. In *Die Hard 3*'s depiction of Harlem, in particular, and blackness, more generally, class issues are reworked and reconfigured in its attempt to unpack racial identity as linked to performance instead of some mythical African or Egyptian homeland. This performance is inextricably tied to class-based markers of difference, markers that make race about doing class as opposed to, say, being a descendent of African ancestors.

Quentin Tarantino, director and writer of commercially and critically successful films such as *Reservoir Dogs* (1993) and *Jackie Brown* (1997), received a lot of criticism for a scene in his Academy Award–nominated movie *Pulp Fiction* (1994) and its infamous "Bonnie Situation" sequence, better known as the "Dead Nigger Storage" scene. In it, Tarantino makes a cameo (an important and motivated casting decision) by playing Jimmy, a suburban white homeowner in Toluca, California, who is imposed upon by the film's black-white buddy pair, Vincent Vega (played by John Travolta) and Jules Winnfred (again Samuel L. Jackson). Vincent and Jules indiscriminately kill people together, they discuss everything from existentialism to fast food together, and they share their lives with one another in a context where race is not so much spoken as very explicitly and specifically performed. Jules, a kind of Zen hit man with an Afro-Jheri-curl hairstyle, is the black English–wielding half of the duo. He walks with a pimp-strut and recites verses from the Bible just because that is "some cold-blooded shit to say to a motherfucker before I pop a cap in his ass." Vincent and Jules work in a kind of color-blind underground world where they both perform certain stereotypical renditions of blackness. Vincent is a "cool" Italian (not a "square") who can dance and speak black slang. In fact, disclosing that indisputable fact takes up a five-minute scene in which Vincent dances erotically with his black boss's white girlfriend, Mia.

After a young black man in his early twenties is shot inadvertently by Vincent in the back seat of the car Jules is driving, the two men are forced to flee to Jimmy's house with the dead body. When they arrive, they both are bombarded by a barrage of racial slurs about "the dead nigger in my garage": "When you came pulling in here did you notice a sign in the front of my house that said dead nigger storage? Did you notice a sign on the front of my house that said dead nigger storage? Do you know why you didn't see it? 'Cause it ain't there. 'Cause storing dead niggers ain't my fucking business." As angry as Jimmy is, he agrees to help them clean up the bloodied car and dispose of the body by calling on the professional services of a Mr. Wolf, played by Harvey Keitel. It is important that the sequence is named after Jimmy's black wife, Bonnie, a nurse working the graveyard shift who will "freak" if she comes home and sees a dead body in their house. Jimmy tells them that she'll divorce him if the men are caught. Jules, Jimmy, Vincent, and Mr. Wolf work diligently and methodically to get the bloodied car and clothes cleaned up before Bonnie returns.

Tarantino was taken to task for his usage of the term *nigger* in this sequence, because it was considered gratuitous, and it caused a big stir in Hollywood. Blacks can use the term *nigger* for one another, the argument goes, as a term of endearment or to make fun of one another's failures and misfortunes, but when they use it, they are not calling on its animus the way, say, white southern slave owners did in the antebellum South. The term *nigger* is that policed parlance of racial specificity that is off-limits for other races. A popularized version of the "nigger question" is the comedian Chris Rock's distinction between "niggers" and "black people." Rock claims that blacks are more racist than whites because whites just hate niggers. But black people, he says, hate whites and niggers. He coats the notion of nigger with a class-coded set of implications, and niggers are seen as those poor and deviant blacks who give other black people a bad name.

Even Samuel L. Jackson was questioned in the media for allowing Tarantino's vitriolic tone and racist slurs in the Bonnie Situation sequence. Jackson was called to defend his blackness for letting Tarantino say *nigger* so prevalently in front of him—since any real black man would have objected to the film's dialogue or even disposed of Tarantino himself posthaste. Jackson dismissed those criticisms as political correctness and claimed that as an actor the integrity of his art form is more important than identity politics.

Tarantino's defense of his work and of the character's dialogue in this scene is particularly interesting. His first argument is about context, intent, and veracity. He didn't mean it as a slur, he claims; it is just the real way the character he played would have spoken. Moreover, he argues that saying *nigger* isn't necessarily racist. He writes his characters truthfully and vows not to curb that truth in the wake of public pressure. But all of these arguments pale in comparison to his most important claim to the word *nigger,* a claim based on his own behavioral blackness. "I went to an all-black school," Tarantino tells actress Jada Pinkett-Smith in a magazine interview. "A woman who is like my mom's best friend, my second mom, is black. Her daughter is like my sister. I grew up among black losers, con-men, you know, those shifty loser asshole guys.

I have more of a connection and a feel or inner personality with black culture than I do with Italian culture. When I get mad or when I get in a fight I talk with a black dialect."[18]

In some ways, Tarantino makes two related but nonidentical arguments here about why it is okay for him to use the word *nigger*. For one, he considers his most important familial ties to be with black people. This interracial kinship grounds his usage of the word *nigger* in a context of his identification with other blacks as relatives. These bonds are formative for him. Tarantino is not only black by virtue of kinship ties, however. He also claims to *do* blackness instinctively, a performance that isn't even self-conscious. It is a semihardwired performance of blackness that he claims to revert to (in terms of speaking "black dialect") whenever he gets worked up. He does blackness, Tarantino argues, more than Italianness, and that is his ultimate defense for using the word *nigger*. Tarantino sets up a notion of race as a performed identity and identification, not explicable without recourse to racialized actions and social networks. Blackness is not about ontology but methodology, not what one is in a precultural, prediscursive sense but rather what one does behaviorally, instinctively, and culturally.

Tarantino's blackness is also linked to place. It is an argument that hovers around race and place in ways that resonate with much of the unpacking of race and class that I have offered in the previous chapters. Tarantino goes so far as to argue (later on in the same interview) that class trumps race: "I feel the whole situation of race is more overplayed than it really is," he offers. "It is more a situation of class. I have always felt that blacks living in the projects in Cabrini Green in Chicago have more in common with white hillbillies living in West Virginia than they have with blacks in Pasadena."[19] Tarantino argues that it is not about race, it is "all about economics."[20] However, it is really not that simple, not even in Tarantino's own discourse. He seems to want it both ways. He has black family ties and a black set of behavioral patterns and that makes him black. But there is no blackness that can connect black people across the chasm of class differences. He says race is reducible to economics but still offers race as the valid grounding for his own sense of self—and as an excuse for using racially charged language in his films. He wants to have his cake and eat it too. Tarantino argues for a kind of two-worldliness (the kind predicated on black class difference) wherein class trumps race—at least insofar as it allows him to slip through that class-based racial difference. In the lacuna between under- and middle-class blacks of Chicago and Pasadena, respectively, Tarantino inserts not just white hillbillies but also his own blackened white self. Race is a mirage for class, he claims, but it is only part mirage. To rephrase the hip-hop song from the group "Goodie Mob" invoked in the previous chapter, you can't say *nigger,* according to Tarantino, just because you are ontologically black; you can say it "'cause of how you act." According to Tarantino, if you act black, if you act like a nigger, you, in an important sense, are one.

In real life, Tarantino has had to stand up for his right to do blackness (and to use the word *nigger*) on at least two separate occasions when people have challenged him and literally fought with him over his depiction of blacks. It seems, moreover, that Tarantino falls victim, in spite of himself, to the assumptions about race and class that link blackness not with multiple class realities but instead with the lives of the black poor exclusively. He invokes middle-class blacks in Pasadena not so much to offer them as another kind of blackness (as some might argue) but rather to maintain that the real black community is only composed of poor folks—whether in Cabrini Green or in Appalachian towns inhabited by poor whites. He does not want to say that class splits blackness up into different socioeconomic realities as much as he argues for the black underclass as a privileged site for blackness over and against the black middle class. Even when he talks about his own black social capital, his argument is not that he knew black doctors and lawyers, so, therefore, he can say *nigger.* He knew the "con-men . . . the shifty loser types." Tarantino provides himself with access to blackness by linking it to a specific class of behaviors (in this case, illicit behaviors of the black poor). He privileges these classed actions as premier sites of black racial difference, sites that define middle-class black Pasadenians out of the black racial fold while kneading himself in.

Seeing Race and Class Onscreen

Tarantino's rhetoric about race and class, and his justification for the Dead Nigger Storage scene in *Pulp Fiction,* are important because they form the cinematic pretext and context for the *Die Hard 3* opening and its departure from traditional action-movie portrayals of race. Both Willis and Jackson had signed up for *Die Hard 3* after first performing together in Tarantino's *Pulp Fiction* (Willis as a boxer who double-crossed Jackson's boss). There is even an explicit reference to *Pulp Fiction* in the dialogue of *Die Hard 3* when Willis, as McClane, says that he's been "smoking cigarettes and watching Captain Kangaroo" (an intertextual reference to a song from the *Pulp Fiction* soundtrack).[21] It is only in this post–*Pulp Fiction,* post–Bonnie Situation, post-Tarantino context that

Die Hard 3 could be made against the grain of traditional Hollywood black-white buddy movies. If race is about performances and practices as opposed to ontology, then the traditional formula of these films (in which the black character is considered mainstream and the white one marginalized) allows for a kind of inversion of the racial order as a consequence of this same behavioral grounding of race. If the white character performs stereotypically black actions in the symbolic logic of the film's narrative, then the white character is (if race is contingent on actions) really the black character. That is, if race is predicated on actions and not ontology, black actions make one black. Moreover, the black character, the more mainstream figure, can be read as white, with all of the baggage that goes along with such a redesignation.[22] Zeus Carver, one of the proverbial rage-filled black middle-class people about whom Ellis Cose has written, can be read as exhibiting a kind of white rage in blackface. Indeed, Zeus is irrationally racist, invoking race to explain just about every single thing that happens between him and McClane. He finds racial difference everywhere. Zeus's black-on-white racism (which can be read as white-on-black racism if we accept that McClane, in a post-Tarantino cinematic world, occupies the racial position of blackness as a function of his deviant behaviors and social marginalization) becomes the cause and not the result of the racial differences between the two men.

Zeus's rage-filled racism does not exempt him from being the victim of racism. For instance, Simon, angry at Zeus's attitude, calls him a "boy" over the telephone early in the film. But Simon quickly apologizes, calling his slur a joke and renaming Zeus the "Good Samaritan" instead. That "boy" reference hints at the racial realities beyond the film that link race to a sociohistorical context of slavery and institutionalized racism. Otherwise in *Die Hard 3,* black is white and white is black—and the historical context of white racism is bracketed out of the story entirely, as little more than a tasteless joke. *Die Hard 3* provides a head-on confrontation with race that is only possible in a post-Tarantino multiracial cinematic world, a world where white subjectivity is not only marginalized but re-racialized as well.

But the film is also important because of its representation of the proverbial black underclass. As McClane emerges from the police truck, it takes off, leaving him standing alone on the Harlem asphalt with his huge racist placard, the black underclass threat blurred off into the background. Finally the threat emerges: all black men, some without shirts, all shooting craps, some with bandanas on heads, oiled-down bodies, fighting one another over money (obviously unemployed because it is the middle of the day and they're not at work). The group only really comes into focus when one of the bunch recognizes the "I Hate Niggers" sign McClane is wearing and exclaims, "What the fuck?!"

The mob quickly surrounds McClane, bounces a basketball against his forehead, takes out switchblades, and even cracks a liquor bottle against his skull. (The synecdochal stereotyping intrinsic to those three items—basketball, switchblade, and liquor bottle—are lost on no one.) Just in time, Zeus swoops in to save the day and rushes the bloody McClane into a serendipitously passing cab as they take off up the street and out of Harlem. And thus the interracial squabbles and strife begin. Many of Wiegman's analyses of white-black buddy movies work within the narrative of *Die Hard 3* (it is an all-male world, except for a knife-wielding German woman; the real threat is located beyond the United States in the form of a money-hungry, accented foreigner, "Simon"). But the explicit racialization of the story line (one that starts with a sign about niggers and foregrounds racial animosity the whole way through) is a peculiar twist on the white-black buddy movie that Wiegman did not necessarily anticipate—at least not fully. It is a post-Tarantino, post-African black moment in which race is unflinchingly addressed in the film's narrative: not so much to say black racism is misguided (which is one interpretation), but more to show that race is simply about behaviors—therefore not as sacred and beyond critique as it has always been considered.[23]

Harlem with Your Eyes Closed

One thing about Harlem and its overdetermined blackness is that it can be used toward any number of ends, for various political projects. Furthermore, places like Harlem have a class structure that one is less able to access without a microlevel analysis that takes what people say with respect to race and place seriously. The sociologist Jean Baudrillard talks about contemporary society being in a state of "radical semiurgy" and hyperreality, where the media-disseminated symbols we have and hold about the world are the only real world we know at all, a kind of mass-marketed and simulated never-never land from which we can never escape. This is just the kind of place where an ethnographer must conduct fieldwork, within what might be called an ethnographic land of make-believe.[24] Any hard and fast "Harlem" is disguised behind the images, impressions, and stereotypes we have about the place and its people: simulations in films, television shows, academic books, or print journalism. But the key question is, how do people use these signs? What does that Harlem on the screen mean to the people who look to it and fight over it? Are these images of Harlem used in a kind of de Certeauian sense in which consumption is a site of potential challenge and agency? Moreover, the connections between real worlds and make-believe worlds can become quite soft. What are anthropologists to see in this simultaneously real and unreal world? That question has always been an issue for the discipline, and this is especially the case when highly mobile and effective images are circulating in the public sphere with a speed and proliferation like never before. How is an anthropologist to deal with this reality? How is one to define one's field site, to make sense of it, to even see it at all?

To answer this I want to backtrack a bit, to a genesis story of sorts. We could debate the early strands of the discipline's lineage, but in one story of anthropology's early years, there was the armchair in which sat an ethnologist, the person who supplied an analytical eye to the haphazardly acquired raw materials of others' observations. It was someone else who did the ethnographic dirty work (say, a traveling merchant with a trusty journal or a proselytizing missionary, diary in hand), and the masterful ethnologist pulled these sordid and motivated tales together into a universally explanatory schema. But this armchair brand of anthropological inquiry gave way as the discipline flung itself into an institutional and accredited distinction between methodologically honed scientific empiricism born of first-hand participant observation and what were considered the shoddy, grossly unscientific, and relatively inadequate writings of nonanthropologists who were also interested in going to the bush to view the primitive. But the anthropologist's expertise came not just from the fact that he had been "there" in person (as was the missionary for the church or the colonial administrator for the state), but rather from the fact that the anthropologist brought along a scientifically trained vision that could pierce through the many details of an otherwise incomprehensible culture to provide the most valuable and scientific formula (be it evolutionism, structural-functionalism, transmissionism, structuralism, or cultural materialism) with which to make sense of it all.

As many have argued, however, this perfect, scientistic picture of cultural critique elides as much as it illuminates. First of all, the "field" contained a culture more dynamic, ephemeral, and far-reaching than the overconfident and omniscient anthropological narrator could completely dismiss. The world, as it worked in a small village (like everywhere else on the planet), was less rigid, more fluid, ever-shifting, and recombining than previously allowed for.[25] It wasn't as isolated, discrete, and monolithic as it was (explicitly or implicitly) assumed to be. In fact, this field site, the empirical ground on which the discipline stood, was even said to be a kind of fabricated region, a made-up space—in more ways than one. This very fabrication resonates most directly with Dexter's attempts at dislodging Harlem from its Manhattan moorings. The anthropologist can be said to create boundaries where there are none, to force and forge distinctions between here and there in an effort to pin down and circumscribe the space within which fieldwork will take place. In order to see "the other" better, the ethnographer has traditionally had to condense and downscale the amount that was to be seen. And that downsizing has often meant a particular gerrymandering of social space. But for the anthropologist to see for himself, of course, was not the ultimate point, and the published monograph distilled the anthropological gaze into a narrative form that solidified the ethnographer's unassailable authority while freezing the other into a perpetual past distinct from the Western world's much more modern present.[26] And so a moment opened up, a meta-ethnographic moment, that would allow for ethnographic texts to be "looked at" as well as "looked through" to some overly reified and supposedly transparent other.

Critiques of ethnography as text abound. What ethnographers see and what they think they get are both fair game for critical engagement. Ethnographies, it is argued, are not just pure and unadulterated reflections of what has been observed but rather crafted and constructed worlds that stand in for the jumbled reality from which often indecipherable field notes are alchemized into realistic narrative accounts.[27] And if that was true for Bronislaw Malinowski's Western Pacific or Margaret Mead's Samoa (or, more self-consciously so, for Zora Neale Hurston's Eatonville or Haiti), and if true then, how much more so now?[28] And in a place like Harlem? Even and especially Harlemworld, "that mecca of black America," "African Americans' Africa," "the queen of all black belts." And how much more so in the here-and-now of the early twenty-first century's transnational trade agreements, international immigration shifts, and first-world deindustrialization? The head-in-the-sand anthropologist of yesteryear was a fiction created, among other reasons, to justify the discipline to itself.[29] Today anthropologists are required to look up, out, and beyond what easy borders they are quick to create, beyond the arbitrary boundaries of the locations they translate into and onto anthropological field sites. They open up the ethnographic view to include international connections that link places through the flow of never-ending, mobile capital and hard-journeying peoples. Anthropologists ask for ethnographic engagement with people

and cultures that take mass media gatekeeping and stereotyping seriously as obstructions to any ethnographic understanding of African
Americans.[30] They lobby for an opening up of ethnographic inquiries
and field sites into an analysis of how television, radio, and motion picture representations inform and co-create our perceptions of the world.[31]
They plea for a transnationalized, transculturally savvy opening up of
our understanding of societies in ways that link the locally specific to
its global context.[32] Where they all agree is in the understanding that
field sites must be opened up into other sites, even "multi-sited." But
how far open? And where does the opening end? Where does it close?
Should we open the anthropological gaze into other nearby neighborhoods only? Into contiguous nations? Into a black Atlantic paradigm
that recognizes the analytical bankruptcy of the nation-state's borders
as valid cut-off points for social and cultural analyses?[33] Even into
Wallersteinian-influenced world-systems theories that ask for center-
periphery models of the entire planet's players on the global market?[34]
Derridean invocations mean opening "the field" up into textuality and
intertextuality, all of which could be interpreted with Geertzian thick
descriptions.[35] Especially in a place like Harlem, a place like Harlemworld, we must open up the field site into that ethnographic land of
make-believe, into the ethnographic imaginary, where fact and fiction,
truth and falsehood, chip away at the walls of demarcation that separate
their shadowing and mutually constitutive worlds: an opening up into
the ideas we hold and are taught to have about places like Harlem, places
whose boundaries are magically malleable and whose people are stereotypically assumed.

Six Degrees

Chuck, twenty-five, a part-time student at a community college on
125th Street, says that "Harlem is like a person you got to take the time
to know. When you know Harlem, she will treat you right. And if you
don't take the time to, she won't. She'll lie to you and you'll be stupid
enough to believe it. 'Cause people do everyday. They think Harlem is
this but it ain't. It's that. And they don't get it. And won't believe you
when you tell them they wrong." Chuck's decidedly gendered Harlem
is a place that, first and foremost, misrepresents itself, that tells tales on
itself. It is a Harlem that might be said to make itself up as it goes along,
a Harlem able to fictionalize itself and keep its pursuers off its hidden
tale.

The artisans, of course, are the first ones there in that make-believe, made-up land of a camouflaged, quotation-marked-off Harlemworld that "is not Manhattan"—the artists, particularly the actors, the professional pretenders, the first to recognize the inevitability of that constitutive intermingling of truth with falsehood when it comes to identity. A case in point is Denzel Washington's carefully measured advice to rapper-turned-actor Will Smith—and the approach Washington thought Smith should take to his role in the film *Six Degrees of Separation* (1993), in which Smith plays "Paul Poitier," a black, homosexual, Walter Benjamin–quoting con artist who lies his way into the home of a wealthy art dealer in Manhattan by claiming to be Sidney Poitier's son. Pretending to be the child of a black film icon, Paul is indeed Harlem's prodigal offspring. In fact, Harlem, as a character in the film, is right there (off camera, of course) portentously in the background all the while—playing itself and providing the distant, aerial-shot backdrop to this tale of class-based posing, passing, and performativity. The separation point, the borderline, is an apartment off Central Park, that last landscaped border post protecting a posh upper-middle-classness of double Kandinskys and handmade English shoes from the presumed racial difference raging uptown.

But *Six Degrees* is only based on one real story made into a stage play and then adapted to the silver screen. The other real story, the real-life story, has Denzel Washington, another icon, this generation's Sidney Poitier (some say), who's played many a Harlemite onscreen, advising Smith not to kiss a white male actor onscreen as called for in the script—Washington suggesting that Smith feign the two kisses (one set in a Boston studio apartment, the other in a hansom cab riding through that very same Central Park borderland).[36] In the film Smith obstructs the kiss from view, faking it (by turning his back away from the screen and the audience and pretending that he and his co-star's lips touch on the other side of the back of his head). Smith must conceal the act, Washington argues, because the black audience wouldn't be able to read that action as made up, as acting. Washington's assessment of black people's mass media decoding capabilities is an interesting model, I believe, for looking at a place such as Harlem, where the line between fiction and nonfiction, as people talk about the neighborhood they know, is blurry indeed. Maybe Washington's point helps unpack the truths and fictions of Cynthia's beggarless and Ms. Joseph's drug-dealerless Harlem, U.S.A. Or Dexter's Harlem, which is not Manhattan. What if that black audience Washington talks about can't tell the difference between fact and fiction because they recognize the often equivalent effects of the shadow and its act? That is, they know a world where stereotyped unrealities have a substantial impact on people's lives, an impact that disproves any easy arguments for the power of some supposed real over the unreal. Indeed, the unreal assumptions about places like Harlem (assumptions that affect the decisions, say, of big businesses about whether to move there) have been powerfully determining factors in the very real lives of the people who reside here.

Remember that in a place like Harlem, what is "real"—what is Harlem, really—becomes a tricky question. I think of Margaret, the thirty-three-year-old City College attendee, and her take on Harlem: "Harlem is no poverty, no immigrants, no trash on streets. Harlem is not any of that. That is not what I think about. I don't. I don't at all. Harlem is nothing bad. Nothing bad like that. And nobody can't tell me any different. Nobody."

Margaret's is a Harlem that surely is not Manhattan, but what people think about Harlem and its boundaries, whether true or not, has true enough consequences, especially when depictions of blacks affect how people theorize and negotiate the place itself. As Dexter put it, "they come up here they don't know us. Think they know Harlem; they think they do, but they don't. They could never know us. They just think they know us from what they been taught from TV and shit for all these years. Nothing but lies." The "they" and "us" of Dexter's pronouncement are only mildly ambiguous, even though both pronouns are asked to do grammatical work without the help of an explicitly stated antecedent. This is most interesting in a Harlemworld of both blackness and whiteness, where the two meet and sometimes switch places, a possibility one must recognize as an ethnographer working in a location where race and class are inextricably bound up with notions of how people behave in the social world.

Hoodlum

Hoodlum (1997), a Laurence Fishburne vehicle, is also post-Tarantino—which wouldn't be as important a note were it not that it also seems overly preoccupied with how often (and with how many different inflections) actors can say the word *nigger* in a two-hour film. *Hoodlum* is set in Harlem circa 1930 and tries to be as much a rumination on black history as it is a depiction of the life and times of protagonist Ellsworth "Bumpy" Johnson, a character based on a real-life numbers runner from early twentieth-century Harlem. In *Hoodlum*, Bumpy (played by Fishburne) battles with Lucky Luciano (Andy Garcia) and Dutch Schultz (Tim Roth) for the underground gambling dollars to be had in upper

Manhattan. As in the movies mentioned earlier, *Hoodlum* is an important example of how race and class are combined and distinguished in Hollywood offerings today. Moreover, the fact that *Hoodlum* is a purposeful and self-conscious reconstruction of the Harlem Renaissance means that it also provides a story line in which race, class, and place are all operative aspects of an overarching symbolic matrix that places the very history of Harlem at the center of the action.

In *Hoodlum*, race, class, and ethnicity fight one another for top billing and ultimate importance in this late twentieth-century reformulation of pre–World War II Harlem. Most important, *Hoodlum* foregrounds historical Harlem as a highly symbolic space. Everything in the film is a very purposefully placed reference to this history. It is a Harlem with rent parties and blues singing, with heavy-handed references to the Scottsboro boys and UNIA nurses. Father Divine signs are prominently displayed on streets, and the camera stays on all of these images just a second or two longer than necessary—just to make sure their historical importance is not missed. The characters pause ever so briefly before they utter the names of historically hallowed locations such as the Cotton Club. However, this is a representation of the past that is cognizant of its constructedness and hardly chained to any absolute sense of historical accuracy. Historical personages (such as Pig Foot Mary, an actual soul food vendor and entrepreneur from Harlem's past) are also depicted in the film, with only the slightest tethering to historical reality, pretty standard in Hollywood history writing. In *Hoodlum* this figure is bloodily murdered at the hands of Dutch Schultz—even though Pig Foot Mary did not meet such a dastardly end. Indeed, it's ironic how some historical references to Harlem's past are made just-so—and with an extraspecial care—while Pig Foot Mary's life is ended in a blatant and graphic historical inaccuracy.

Ellsworth "Bumpy" Johnson's life is equally manipulated and massaged by the filmmakers. Most specifically, it is reduced to yet another rags-to-riches biographical account of an ex-convict who becomes a middle-class success story dressed in three-piece suits, donning expensive fedoras, and residing in a huge loft furnished with the finest rugs and furniture. Bumpy wears silk pajamas at night as he sleeps on king-size beds in bedrooms with expensive oil canvasses filling the walls. His bathroom is larger than some Harlem tenement apartments. Bumpy, the ex-con, even behaves like a member of the middle class. He frequents Italian operas downtown, speaks Standard English, and takes his hat off whenever passing a lady. Even his bodyguards have pin-striped three-piece suits and class etiquette. They are all chess-playing, leg-crossing men. Bumpy and his criminal cronies drape trench coats around ladies as they run through the rain. They have white handkerchiefs peeking out of their breast pockets. These are all the attributes of a kind of behavioral middle class. But this is a middle-class sensibility that is tempered by the fact that Bumpy is a cold-blooded killer and criminal. He could easily pass, in his mannerism, for a colored doctor, lawyer, accountant, or some other decidedly middle-class Harlemite of the era, only he's a numbers runner and an ex-con.

Of course, even with all of his material success, Bumpy hasn't forgotten where he came from. In one scene, Bumpy's connection to the black poor is cemented and verified by his throwing money out to the masses (Robin Hood–style), money he stole from the Jewish interloper Dutch Schultz. On another occasion, he walks down a fairly deserted block with his love interest (played by Vanessa Williams) at his side and takes the time to offer money to a Harlem panhandler. Bumpy is shown as someone who, though middle-class in lifestyle, still allows himself to think about the interests of the black poor and about uplifting the race.

One of the most telling scenes in the film shows Bumpy and Luciano in the back seat of Luciano's chauffeur-driven limousine. The two men are talking about what is wrong with Dutch Schultz, especially the way he lives his life and runs his crime syndicate. Of course, Dutch is deemed crazy (a psychological problem), but this becomes most problematic in the way it translates into specific performances of class(ed) identity. Luciano makes a point of mentioning to Bumpy that Dutch is worth "about three million dollars" and still "buys his clothes off the rack." The film audience can believe this. We've seen Dutch's behavior for about an hour by that time. Dutch is vulgar, gulps down food like an animal, and generally acts like a criminal from the streets (which he is)—and not the millionaire that he also is. Luciano and Bumpy (another interracial duo) agree that Dutch doesn't have class, and that, they decide, is his biggest problem. Tellingly, the two men discuss all of this (and plot Schultz's "demise") in calm and cool ways, donning three-piece suits, with very few of the grand gestures found amid conversations of common folks. Moreover, Johnson responds to Luciano's class-based critique of Schultz by saying, calmly and coolly, "If you don't know, you don't know." And evidently Lucky Luciano and Bumpy Johnson know something that Dutch Schultz does not. They know how to perform class in a way that transcends the racial divide that could potentially separate them. Just as Vincent and Jules can find commonality in their performance of a Tarantino-esque kind of blackness in *Pulp Fiction*, Luciano and Bumpy find common ground in their equivalent performances of middle-classness. It is Dutch's inability to fit into their class mandates, his inability to perform class in ways that satisfy Luciano and Bumpy, that supposedly cause the two men to plot the assassination of their nemesis. One can read Bumpy and Luciano's class-inflected critique as a mask for anti-Semitism in the context of Nazi build-up in Europe and concomitant Jewish immigration to the United States. However, Schultz's Jewishness is not offered as the explanation for his inassimilable difference. Bumpy, Luciano, and Schultz are all pummeled by insensitive racist and ethnic slurs throughout the film, and it is not such difference that explicitly grounds Bumpy and Luciano's pact. Instead, class markers serve as a proxy for Jewish difference, justifying the assassination as a function of class-based behavioral differences that distinguish Schultz from the other two gangsters.

Luciano and Johnson are middle-class because they act middle-class at home, regardless of the fact that they are criminals, killers, bootleggers, pimps, and number runners on the job. In fact, Bumpy has a black nationalist economic argument that justifies his illegal exploits in the numbers racket as a valid means of employing Harlemites and offering them a little opportunity for economic achievement and success in a racial world that forecloses most legal outlets for black people. Laurence Fishburne's *Hoodlum* flies in the face of contemporary understandings of black criminality, especially the kinds of "hoods" referenced in John Singleton's *Boyz 'n the Hood*. *Hoodlum* plays against the black criminal stereotype, offering criminals that aren't poor, destitute, and underclass miscreants. The film argues for an understanding of class location and identity as contingent not only on occupation per se, or even income, but also on how successfully one performs the requisite personal behaviors that go along with a higher income and status—that is, how well one *does* class in the everyday world. *Hoodlum* offers a certain performance of middle-classness as a logical mechanism for the acceptance of racial difference—that is, as long as it does not also reflect class differences linked to behavior. Schultz was the threat to this symbolic order of class-based practices and performances, not Bumpy. If anything, Schultz is marked for death by these two men in the back of Lucky's limousine because his lack of class stunted his ability to form alliances with his fellow crime bosses that supersede the racial and ethnic partitions that could divide them.

Moreover, *Hoodlum* uses an understanding of race in Harlem that plays with national and diasporic differences. The film starts with Fishburne and his cousin working for a number-running cartel led by Caribbeans whose accents are emphasized to distinguish them from the

African American members of the clique. Bumpy and the other African American Harlemites make jokes about (and take note of) the linguistic differences that distinguish West Indian English from their own. In fact, it is only after this foreign-tongued blackness is eradicated (an ambush by Dutch Schultz kills all the foreign tongues on a downtown street) that Bumpy and his decidedly native-born gang can redouble their efforts to get rid of Dutch Schultz for good. Indeed, the Caribbean leaders of the group had spent the entire film up to that point staunchly opposing a proactive strike against Schultz and his crew. Their mass murder on a midtown street marks the opportunity for another kind of post-diasporic black moment, a performance-based black moment that eventually is to eliminate the Schultz threat, the point being that black American gangsters do what they do differently than their Caribbean counterparts.

Anachronistically, the chart-topping soundtrack for this period piece sold hip-hop music (instead of blues and jazz from that era) to the hundreds of thousands of music fans who purchased it. The make-believe land that is *Hoodlum*'s Harlem transcends the early twentieth century, playing with time and space by offering contemporary hip-hop songs as the tool for promoting this historical film to its contemporary audience. As usual, it is a history in service to the present, a history where Bumpy Johnson can act as a kind a role model for how class is done, demonstrating middle-class behavior for the young hoodlums of today said to be abandoned by the black middle class. Even criminals had "class" back then, when the high-class criminals stayed in Harlem. The choice of hip-hop is important because it emphasizes the pressure of the present-day impulses on any and all representations of the past. I want to use this history-bending invocation of hip-hop music to move from a Harlem of the past to a certain rendition of Harlem's present and future.

Harlemworld, the Music

My ethnographic fieldwork was based in the upper Manhattan community of Harlem. Using formalized interviewing techniques and participant observation, I am trying to make an argument about how contested perceptions and performances of race and class intersect in the lives of contemporary African Americans. Not only is Harlem a class-variegated community (and hardly in terms of easy binaries between equally reified underclasses and middle classes), but residents constantly use class-, race-, and gender-inflected arguments as a way of tampering with the boundaries of belonging. But Harlemworld is not Harlem in any easy sense of the place. Rather, it exemplifies an explicitly imagined community, a "quotation-marked-off place," an ethnographic land of make-believe predicated on a reconfiguration of the connections between race and class today. Harlemworld is a decidedly hip-hop-based space, a land where race and class and their interconnective, cross-constitutive tissue challenge some of the assumptions we have about what places like Harlem can mean and represent.

My interest is in place (in this case Harlemworld as extension of Harlem, New York) and its linkages to racial identity. Lately, this gambit is my own preoccupation, but it is also a bedrock concern of the hip-hop music I'm interested in discussing a bit here. Place and race have always been important in hip-hop culture. In one corner, academic analyses of hip-hop as cultural production began in earnest with debates pivoting most explicitly on different origin stories: some posit its birth, fully formed, within the political economy of the postindustrial inner-city landscape of the South Bronx (rife with slum clearances of more than 100,000 people for the Cross Bronx Expressway and a fiscal crisis on Mayor Beame's watch). In another corner, academics offer a more dispersed placing wherein the operative unit of geographical analysis for locating the origin story of hip-hop culture outstrips the nation-state, favoring, instead, a topography of ocean currents and the ships that traverse them.[37]

But "place" isn't important only to scholars in academia writing about hip-hop music and its beginning. Place is also a seminal thematic for the hip-hop artists themselves. As rap music first gained a mass-market appeal, the clearest allegiances (and most important references) found in the music were to place: specifically the boroughs of New York City where artists lived. Early rappers battled in their songs by entering an ongoing conversation about the important attributes distinguishing boroughs. One's loyalty was to Queens or Brooklyn or the Bronx or Manhattan, and each evocation of place codified a series of attributes that made hierarchical sense of hip-hop's delimited geographical landscape.[38]

Once rap acts began to consist of members from across the boroughs and hip-hop went national, the borough-based differences became less significant than the distinction between East Coast (read: New York) hip-hop and the brand of hip-hop found on the West Coast, most especially southern California. As hip-hop went national it paradoxically became regional as different emceeing and musical styles began to distinguish different chunks of the country.[39] As the reach of the music increased, place remained important, but the meaningful interpretive unit changed from specific boroughs, to all of New York City, to the entire East Coast. There was an East Coast sound, a West Coast sound, a Chicago sound, a southern sound, a Houston sound. Moreover, these distinctions between places came with often sophisticated analyses about the aesthetic differences linked to regionality within that musical genre. For example, the historian Tricia Rose paraphrases Chuck D, lead man for the group Public Enemy, as saying, "the music coming out of New York is often produced with the walkpeople's earphone acoustics in mind, whereas, the more auto-based cities of Miami and Los Angeles produce music that reflect automobile cultures and acoustics."[40] Here, an analysis of place connects to another analysis of how places are differently designed and negotiated social spaces predetermining location-specific aesthetic necessities—and linked to detailed differences between the technologies of choice (SP1200s, TR 808, MPC-60s) used to create differing kinds of sound possibilities.

Amid all of the contemporary regional differences within this musical genre stands "Harlemworld," a symbolic construct that comes out of Bad Boy Entertainment, the New York–based hip-hop company headed by artist, producer, entertainer, and entrepreneur Sean "Puff Daddy" Combs. Combs and his erstwhile partner in crime Mason "Mase" Betha (spelled M-A-$-E) are prime residents—maybe even crowned princes—of Harlemworld, and they use their songs and music videos to disseminate a specific depiction of this place and the people who reside there. Both men, about ten years apart in age, claim Harlem as their home. Combs's father, an alleged hustler, was shot in Central Park in the early 1970s, and his mother moved the family from their rather middle-income place on Lenox Avenue to Mount Vernon, New York, an area sandwiched between New Rochelle (another breeding ground for several contemporary hip-hop artists) and the Bronx. Betha, from the South, grew up in Harlem with his mother, father, and six siblings. He rapped around Harlem in the early 1990s under the name "Murder," spitting out gangsta rap lyrics before Combs signed him to a record deal at Bad Boy and helped change the young rapper's image.[41] Combs had a long history of discovering and marketing "ghetto fabulous" artists able to split the difference between street authenticity and bejeweled material wealth. Fired from Uptown Records in 1993, Combs launched Bad Boy Entertainment, bankrolled by Arista Records executive Clive Davis, and hit the ground running with rapper Biggie's debut album *Ready to Die*.

Mase's first album, *Harlem World,* debuted in 1997 and sold more than four million copies for Bad Boy Entertainment. Mase parlayed that success into his own record label, All Out Records, a separate recording deal for some of his old Harlem crew, and a management offer from Ervin "Magic" Johnson himself. During my fieldwork stint, Betha and Combs were at the height of their fame and popularity, and in 1997 Bad Boy Entertainment grossed more than $100,000,000 in sales. Combs's empire branched out into restaurant chains, a clothing line, and a film and television division. By 1998, however, after the murder of Biggie Smallz (a murder linked to hip-hop-based regional rivalries), Bad Boy Records took a substantial hit in the pocketbook, sales receipts dropping by more than 75 percent the following year. In 1999, things seemed to go from bad to worse, as Combs found himself in trouble with the law, first for assaulting a record executive and then for his involvement in a shooting at a New York City nightclub. Before some of these recent snags, Puff Daddy's Harlemworld could do no wrong, selling millions of albums and fascinating white and black fans alike.

There is much more history of hip-hop in Harlem that can be unearthed, from clothing stores like Dapper Dan's on 125th, which dressed early New York freestylers, to rap group Run DMC's internationally canonized reference to wearing shell-topped "Adidas on 2-5th street."[42] One of the earliest hip-hop-related references to a Harlem World is a "cultural and entertainment complex" by that name located on Lenox and 116th Street in the late 1970s and early 1980s. There, young people would hear the latest from hip-hop deejays, girls might be admitted free before a certain time, and of course proper attire was always required (sometimes with cash awards for the best dressed). There were a lot of these kinds of early venues for the development of hip-hop music and culture in New York at that time.

What is most interesting about the visual and discursive depictions of Harlemworld found in Mase and Puff Daddy's early albums and music videos is how stunningly absent Harlem, the place, seems to be. Mase makes particularly extended use of "Harlemworld" as the name not only of his first album but of what he calls his "movement," and also for his old Harlem crew, which was signed to All Out Records. For Mase and Combs, Harlemworld is a world of high-class, top-dollar material culture and accoutrements. Rolex watches are on wrists, and Mercedes-Benzes, Lamborghinis, and Rolls-Royces are the cars of choice. Bikini-clad women fill the pools and bubbling Jacuzzis that flank every mansion-like suburban home shown on screen and mentioned on CD. This was a Harlemworld without any specific images of Harlem streets, a musical derivation of the place without any recourse to Harlem, New York, at all. This is a particularly conspicuous absence because most earlier rappers had simply taken film crews to their old haunts and immortalized their neighborhoods on celluloid or video. Even equally materialistic gangsta rappers from the West Coast (folks like Dr. Dre and Snoop Doggy

Dogg) used music videos with landscapes linked specifically to areas where they lived. This was not the case for Harlemworld. In its music videos, interior scenes are shot in fairy-tale studios, with otherworldly lights, gadgets, flares, fire, sparkles, and mirrors. These videos project a kind of anywhere-place that is supposed to capture the glitz and glamour on the invocation of which Harlemworld's main residents, Puffy and Mase, stand.

The exterior representations of Harlemworld are equally conspicuous for their lack of 125th Street charm. It is a Harlemworld of open desert plains, of sandy beaches and dirt highways spread out for miles without end. Mase and Puff Daddy are in Tunisia, Libya, Las Vegas, or a variation on Disney's Celebration, U.S.A. Never the actual streets of Harlem. Within the first ten music videos that Mase and Puff Daddy have made (the majority of which contain lyrics that invoke this place called Harlemworld or even Harlem—"Harlem on the rise / and you don't want no problem with us guys") one would be hard pressed to find depictions of anything within the actual region of Harlem. No Apollo Theater. No Sylvia's restaurant. Not even, more generally, urban landscapes and tenement buildings; instead, one finds mostly huge mansions and jet planes that take them to other exotic locales even farther away from Harlem. Times Square gets a shot or two, but that's the extent of the urban topography. Indeed, Mase and Puffy's Harlemworld represents everyday realities that few of the people in Harlem ever see or experience.

Not only is the lack of Harlem imagery in early Harlemworld important, so is the discourse constructed about Harlemworld itself. It is a place where poverty is always situated in the past tense, not just in some other place but in another time as well. Puff Daddy, dancing with Mase on a sand dune that could be anywhere in the world save Harlem, raps about his own past in these very terms:

> I was a one-bedroomer, dreaming of a million
> Now in beach houses, cream to the ceiling
> I was a gentleman living in tenements
> Now I'm swimming in all the women that be tens
> Went from Bad Boys to the Crushed Linen Men
> Now my dividends be the new Benjamins.

But that former poverty (those "tenements") existed in Harlem. Harlemworld is peopled by individuals who are "young, black and famous / with money hanging out the anus." Mase concretizes the grounding of place in economic success when he says that if there is "one thing about Harlemworld, we all got dough." This representation of Harlemworld is interesting because it works to make class achievement a kind of prerequisite for spatial and racial belonging. To have access to Harlemworld, one must be making incredible amounts of money, one must be able to take jet planes to exotic places, battle sheiks in remote locations, and drive six-figure automobiles. If Tarantino can exempt the black middle class from a certain version of racial authenticity vis-à-vis black poverty, Harlemworld is posited as a place where, to the contrary, not having money jeopardizes one's racial status and degree of belongingness. In Harlemworld, identity is predicated on having "dough." Whereas Harlem is usually offered as the stereotyped landscape of black inner-city poverty, Harlemworld brackets that poverty out and argues for a blackness based on a high class position, fancy cars, expensive clothes, and lush scenery.

Just like the black ghettos depicted in the social science literature concerning black America, Harlemworld was initially constructed as a kind of class-homogenous space. Whereas ghettos like Harlem are usually viewed as unilaterally poor (class variety being downplayed or ignored outright), Harlemworld is all riches and wealth, all trips around the world and Rolex watches. In a sense, Harlemworld is a hip-hop-based critique of the underclass model of contemporary black America, a critique that makes "racial authenticity" a function of class achievement as opposed to social marginality, poverty, and failure. It is a world (as we've seen in other contexts) without beggars on the street, without the homeless, without poverty or filth. Instead, Harlemworld writes race and class in such a way that economic achievement does not relegate one to the mainstream and keep one beyond the protective cover of blackness. Instead, here class achievement actually reinforces and shores up one's racial and social self. In this early Harlemworld, the performance of class-based success translates into the performance of an authentic black racial identity. Much of the contemporary social science literature on black America creates another kind of Harlemworld, one that is also without a truly accurate image of Harlem in it, one of utter poverty and despair. The "real" Harlem is located somewhere between those two extremes—at a point where people are negotiating class-stratified social spaces by way of class-specific and racialized social performances that help them navigate the contested terrain of place in their everyday lives.

Recently, hip-hop's Harlemworld has become a little grittier and more urbanized. There are now specific music video images set in Harlem where one spots landmarks such as M & G's Soul Food, the Apollo Theater, and Mart 125. In 1999, Mase rededicated his life to Jesus Christ,

left hip-hop music, and relocated from glitzy Harlemworld to a historically black college in the South. Simultaneously, as Puff Daddy's street
credibility waned and his sophomore project's sales sagged, he moved
not just into a more hard-lined rhetoric (calling himself "public enemy
number one" and screaming on record, "Die motherfucker die; you
don't give a fuck; I don't give a fuck") but also into a decidedly more
militarized landscape specifically located in Harlem proper—and when
not in Harlem, in a clearly cement-and-glass-enclosed cityscape. There
are few invocations of the term *Harlemworld* in Puffy's most recent songs.
And this provides fodder, perhaps, for the ultimate question about the
limitations inherent to behavioral notions of identity. Combs and Mase
tried to resignify racial authenticity in a Harlemworld of material wealth
and economic overachievement. As soon as it was questioned, as soon
as Combs became the butt of web sites questioning his sexuality as well
as his street authenticity, Combs returned to the same overused images
of urban poverty that bolster most commonsense and academic versions of black racial particularity. But that former Harlemworld of 1996
and 1997, for all its classism, sexism, and unabashed materialism, still
opened the door to a slightly different version of race and place in contemporary black America, a version that linked ghetto fabulousness to
high-profile socioeconomic success. That initial formulation (as well as
Puff Daddy's more recent return to urbanity's most obvious stereotypes)
provides interesting lessons about (1) the arbitrariness of class-based representations of racial authenticity and (2) the tremendous social pressure
exerted against those who go against the grain of contemporary equations about race's most obvious connection to class in contemporary
black America.

UNDOING HARLEMWORLD

BET Comes to Harlem

In late summer of 2000, Black Entertainment Television (BET) hyped the relocation of several of its key shows and production facilities to Harlem from Washington, D.C., where most of that cable network's programming had previously been produced and recorded. The network ran a daily countdown to *Harlem Block Party*, a televised event organized on the streets of Harlem in celebration of this interstate move. *Harlem Block Party* included a series of hip-hop and R&B performances on the Apollo stage, along with dancing, interviews, and entertainment in the street outside. In the days immediately following that BET broadcast, many of the network's VJs could be found on-air touring the community, identifying landmarks such as the Apollo Theater and the Hotel Theresa, while explaining some of those landmarks' historical lore for viewers in other places.

This book is not about gentrification per se, but BET's move highlights some of the massive changes that affected Harlem during the last decade of the twentieth century, catapulting Harlem back onto a certain national radar screen. Businesses are returning. Capital has been found to finance a variety of neighborhood improvements. For instance, that once-weathered and worn 1940s Apollo marquee with dangling and haphazardly combined letters is not quite so weathered and worn anymore, especially after New York State's Department of Parks, Recreation, and Historic Preservation supplied $325,000 toward its restoration in 1999. Governor George Pataki and Empire State Development Corporation head Charles Gargano have provided even more financial assistance for the famed entertainment facility built in 1913—as have Time Warner and its new Apollo Theater Foundation board members.[1]

But more than just the look of Harlem's buildings has changed over the past few years. The black middle class is moving into the area with renewed speed, capped off by an 80 percent increase in the number of neighborhood households earning more than $75,000 per year between the beginning and end of the 1990s.[2] Harlem's housing stock is also rising dramatically in worth, as refurbished brownstones on Fifth Avenue and 125th Street sell for well over $800,000 in New York's competitive real estate market. Indeed, the Harlem of my fieldwork in 1994, 1996, 1997, and 1998 is already and decidedly a remnant of the past, but it can still tell us something useful about what the intersections between race and class mean as social categories in contemporary black America—and, with careful extrapolation, in American culture more generally.

As the United States eases itself into the beginnings of a new millennium, all of its citizens continue to grapple with age-old concerns about solidarity, nationhood, and identity. These concerns have changed characteristics and even terminology throughout the years without losing any relevance in terms of implications for the smooth functioning of American society. More specifically, issues of racial and ethnic identity and solidarity have been drastically reconfigured in the wake of 1960s civil rights struggles, which forever changed the nature of race relations in this country, fostering a public outcry against the harsher injustices of legalized segregation. According to various analysts, however, the civil rights movement's measured attacks on the most conspicuous excesses of a segregated society left to subsequent generations the complex task of challenging tacit and "camouflaged" forms of racism, forms more difficult to see and less easy to combat. Indeed, many have argued about the continuing importance of race and racism in an era when civil rights legislation has supposedly made all citizens equal in the eyes of the law.[3]

I enter these debates on race and class in post–civil rights America by looking specifically at the implications of class stratification for African Americans and their social interactions. Many social scientists assume class isolationism between two seemingly discrete and estranged socioeconomic groups as the defining feature of contemporary black America's class structure. Yes, there is social mobility in people's lives (not to mention a social mobility literature in the social sciences), but this ongoing discussion about how people's class realities change over time is often left out of mutually exclusive, sensationalized, and sealed-off constructions of the black underclass and middle class. Instead of assuming that class-based isolation and social bifurcation, I've looked at the permeability of class boundaries in black America by focusing on familial and friendship networks—as well as more ephemeral public interactions—to examine how people make sense of class differences that affect their everyday relationships. I was interested in moments when socioeconomically different lives and lifestyles touch, what people say about that contact, and what they do (or say that others do) in those instants. Poverty has spread, and spatial segregation of the black poor is an undeniably real phenomenon, but the black middle class is caught up in a racially segregated housing market that tends to keep its members decidedly closer to the black poor than the white middle class is to the white poor.[4] This same spatial and economic reality promotes opportunities for cross-class interactions within black communities, interactions that African Americans think about and argue over in their daily lives.

Harlem is something of a statistical outlier in terms of typical black communities' levels of class stratification. As "the capital of black America," Harlem has always held a special place in the hearts and minds of middle-class African Americans otherwise preoccupied with the lure of suburbanization. Still, the reclamation of urban landscapes is a national trend, as residential gentrification and corporate reinvestment in previously underserved and discarded urban markets across the country have tended to push many of the poor from formerly ravaged urban communities. Class warfare (both subtle and not-so-subtle) is being waged through business improvement districts in American cities, Harlem's massive vendor relocation in 1994 being only a more dramatic example of the Disneyfication intrinsic to most urban renewal schemes.[5] With these urban improvements, questions remain: Who are these spaces being constructed for? Who still belongs and who is no longer welcome? And what part do class and race play in determining answers to these kinds of inquiries?

It is in the context of such Disneyfications of urbanity that Harlem's connection to Harlemworld is most structurally grounded. Harlemworld isn't just about the ideas and assumptions people truck into discussions about the actual place. It also underscores the battles for valid belonging within a changing community of dislocation and conflict. Moreover, as atypical as Harlem's class variation may appear, these same theories of class variation and racial performativity can be unpacked in the context of a larger imagined community peopled by inhabitants who need not leave the comforts of their homes. Passage is booked through remote controls and *TV Guides* over and against tour buses, airplanes, and moving vans. In this mass-mediated context, class variation is part and parcel not only of the geographical expanse that defines the borders of northern Manhattan but also of the class-stratified representations of blackness within the funhouse mirror reflections that people experience vicariously through television sets and film screens. Just as people make claims about identity and belonging based on the actions of neighbors, friends, family members, and passersby whom they engage in the public sphere, people also look to the representations of place and identity offered up by infotainment outlets such as BET to draw the farthest limits of their community's symbolic boundaries.[6]

Reading Behavior

There are many reasons why interpretations of people's everyday behaviors are potentially useful starting points for discussions about social differences organized around race and class in black America. For one thing, the supposed distinction between the black underclass and the black middle class has always been predicated on behavioral specificities. Social scientists analyzing poverty almost exclusively draw on behavioral disparities to define and describe America's poor: Ken Auletta uses "antisocial behavior" as an essential feature of the underclass; Lawrence Mead talks of "functioning problems" (people's inability to perform certain basic social skills) as the central definition of underclassness; Charles Murray foregrounds what he sees as shiftlessness and a disregard for the work ethic (unwillingness to do anything productive) as the major characteristic of America's welfare-dependent underclass. In all of these instances, the underclass is defined by what its members do or don't do, and the black middle class is counterfactually understood in action-based opposition to these supposed behavioral proclivities.[7]

Social scientists aren't the only ones who use behavior to parse class-specific social distinctions. Many of the people I met in Harlem interpret everyday actions as important class-based distinguishers within multi-classed social worlds—worlds they know intimately in Harlem or as part of the Harlemworld racial imaginary that surrounds it. These contemporary folk theories link class to behavioral variables, and these quotidian behaviors (the way people walk, talk, stand, sit, smile, laugh) serve as a proxy for what are understood to be class-related differences. Assumed economic differences are gleaned from seemingly noneconomic activities. These behaviors are not necessarily classed in intrinsically obvious ways, but rather are rhetorically glued to particular social positions within a larger symbolic and discursive universe of public contestation. People use these behavioral variables to translate back and forth between gradational and relational notions of class in strategic and context-specific ways.

Contrary to popular belief, African Americans aren't always simply blind to class, but rather are sometimes quite stringent about when, where, and how they link specific social actors to particular social classes. The translation of lived experiences into class formations often entails the invocation of behavioral differences as endemic to any identifiable indicator of "objective interests." The fact that this feat is discursive and performance-based doesn't make the divisions constructed any less powerful for the people who espouse them. And the ultimate arbitrariness of such class-inflected sign systems (walking fast can be indicative of both underclassness and middle-classness) may make it more amenable to debate, to change, and to potentially empowering reinterpretations.

The simultaneity of race and class is more than just an easy academic mantra. Behavioral models of difference show how and why race and class are mutually constitutive social facts. People theorize race in similarly behavioral ways; that is, race, like class, is said to be expressed through behavioral differences that are loaded down with racialized significances. Raced behaviors constrain and structure the conceptual possibilities that people bring to bear on their sense of themselves and their social identities. However, race's structuring hegemony is only "partial" within such a decidedly performative matrix. This a performative matrix not just because behaviors are key variables in folk definitions of racial difference, but even more important, because performances and practices of race are the only real grounding on which hierarchical notions of race in the United Stands can ultimately stand. It is not just Africa or Harlem or black skin or any other such hard-and-fast anchor that steadies the mobile possibilities of racial identity. Instead, performances of race define and constitute the substance from which all racial distinctions are crafted, especially in *intra*racial contexts. Of course, there are limits and pitfalls to racial performativity, to the progressive possibilities of race as performance. The intersections between race and class are often used to disparage and de-authenticate persons based on the things they do. Also, as Katya Gibel Azoulay argues, in *inter*racial spaces blackness "is less a matter of doing than of being done to . . . one need not work at being black to be reminded of it."[8] One's body can be marked as if that marking provided irrefutable evidence of social difference.

Still, many of the Harlemites I met play with interpretations of actions to define social sameness and difference in interesting and even idiosyncratic ways. Likewise, they use behavioral variables as an explanation for racial authenticity or inauthenticity. I am less interested in the behaviors themselves than in the discourses and rhetorical high-wire acts that give otherwise meaningless behaviors sociocultural intelligibility. We "do" race and class not necessarily because there are some behaviors that best index them (that are somehow transparent reflections of what race and class actually are), but because it gives us a sense of power in our ability to mold, remold, and challenge the cues we use to determine social identities. These performative moves can be either liberating or oppressive, depending on the use to which we put them. There is the potential for allowing white bodies to read as black, which Tarantino argues through his behaviorally blackfaced cinema. There is the possibility for using behavior to narrowly police other people's claims to belonging and identity, using behavior as prescription and racial dogma—action-based notions of identity that theorize behaviors as the only real signs (over and against phenotype and biography) of social authentication. Tarantino and the other Hollywood examples from chapter 6 show the excesses of such a position, excesses wherein social context is bracketed out for an overly voluntaristic rendition of racial difference and authenticity.

Race is what you do, but it is not only what you do. Moreover, people don't just "do" race and class in some kind of social vacuum. Race and class are also done *to* people in the form of racism and class-based exploitation—with gender, sexuality, and ethnicity always operative in parallel ways. In the folk theories of race I've highlighted here, biology is necessary but not sufficient for making sense of racial identity. Biography (growing up in the hood) is also not enough. Interpretations of social actions serve as the third side of a triangular articulation of identity. These social actions don't simply trump biography or biology, genetics or sociality. They don't allow people complete freedom to successfully "do" any kind of racial self they desire. However, factoring in these performances complicates the equation, alternately allowing for biology to be less than sufficient and for less-than-compelling performances to be critiqued as inauthentic.

The Ends of Race

Obviously, there is much at stake in this discussion of race as behavior, much to be unpacked and explored, both personally and politically speaking. Some scholars argue for the end of race as a meaningful and affect-laden social category.[9] Other academics take various places along a continuum of deconstructionist notions of race, many stopping far short of its complete disavowal.[10] These theories of race are often difficult to graft onto people's everyday social relations. What might the deconstruction of race look like in a social world where nationalism is historically carried atop the arched back of white racism? Where rapper Eminem and actors Michael Rapaport and Danny Hoch prove that ostensibly white men can act black in seemingly authentic ways—or that acting black may not be an exclusively black-bodied thing? Where a growing mixed-race movement takes census-based shots at the phenotypic and heritable ends of hypodescent?

For me, as an American-born black male of part Caribbean and part southern ancestry, many of these issues of racial identity are permanently melded to ethnicity and gender. Moreover, I look to my own social networks for the kinds of class isolationism described in the social science literature. I examine my personal history to find explanations for the different degrees of academic and social achievement experienced by the African American and Caribbean American kids I went to school with as a youngster. I wonder about my own social trajectory; what does it explain, and what does it explain away? What does differential access to socioeconomic success mean for the ways in which African Americans discuss racial solidarity across class lines?

Paraphrasing white racial ignorance about blacks circa 1903, W. E. B. Du Bois asked, "How does it feel to be a problem?"[11] That is, how do black people deal with a second-class citizenship predicated on the enforcement of a strict racial caste system that pathologizes their very existence? One hundred years later, that same question still holds. But many people are equally fascinated by its converse: How does it feel to be a socioeconomically successful black person amid an assumed sea of black poverty? Do all black Americans embody the same exact Duboisian problematic? If not, what does that difference mean for the ways in which black people think about their connections to one another?

Some scholars might believe themselves and their colleagues to be the only folks contesting essentialist social identities, while ordinary people out there in the world just go around essentializing their identities left and right—and in exactly the same ways each time. The people I met in Harlem challenge one another's definitions of identity at every turn. They construct different linkages between identity (as predicated on class or race) and the social practices said to reflect them. These same actions are less a reflection of some pre-existent social identity than of the empirical engine used to power that identity's very insertion into categorizable social space. The details justifying social hierarchies and racial chauvinism are immaterial, irrelevant, and arbitrary.[12] Once that difference is projected onto the world, just about any set of characteristics will do to explain it.

One can use this understanding to dismiss any serious intellectual engagement with the context-specific attributes people invoke to justify xenophobia, racism, and social differentiation. Instead, I've tried to look at how these attributes are talked about and challenged within everyday discussions about racial and class-specific categories of difference, how these links from identity to activity provide room in the debate about the categories we use as social filters. The first step is to de-essentialize our notions of essentialism and to move beyond the flippant and dismissive "there is no there there" variants of antiessentialist discourse. I take my cue from some of the more pragmatic impulses of Du Bois, treating seriously his politically relevant mandate to use race to transcend itself.

This is not a book about white racism—or an argument about how blacks in Harlem, Harlemworld, or any place else get duped by American racial discourse into re-creating that same white racism in minstrelled form. Moreover, black people's folk critiques of class-based and racial differences should not be dismissed as anti-intellectualism, white bashing, or reverse discrimination, which some readers may want to do. The particular ways in which people theorize social difference with recourse to behaviors—or challenge others' theories along those lines—constitute the ground floor of antiracist folk analyses of identity. Behavioral generalizations made about social groups anchor racist belief systems, but their recognizable arbitrariness and inexhaustiveness create spaces for people to chip away at the most reactionary and essentialist variations. More and more people are arguing that racial difference is not coterminous with a single set of behavioral traits, and such arguments challenge the very core of racialist reasoning.

In the context of debates about the human genome project and the browning of America, many people argue that racial differences are doomed to nonexistence by the mid-twenty-first century—that race is a thing of the past and present but certainly will not survive the near future. But the social fact of race isn't just about genes and biology, skin color and nationality. Race is also adduced in important ways through what people do in the social world. And as long as different people do different things, there is always the potential for linking such behavioral differences to a framework of hierarchical social groups verifiable through examinations of such divergent social practices. More encouragingly, as long as people use behaviors to verify and justify their assumptions about social differences, the arbitrary and partial nature of such linkages can grease the wheels of progressive politicking by allowing individuals to contest groupings based on those same empirically assessed behavioral grounds. If, as I say here, racial essentialism is based on what people do in the social world, it might possibly be undone with recourse to analyses of those same action-identity arguments, analyses that highlight the contrived nature of the connections we make between *being* and *doing, identity* and *activity, race* and *culture.* People observe how other people do race and class, and they also battle over how these behaviors should be classed and racialized. As long as folks continue to link supposed racial differences to behavioral differences, they set up empty spaces where the links don't really hold, where other people can contest such linkages on empirical grounds and challenge any such argument about absolute group differences in contemporary society.

Many years ago, Melville Herskovits and E. Franklin Frazier carved out the fault lines of a much-rehearsed discussion about African American cultural specificity.[13] Herskovits, along with Carter G. Woodson and Lorenzo Turner, argued that African cultural particularity could be seen in contemporary black cultural life-ways, whereas Frazier and fellow sociologist Robert Park dismissed such supposed links between African American and African cultural patterns, arguing that the harsh mandates of chattel slavery caused subsequent generations of black slaves to lose all former cultural ties to their African homelands. These debates were often extended to arguments about how race-specific cultural differences (whatever their etiology) explain racial discord and miscommunication. Black cultural styles and white cultural styles were considered to be in "conflict," and this conflict was used to explain the dire state of race relations in America.[14] I am not trying to marshal ethnographic evidence for an argument about clear-cut or absolute black-white cultural divergence, but I do want to offer folk theories of identity as predicated on the same kinds of arguments that Frazier, Park, Woodson, and Herskovits canonized and that Mintz and Price superseded. Whether the supposed cultural chasm between blackness and whiteness is linked to ancient Africa, class differences, or racist oppression, ordinary people anchor their notions of identity to behavioral arguments that place the onus for that difference not just on the surface of the body but in bodies' motions and activities in the everyday world. Whether or not actual race-based cultural and behavioral differences create space for racial conflicts may be less important than the fact that people mobilize those supposed differences to explain such conflicts—and to make sense of their connections to other social actors. If people define racial difference as a function of what individuals do, then racial essentialism can be slowly undone by challenging the behaviors that others invoke to explain social hierarchies of all stripes. This dialectical process goes on every single day in Harlem and all around the world.

NOTES

Introduction

1. All names and anonymity-compromising details have been changed, a standard urban ethnographic practice that I use although it is being challenged by a few recent ethnographic endeavors. Mitchell Duneier, *Sidewalk* (New York: Farrar, Straus, Giroux, 1999) and Steven Gregory, *Black Corona: Race and the Politics of Place in an Urban Community* (Princeton, N.J.: Princeton University Press, 1998) are a couple of the most highly touted contemporary examples. *Harlemworld: Doing Race and Class in Contemporary Black America* started out as a doctoral research project and entailed confidential consent forms specifically aimed at protecting participants' privacy and anonymity. With that in mind, I have tried to ensure that the details provided do not compromise the confidentiality promised. Also, by way of introductory remarks, I should point out that I purposefully use the terms *black, black American,* and *African American* interchangeably in this book. A definitive resolution to questions of appellation is precisely what is up for grabs in this work and should not be decided on beforehand or imposed for textual consistency. This decision is part and parcel of a broader anthropological angst about the politics of cultural representation and ethnographic writing. Thus, I have also tried to mix and blur various literary genres in drafting this narrative: ethnographic realism, fiction, film criticism, and cultural theory. I hope this does not seem too self-indulgent—and that it will not overtax the reader's patience. Instead, I intend this combining of genres to subtly underscore the constructedness of the text and to stylistically mirror the diversity of voices represented. George E. Marcus and Michael M. J. Fischer, *Anthropology as Cultural Critique: An Experimental Moment in the Human Sciences* (Chicago: University of Chicago Press, 1986), James Clifford and George E. Marcus, eds., *Writing Culture: The Poetics and Politics of Ethnography* (Berkeley: University of California Press, 1986), and James Clifford, *The Predicament of Culture: Twentieth-Century Ethnography, Literature, and Art* (Cambridge: Harvard University Press, 1988) are canonical syntheses of these writerly anxieties, which concern many anthropologists.

2. James C. Scott discusses "infrapolitics" as a kind of "hidden transcript" employed by the oppressed to resist social marginalization. See *The Moral Economy of the Peasant* (New Haven, Conn.: Yale University Press, 1976) and *Weapons of the Weak: Everyday Forms of Peasant Resistance* (New Haven, Conn.: Yale University Press, 1985). The historian Robin D. G. Kelley uses this notion of infrapolitics to describe how southern radicals and entry-level service sector employees oppose class exploitation through other than formal and unionized channels. *Race Rebels: Culture, Politics, and the Black Working Class* (New York: Free Press, 1994) opens with Kelley's past employment stints at fast food restau-

rants rife with examples of infrapolitical tactics. Pan-toting, wearing McDonald's baseball caps to the side, turning the manager's piped-in music from easy listening to Rick James, and extending fifteen-minute breaks by fifteen more minutes are some of the infrapolitical strategies his crewmates used. I invoke Kelley's specific examples here because they shadow this book's McDonald's-based opening. George Ritzer, *The McDonaldization of Society: An Investigation into the Changing Character of Contemporary Social Life* (Thousand Oaks, Calif.: Pine Forge Press, 1996) and Robert Leider, *Fast Food, Fast Talk: Service Work and the Routinization of Everyday Life* (Berkeley: University of California Press, 1990) offer more substantive engagements with McDonald's as an important force for societal change and space for interpersonal negotiations.

3. For an analogous sealing-off of social space as a decidedly racialized place in a Liverpudlian context, see Jacqueline Nassy Brown, "Enslaving History: Narratives on Local Whiteness in a Black Atlantic Port," *American Ethnologist* 27, no. 2 (May 2000): 340–70. For an analysis of how people are taught to view geographical space in such racialized terms, see Stephen Nathan Haymes, *Race, Culture, and the City: A Pedagogy for Black Urban Struggle* (Albany: State University of New York, 1995). Randall Kenan, *Walking on Water: Black American Lives at the Turn of the Twenty-first Century* (New York: Vintage, 1999) embarks on a national journey in search of the blackened significances of places like Harlem.

4. Jonathan Reider, *Canarsie: The Jews and Italians of Brooklyn Against Liberalism* (Cambridge: Harvard University Press, 1985) puts some of that subjective distance into its sociohistorical context. In the 1970s and 1980s, Canarsie was a predominantly white section of Brooklyn, and many of the residents there fought adamantly against the black residential influx that families like mine represented.

5. This "something else" is reminiscent of the "something else" in Ralph Ellison's critique of abstract sociological depictions of Harlem as little more than "hardship," "poverty," "ruggedness," and "filth." He writes: "[T]here is something else in Harlem, something subjective, willful, and complexly and compellingly human. It is 'that something else' that challenges sociologists who ignore it." For the context of this statement and its measured critique of social scientific excess, see Ralph Ellison, "A Very Stern Discipline," *Harper's*, March 1967, 76–77.

6. J. Martin Favor, *Authentic Blackness: The Folk in the Negro Renaissance* (Durham, N.C.: Duke University Press, 1999) argues that the black literati have always used lower-class black cultural repertoires as the deciding criterion for racial legitimacy. He looks at the work of W. E. B. Du Bois, James Weldon Johnson, Nella Larson, and others in that very light. Favor also invokes the provocative theoretical work of Judith Butler concerning issues of gender performativity to ground his argument. *Gender Trouble: Feminism and the Subversion of Identity* (New York: Routledge, 1989) and *Bodies That Matter: On the Discursive Limits of "Sex"* (New York: Routledge, 1993).

7. *Behaviors, practices,* and *performances* are not identical terms, but they can be thought of as in cahoots—calling for a measured cobbling together of theoretical strands from Erving Goffman's notions of self-presentation, Pierre Bourdieu's "practice theory," Michel Foucault's "discourse analysis," and Butlerian "performativity."

8. See George Gilder, *Wealth and Power* (New York: Basic, 1981); Charles Murray, *Losing Ground: American Social Policy, 1950–1980* (New York: Basic, 1984); and Lawrence Mead, *The New Politics of Poverty: The Non-working Poor in America* (New York: HarperCollins, 1992) as the most cited examples of this position. For a critique of these behavioral explanations for perpetual poverty, see Adolph Reed Jr., *Stirrings in the Jar: Black Politics in the Post Civil Rights Era* (Minneapolis: University of Minnesota Press, 1999), pp. 179–96.

9. See Philippe Bourgois, *In Search of Respect: Selling Crack in El Barrio* (Cambridge: Cambridge University Press, 1995); Carol Stack, *All Our Kin: Strategies for Survival in Black America* (New York: Harper and Row, 1975); and William Julius Wilson, *The Truly Disadvantaged: The Inner City, The Underclass, and Public Policy* (Chicago: University of Chicago Press, 1987).

10. See Philip Moss and Chris Tilly, "Growing Demand for 'Soft' Skills in Four Industries: Evidence from In-Depth Employer Interviews (Russell Sage Foundation Working Paper #93, 1996); Harry Holzer, *What Employers Want: Job Prospects for Less-Educated Workers* (New York: Russell Sage, 1996); and Peter Gottschalk, ed., *Generating Jobs: How to Increase Demand for Low-Skilled Workers* (New York: Russell Sage, 1998).

11. See Pierre Bourdieu, *Distinctions: A Social Critique of the Judgment of Taste* (Cambridge: Harvard University Press, 1984).

12. See Elijah Anderson, *Streetwise: Race, Class, and Change in an Urban Community* (Chicago: University of Chicago Press, 1990) and *Code of the Streets: Decency, Violence, and the Moral Life of the Inner City* (New York: Norton, 1999). For a discussion of the "cool pose" as black male public posturing, see Richard Majors and Janet Mancini Billson, *Cool Pose: The Dilemmas of Black Manhood in America* (New York: Touchstone, 1992).

13. This position owes much to the influential arguments of William Julius Wilson, *The Declining Significance of Race: Blacks and Changing American Institutions* (Chicago: University of Chicago Press, 1978) and *Truly Disadvantaged*.

14. Signithia Fordham has conducted one of the richest anthropological analyses of "acting white" in *Blacked Out: Dilemmas of Race, Identity, and Success at Capital High* (Chicago: University of Chicago Press, 1996). Also see Signithia Fordham and John U. Ogbu, "Black Students' School Success: Coping with the 'Burden of Acting White,'" *Urban Review* 18, no. 3 (1986): 176–206. And most recently, see Prudence Carter, "Balancing 'Acts': Issues of Identity and Cultural Resistance in the Social and Educational Behaviors of Minority Youth," (Ph.D. diss., Columbia University, 1999).

15. Examples of this can work in any number of ways: whites can attack any person of color for cultural and behavioral differences that supposedly bespeak racial inferiority: doing poorly in school, speaking black English, and so on. And blacks can do the same thing, challenging other blacks who speak proper English or black English, considering gay blacks not "down" enough because of their sexuality, dismissing blacks in interracial relationships as "sellouts," belittling black youngsters who excel at school, or belittling black youngsters who fail out—all depending on context and speaker.

16. See Charles Mills, *Blackness Visible: Essays on Philosophy and Race* (Ithaca, N.Y.: Cornell University Press, 1998) for a discussion of vertical systems of racial difference in comparison to hypothetical horizontal ones.

17. Vernon J. Williams Jr., *Rethinking Race: Franz Boas and His Contemporaries* (Lexington: University of Kentucky, 1996) makes it quite clear that even Franz Boas used anthropometrics to argue for aggregate differences between races. Boas also believed that those group distinctions did not necessarily tell us anything about the differences between any two particular representatives of the races in question. This same argument has been updated, without Boas's liberal leanings, in Charles Murray and Richard Herrnstein, *The Bell Curve: Intelligence and Class Structure in American Life* (New York: Free Press, 1994).

18. Folk theories of race declare that different racial groups do measurably different kinds of cultural things, and this carves out a space for dissenting voices to disprove that very link, especially when posited connections between racial categories and their alleged behavioral manifestations (essentialism's baseline proposition) are subjected to scrutiny. Racial categories need these behavioral groundings if they are to obtain any kind of hierarchical social significance, but those same groundings, owing to their arbitrariness and partiality, can potentially bring about race's metaphysical self-destruction as an overly reified and essentialist social category.

19. I try to make this point a bit more directly in chapter 6, looking at the work of rappers Mason "Mase" Betha and Sean "Puff Daddy" Combs as musical and visual architecture for Harlemworld's hip-hop landscape.

20. The material for this section comes from various sources, including the 1995 Columbia University Urban Planning Program's *Lower Manhattan Economic Development Guide,* the 1990 Columbia University Urban Planning Studio for Central Harlem, and the *Community District Needs: Fiscal Year 1995 Reports,* and many of the figures are based on 1990 dollars. What is important about the numbers I use here, however, is that they speak to the demographic realities of the Harlem community I worked in from 1994 to 1998, a community rapidly changing on every socioeconomic indicator. For an indication of the kinds of demographic shifts taking place in Harlem during the last decade of the twentieth century, see "Harlem Rising," *The Kip Business Report,* August 1998.

21. The community-galvanizing work of the West Harlem Environmental Action group has been integral to protecting Harlem as an ecologically healthy area since 1988, when the group was formed as a response to the health threat posed to residents by the North River Sewage Treatment Plant, located on Riverside Drive.

22. Again, these numbers go back to the mid-1990s, before Temporary Assistance to Needy Families (TANF) and its replacement of Aid to Families with Dependent Children (AFDC) could be fully felt, as stricter welfare timetables and block grants spelled the end of welfare as entitlement and the slashing of the welfare rolls.

23. These income figures changed a great deal with increased gentrification in the 1990s. Local activists dispute what median income really represents in the residents' economic realities. On a slightly different note, during my research project, 24 percent of the area's land was actually vacant, a figure that the Empowerment Zone effort has slowly decreased. One of the major new advancements on the horizon for East Harlem and its residents is the influx of new corporate ventures in the community—for example, the recent opening of a million-dollar Pathmark supermarket on 125th Street. Much is ex-

pected of these kinds of entrepreneurial endeavors in terms of improving living conditions for Harlem residents adversely affected by the suburbanization of employment opportunities after the 1960s. Part of the argument about these projects has pivoted on community activists rallying to ensure that local residents are actually the ones slated to work at places like Pathmark—and for a living wage and substantive employment benefits. Suburbanized jobs that leave urban residents to fend for themselves in underserved inner cities (the spatial mismatch theory) isn't the end of the story of how and why many urban residents have a hard time finding employment. Many researchers have shown that the employers who remain in poorer minority neighborhoods often actively discriminate against local residents, a fact that has forced Empowerment Zone businesses to earmark a certain number of jobs for the local community, even for specific zip codes. For further discussion of employer biases against urban African American residents, see Mercer Sullivan, *"Getting Paid": Youth, Crime, and Work in the Inner City* (Ithaca, N.Y.: Cornell University Press, 1989); William Julius Wilson, *When Work Disappears: The World of the New Urban Poor* (New York: Knopf, 1996); and Katherine S. Newman, *No Shame in My Game: The Working Poor in the Inner City* (New York: Russell Sage and Knopf, 1999). Mary C. Waters, *Black Identities: West Indian Immigrant Dreams and American Realities* (Cambridge: Harvard University Press, 1999), shows that African Americans are sometimes less desired potential employees than English-speaking Caribbean residents regardless of relative distance from the place of employment.

24. Again, these numbers have changed fairly significantly in the years since I began my fieldwork, due to rising rates of black and white middle-class inmigration.

25. Higher-than-average mortality, asthma, and tuberculosis rates are also significant issues for the community, as well as for other minority neighborhoods more generally. See Phyllis Y. Harris, "Impact of Social factors on Health," in *Growing Up . . . Against the Odds: The Health of Black Children and Adolescents in New York City,* ed. June Jackson Christmas (New York: Urban Issues Group, 1997).

26. Columbia's 1968 uprising was about just such a boundary. Columbia wanted to build a gymnasium on the site of Morningside Park with separate entrances and times of operation for students and community residents living in Central Harlem on the other side of that park.

27. See Katherine G. Morrissey, *Mental Territories: Mapping the Inland Empire* (Ithaca, N.Y.: Cornell University Press, 1997). Her work is based in the Pacific Northwest and shows how some pioneers from that region created an alternate sense of regionality not reducible to state borders. Following the work of Otis Pease and Anthony Cook, Morrissey calls this a kind of "vernacular landscape"—one akin, in many ways, to what Robert Park labeled a "natural area" not strictly coterminous with officially assigned spatial designations. See Robert Park, "Human Ecology," *American Journal of Sociology* 42 (1936): 1–15. For a discussion of the "multi-sited ethnography" as a kind of "mobile ethnography" capable of linking local specificity to global embeddedness, see George E. Marcus, "Ethnography in/of the World System: The Emergence of Multi-Sited Ethnography," *Annual Review of Anthropology* 24 (1995): 95–117.

28. For a discussion of contemporary "Cyberia" see Douglas Rushkoff, *Life in the Trenches of Hyperspace* (San Francisco: HarperSanFrancisco, 1994), which connects chaos theory, cybernetics, acid trips, personal computers, MTV, cyberpunk novels, and house music into what he calls an "invisible" and "boundless territory" peopled by hackers who self-consciously and literally create their own social realities. Rushkoff's Cyberia is not quite reducible to the racialized inflections of Harlemworld, especially when the much-discussed "digital divide" stalls the analogy far short of completion. Still, there are several interesting virtual Harlems on the Internet. Some sites allow for web-based tours and historical information, for example, the Abyssinian Development Corporation of Harlem's Abyssinian Baptist Church and one-time Apollo Theater owner Percy Sutton's Inner City Broadcasting Corporation maintain http://hr2k1.adcorp.org/ and http://www.discoverharlem.com/, respectively. There are also many more Harlem-based web sites that are online as I write these notes: see http://www.arch.carleton.ca/ARCH/Harlem/main.html; http://www.hometoharlem.com/Harlem/hthadmin.nsf/harlem/homepage; http://www.hatt.org/ and http://www.atc.missouri.edu/vr/harlem/main.html.

29. Without a doubt, class stratification is important within Harlem. The demographic difference between the top and the bottom of Morningside Park is one blatant example of how that stratification is often spatialized. Manmade and natural barriers (such as Morningside Park or the hills leading up to Hamilton Grange) are used to separate the rich from the poor. It is important to remember that there are clearly class-related differences from block to block in Harlem, and there are people all along the class ladder, from poor to very rich, who live in different parts of the neighborhood.

30. Assessments of phenotype may be necessary, but they are hardly sufficient here. And even their necessity is called into question by certain invocations of race as behavior that I try to draw out in chapters 5 and 6. I intend for this to complicate more epidermalized renditions of race.

31. For a discussion of "racial realism" see Charles Mills, *Blackness Visible: Essays on Philosophy and Race* (Ithaca, N.Y.: Cornell University Press, 1998).

32. For entry into Jean Baudrillard's simulacrascape, see *Simulations* (New York: Semiotexte, 1983); *America* (London: Verso, 1989); and *Cool Memories* (London: Verso, 1991). For a more exegetical and accessible scaffolding around Baudrillard's often impenetrable hyperworlds, see Chris Rojek and Bryan S. Turner, eds., *Forget Baudrillard* (New York: Routledge, 1993).

33. For a literary critic's discussion of the similarities and differences between *signifying* and *signifyin'*—or more specifically, *signifyin(g)*—see Henry Louis Gates Jr., *The Signifying Monkey: A Theory of African-American Literary Criticism* (Oxford: Oxford University Press, 1988).

34. Issues of gender are equally important in discussions of identity as issues of race and class. And the gendered implications of the work that follows should not be dismissed. When I started this project, it was framed as an intervention in a sociological debate about the impact of post–civil rights changes in black America's class structure on the contemporary significance of racial difference. As such, gender was given short shrift. Yet the book does extend several strands of a theoretical argument about gendered performativity into an analysis of racial identities and identifications. In that sense, a certain seg-

ment of gender theory is the implicit foundational model on which I build my own race-based claims. This doesn't make up for many of the sometimes loud silences of gender's present absences throughout parts of this text, but it does begin to explain my own emphasis on race and class as two components of a grocery list of meaningful social categories.

35. The "Game Room" is a reference to a main location found in Bourgois, *In Search of Respect*. Valois can be found in Mitchell Duneier, *Slim's Table: Race, Respectability, and Masculinity* (Chicago: University of Chicago Press, 1992). Also see Elliot Liebow, *Tally's Corner: A Study of Negro Streetcorner Men* (Boston: Little, Brown, 1967). Harlemworld is Slim's table, Tally's Corner and the Game Room writ large, and each chapter recursively and implicitly tries to argue that very point.

36. For a discussion of contact zones, see Mary Louis Pratt, *Imperial Eyes: Travel and Transculturation* (London: Routledge, 1992).

37. See Ruth Behar, *The Vulnerable Observer: Anthropology That Breaks Your Heart* (Boston: Beacon, 1996) for a poetic and persuasive take on a different kind of human vulnerability plaguing all ethnographic observers. In this context, I'm also drawn to James Baldwin's important distinction between an "observer" and a "witness," as explained and exemplified in E. Ethelbert Miller, *Fathering Words: The Making of an African American Writer* (New York: St. Martin's, 2000).

Chapter 1

1. With the expression "imaginative grandeur" I add my name to that "imagined community" of academics who use Benedict Anderson's oft-quoted phrase as a theoretical foil for explorations into the social construction of affect-filled nationalities and solidarities. Anderson shows specific relations between literacy and industrialization spawning the discursive and extradiscursive foundations on which contemporary notions of nationalism were first made to stand. With the advent of mass-produced, print culture capitalism, he argues, people became better able to envision a connection to personally unknown others across the daunting obstacles of space and time. *Imagined Communities: Reflections on the Origin and Spread of Nationalism*, 2nd ed. (London: Verso, 1992). One would be hard-pressed to find an ethnographic account these days that does not mobilize Anderson's phrasing, usually not more than a quick citation that assumes a readership familiar with the term. Andersonian assessments of imagined and imaginable communities speak most directly to the place where I conducted my own ethnographic field research and to the issues I most wanted to address there. If "the black community" is, at least partially, an imagined one, many African Americans readily gesture to Harlem as the capital city of that racialized place. With this point, I am not trying to make an argument about nations within a nation, or about reparations, or about a justification for black nationalism's ideologies. Even individuals without particular leanings toward black nationalist thinking often suggest Harlem as a kind of symbolic pivot-point for black America. The African Americans who gesture to Harlem in this way sometimes live in places like Cleveland, Seattle, or Atlanta, imagining a racial community across the very real geograph-

ical distances that prevent many of them from ever meeting, talking, or comparing racial commonalities face to face. Moreover, it is not exclusively African Americans who so gesture, and not solely in the United States where such gestural moves take place (as this example from Jamaica signifies).

2. Although Harlem's symbolic import jumped out at me during that trip to Jamaica, its viability as a field site was most directly facilitated by the methodological training and community entrée I received from Katherine S. Newman's research project on the working poor in Harlem, which culminated in *No Shame in My Game: The Working Poor in the Inner City* (New York: Knopf and Russell Sage, 1999).

3. See James Clifford, *Routes: Travel and Translation in the Late Twentieth Century* (Cambridge: Harvard University Press, 1997); David Harvey, *The Condition of Postmodernity: An Inquiry into the Origins of Cultural Change* (Oxford: Basil Blackwell, 1989); Derek Gregory, *Geographical Imaginations* (Oxford: Basil Blackwell, 1994); Edward Soja, *Postmodern Geographies* (London: Verso, 1989); Paul Gilroy, *The Black Atlantic: Modernity and Double Consciousness* (Cambridge: Harvard University Press, 1993). For examples of two specific trajectories of contact, see Michael Fabre, *From Harlem to Paris: Black American Writers in France, 1840–1980* (Urbana: University of Illinois Press, 1991), and Anna Scott, "It's All in the Timing: The Latest Moves, James Brown's Grooves, and the Seventies Race Consciousness Movement in Salvador, Bahia-Brazil," in *Soul: Black Power, Politics and Pleasure* (New York: New York University Press, 1998).

4. Specifically, the diverse work on cross-cultural intersections and communication include important offerings from Arjun Appadurai, *Modernity at Large* (Minneapolis: University of Minnesota Press, 1992); Paul Gilroy, *Against Race* (Cambridge: Harvard University Press, 2000); Ulf Hannerz, *Transnational Connections* (New York: Routledge, 1996).

5. Admittedly, my Jamaican interlocutors could have been disingenuously manipulating notions of "Harlem" to entice me into plying them with my American goods and monies, especially the disposable kind brought on typical tourist vacations. Even if that were true in this case, which it very well could be, this kind of subterfuge is still predicated on their recognition of how to use Harlem as an essentialized black space—and on their cognizance of its importance to black Americans.

6. This notion of Harlem as capital of black America can be found in many different works, for example, David Levering Lewis, *When Harlem Was in Vogue* (New York: Vintage, 1981); Jack Schiffman, *Harlem Heyday: A Pictorial History of Modern Black Show Business and the Apollo Theater* (Buffalo, N.Y.: Prometheus, 1984); Andrew Dolkart and Gretchen Sorin, *Touring Historic Harlem: Four Walks in Northern Manhattan* (New York: New York Landmark Conservancy, 1996); Claude McKay, *Home to Harlem* (New York: Harper and Brothers, 1928).

7. Harlem's taken-for-granted blackness is often cited as if that very appeal to the racialization of space exhausted all constitutive possibilities for the policing of place in contemporary black America, as if black Harlemites concretize a singularly black perspective: "What would people in Harlem think?" Undoubtedly, the assumption is, they would think one uniform thing.

8. Marjorie Garber, ""(Quotation Marks)," *Critical Inquiry* 25, no. 4 (1999): 659. For a discussion of the "quotation-marking-off" of place, see John L. Jack-

son Jr., "Toward an Ethnography of a Quotation-Marked-Off Place," *Souls: A Journal of Black Culture and Politics* 1, no. 1 (1998): 23–35.

9. Monique Michelle Taylor, "Home to Harlem: Black Identity and the Gentrification of Harlem" (Ph.D. diss., Harvard University, 1991).

10. Peter A. Bailey, *Harlem Today: A Cultural and Visitor's Guide* (New York: Gumbs and Thomas, 1986).

11. Arjun Appadurai, "Disjuncture and Difference in the Global Political Economy," *Public Culture* 2, no. 2 (1990): 1–24, delineates the various "scapes" applicable to contemporary social analysis.

12. But who invokes this history, and toward what kinds of ends? It is not just the everyday people I talk with and about in this book. It is also the empowerment zone brokers, the Business Improvement District of 125th Street (and the store owners it represents), local school boards, and, of course, local political figures.

13. Ironically, for a place so steeped in consciousness of its own history, far less of Harlem is officially landmarked for historical preservation than other parts of Manhattan. Landmarking is a fraught issue in Harlem because many of the buildings that residents want landmarked would entail changing landmarking criteria and make future renovations more costly. See Sharon Zukin, *The Cultures of Cities* (Malden, Mass.: Blackwell, 1995).

14. Lewis, *When Harlem Was in Vogue,* and Jervis Anderson, *This Was Harlem: 1900–1950* (New York: Farrar, Straus and Giroux, 1987) are both useful treatments of Harlem's cultural history that exemplify the past-tenseness that I want to stress here. The temporal framing of their respective titles speaks to an implicit privileging of the present's distance from a past that was but is no more.

15. For an interesting and humorous critique of black racial stereotypes offered up for public display, see George C. Wolfe, *The Colored Museum* (London: Methuen, 1987).

16. I bring up colonial Williamsburg because of the interesting ethnographic work on how history is (re)created there in a very purposeful projection of the past into the present. Richard Chandler and Eric Gable, *The New History in an Old Museum: Creating the Past at Colonial Williamsburg* (Durham, N.C.: Duke University Press, 1997).

17. Recent concerns about gentrification in Harlem mean that any improvements to the Apollo Theater can be considered a bit suspicious. Since it wasn't fixed up for several decades, some residents argue, any current renovation is probably related to impending white and black middle-class displacement of poorer black Harlemites.

18. The major newspaper articles in the popular press focusing on contemporary issues in Harlem overemphasize the past and its preservation. Recent *New York Times* articles on Harlem usually pivot on a discussion of its mythic history—and often invoke that history explicitly in their titles: "To Open A B&B, She Takes the A Train," *New York Times,* 7 March 1999, 11:4; "Can Harlem's Heritage Be Saved?" *New York Times,* 7 February 1999, 14:1, 10; "30 Years after Battle, Uneasy Truce on Heights," *New York Times,* 19 April 1998, 12:3.

19. This history of Harlem is pulled together from several sources, including Edwin G. Burrows and Mike Wallace, *Gotham: A History of New York City to 1898* (London: Oxford University Press, 1999); James Weldon Johnson, *Black

Manhattan (New York: Arno, 1968); Gilbert Osofsky, *Harlem: The Making of a Ghetto: Negro New York, 1890–1930* (New York: Harper & Row, 1965); Lewis, *When Harlem Was in Vogue;* Anderson, *This Was Harlem;* Cheryl Lynn Greenberg, *Or Does It Explode? Black Harlem in the Great Depression* (London: Oxford University Press, 1991); Samuel Charters and Leonard Kunstadt, *Jazz: A History of the New York Scene* (New York: Da Capo, 1981); Ann Douglas, *Terrible Honesty: Mongrel Manhattan in the 1920s* (New York: Farrar, Straus and Giroux, 1994); Claude McKay, *Harlem: Negro Metropolis* (New York: Harcourt Brace Jovanovich, 1940); James Cone, *Martin and Malcolm in American: A Dream or Nightmare* (New York: Orbis, 1991); Nicholas Lemann, *The Promised Land: The Great Migration and How It Changed America* (New York: Random House, 1991); and Judith Weisenfeld, *African American Women and Christian Activism: New York's Black YWCA, 1905–1945* (Cambridge: Harvard University Press, 1997).

20. "Negro Districts in Manhattan," *New York Times,* 17 November 1901. For a compilation of news clippings that chart the emergence of Harlem as black Harlem, see Allon Schoener, *Harlem on My Mind: Cultural Capital of Black America, 1900–1968* (New York: New Press, 1995).

21. The fact that differently classed blacks shared the same public space didn't mean they had positive interactions. This was not some ghetto "Golden Age" in which relatively rich, middle-class, and dirt-poor blacks all lived together in perfect harmony. See Elijah Anderson, *Streetwise: Race, Class, and Change in an Urban Community* (Chicago: University of Chicago Press, 1990), and Ulf Hannerz, *Soulside: Inquiries into Ghetto Culture and Community* (New York: Columbia University Press, 1969) for critiques of overly romanticized notions of a ghetto past wherein class differences are rendered inconsequential by residential proximity. Hannerz shows how class-based (i.e., lifestyle) differences in the ghetto created class antagonisms between "swingers" and "mainstreamers." Elijah Anderson's much more recent work discusses the defensive public posturing of middle-class blacks in contemporary urban communities.

22. Striver's Row was the name given to the Stanford White–designed townhouses on 138th and 139th Streets between Seventh and Eighth Avenues. Astor Row, a similarly middle-class stretch of homes built by William Astor in the 1880s, sits between Fifth and Lenox Avenues on 130th Street. Sugar Hill names a winding strip from 138th to 155th between Edgecombe Avenue and Riverside Drive.

23. As one prominent resident, the Rev. Dr. Robert Bruce Clark, pastor of the Church of Puritans, argued, "we, the white people, are entitled to say who shall live next door to us." *Harlem Home News,* 28 January 1914, a local paper that championed the causes of white residents in Harlem. These kinds of statements were the norm in early twentieth-century Harlem.

24. Black migration to Harlem was variously called "untoward" and "inexplicable" by many whites at that time. For example, see the *New York Herald,* 24 December 1905.

25. For specific details on how this gendered calculus worked, see Hazel Carby, "Policing the Black Woman's Body in an Urban Context," in *Identities,* ed. Henry Louis Gates Jr. and Kwame Anthony Appiah (Chicago: University of Chicago Press, 1995).

26. William Julius Wilson has championed this black middle-class out-

migration model of perpetual black poverty linked to macrostructural economic forces in *The Truly Disadvantaged: The Inner City, the Underclass, and Public Policy* (Chicago: University of Chicago, 1987) and *The Declining Significance of Race: Blacks and Changing American Institutions* (Chicago: University of Chicago Press, 1978). This out-migration model has been challenged on several levels. Douglas Massey and Nancy Denton, *American Apartheid: Segregation and the Making of the Underclass* (Cambridge: Harvard University Press, 1993), contend that Wilson's picture of black middle-class flight from the ghetto is a highly exaggerated one. They argue that racial segregation keeps the black middle class a lot closer (residentially speaking) to the black underclass than it keeps the white middle class to the white poor. And it is this same segregation, they claim, with its extremes of "hypersegregation," that creates the disturbing and abject poverty of the black underclass—not dependency-inducing government handouts or some conjectural black middle-class desertion (and forsaking) of lower-class race-mates. Paul Jargowsky, *Poverty and Place: Ghettos, Barrios, and the American City* (New York: Russell Sage Foundation, 1997) takes on Massey and Denton (partially vindicating some of Wilson's claims) by arguing that the concentration of poverty in certain areas increases independent of the level of racial segregation. Elijah Anderson, in *Streetwise,* offers a sociological portrait of cool-posing middle-class blacks who act "streetwise" on the sidewalks of their gentrifying community whenever threatened by lower-classed race-mates who have not *yet* been completely displaced by urban renewal. Mitchell Duneier, *Slim's Table: Race, Respectability, and Masculinity* (Chicago: University of Chicago Press, 1992), criticizes Wilson's conflation of black middle-class flight with a loss of progressive and empowering ethical values in urban communities. Duneier uses fieldwork among black males at a Hyde Park cafeteria on the South Side of Chicago to argue that values like perseverance, industriousness, and honesty are indeed cherished and exhibited by black males living in the inner city. Micaela di Leonardo, *Exotics at Home: Anthropologies, Others, American Modernity* (Chicago: University of Chicago Press, 1998) complains about Wilson's "passive voice" invocation of impersonal macrostructural forces without any specific and purposeful agents positioned behind them.

27. For a take on southern black power, see Tim Tyson, *Radio Free Dixie: Robert F. Williams and the Roots of Black Power* (Chapel Hill: University of North Carolina Press, 1999).

28. Glosses on Harlem's prestigious history also underpin more formal and institutionalized political voices in the community (including Tammany Hall's fox, J. Raymond Jones, both Adam Clayton Powells, Congressman Charles Rangel, and even former mayor David Dinkins), people who often leveraged that racialized lore as a tool for community galvanization. See John C. Walter, *The Harlem Fox: J. Raymond Jones and Tammany, 1920–1970* (Albany: State University of New York Press, 1989) for a discussion of J. Raymond Jones, maybe the least widely known of these political figures. Toward the end of my fieldwork stint, John Henrik Clarke, one of Harlem's long-time intellectual figures, political leaders, and community resources, died at the age of eighty-three. For Clarke's experiences in Harlem (and his take on Harlem's diasporic context and symbolic importance), see Barbara Eleanor Adams, *John Henrik Clarke: Master Teacher* (Brooklyn, N.Y.: A&B Publishers Group, 2000).

29. Anthropologists have a great deal to say about how space and time get rearranged in contemporary societies. See Arjun Appadurai, "The Past as a Scarce Resource," *Man* 12 (1983): 201–9; Partha Chatterjee, *The Nation and Its Fragments: Colonial and Postcolonial Histories* (Princeton, N.J.: Princeton University Press, 1993); James Clifford, *Routes: Travel and Translation in the Late Twentieth Century* (Cambridge: Harvard University Press, 1997); Kathleen Stewart, *A Space on the Side of the Road: Cultural Poetics in an "Other" America* (Princeton, N.J.: Princeton University Press, 1996); Amitav Ghosh, *In an Antique Land* (London: Granta, 1992). Moreover, the discipline itself has been complicit with a certain temporalization of social space wherein "differences residing in geographical space . . . became differences residing in developmental time," an anthropological discourse that relegates the primitive "other" to distant pasts, leaving only the anthropologist to negotiate a truly present-day world. Bernard McGrane, *Beyond Anthropology* (New York: Columbia University Press, 1983), p. 94; Johannes Fabian, *Time and the Other: How Anthropology Makes Its Object* (New York: Columbia University Press, 1983); William Roseberry, *Anthropologies and Histories: Essays in Culture, History, and Political Economy* (New Brunswick, N.J.: Rutgers University Press, 1988). One might reconfigure the discussion of Harlem's history as a popularized version of that very procedure. Recasting Eric Wolf's magisterial work and projecting it onto a different spatial scale, one could argue that Harlemites are not so much a "people without history" whose cultural development is seen as arrested in some antiquated European past, but rather an internal, non-European "other" posited with nothing but a rich history—that is, with no viable present or future to speak of, only a splendid and fleeting racial past. Eric Wolf, *Europe and the People without History* (Berkeley: University of California Press, 1982), critiques a historical understanding of the globe that denies historical agency to non-Western people. These people without history are only historyless on a global stage, but by reconfiguring the economy of scale, we can begin to see how the granting of history can do the same job Wolf chronicles through its denial. Harlemites become a people without a present—that is, more polemically put, Harlem is reconstructed as a lost cause in need of redemption and, some would say, just ripe for the corporate picking. This is an overly polemical phrasing but still useful in discussions of history and its use in contemporary Harlem. Empowerment zones and gentrification concerns are fueled by this rhetoric of salvaging a "once great" Harlem, although they can undoubtedly happen without such maneuvers. Harlem is not only a kind of "space on the side of the road" but a space on the outskirts of modern time, waiting to be reincorporated into the temporal fold by Magic Johnson Theaters and Walt Disney Stores. Of course, history is also invoked to fight such gentrification. See Mamadou Chinyelu, *Harlem Ain't Nothin' But a Third World Country: The Global Economy, Empowerment Zones, and the Colonial Status of Africans in America* (New York: Mustard Seed, 2000), and Dorothy Pitman Hughes, *Wake Up and Smell the Dollars! Whose Inner City Is This Anyway? One Woman's Struggle Against Sexism, Classism, Racism, Gentrification, and the Empowerment Zone* (Los Angeles: Amber, 2000). In order to glimpse the Harlem of today, people focus on the Harlem that is no more, teasing whatever there is of a present out from the recesses of that overstated past. But Harlem's assumed and historical blackness is constantly

redefined today with recourse to decidedly nonracial criteria as folks battle with one another about belonging and not-belonging in a world-famous, historical, and quotation-marked-off place like Harlemworld, U.S.A. For a detailed ethnographic and macrostructural discussion of a particular Queens, New York, neighborhood's changes over time, see Roger Sanjek, *The Future of Us All: Race and Neighborhood Politics in New York City* (Ithaca, N.Y.: Cornell University Press, 1998).

30. The books spread out on the table included the following: Cheik Anta Diop, *Civilization of Barbarism: An Authentic Anthropology* (Brooklyn, N.Y.: Lawrence Hill, 1991); Frances Cress Welsing, *The Isis Papers: The Keys to the Colors* (Chicago: Third World, 1991); George Jackson, *Stolen Legacies: Greek Philosophy Is Stolen Egyptian Philosophy* (New York: Philosophical Library, 1954); John Coleman, *Conspirators' Hierarchy: The Story of the Committee of 300* (Carson City, Nev.: America West, 1992); A. Ralph Epperson, *The New World Order* (Tucson, Ariz.: Publius, 1990); A. Jan Marcussen, *National Sunday Law* (Thompsonville, Ill.: Amazing Truth, 1995); Mustafa el-Amin, *Freemasonry, Ancient Egypt, and the Islamic Destiny* (Jersey City, N.J.: New Mind Productions, 1988)—along with various romance novels, children's books, and crossword puzzles with a racial twist. These texts create an alternate discursive space akin to the kind Benedict Anderson highlights in *Imagined Community: Reflections on the Origin and Spread of Nationalism* (New York: Verso, 1995). For a politico-theological critique (from within this alternative discursive community) of one of Harlem's most controversial religious figures, see Elder Paul E. Hunter, *Prophets and Profits: And What's to Be Learned from Daddy Grace and Others Like Him* (New York: Revelation Books, 1995).

31. In Dawn's assessment of her life-long connection to Harlem, she brackets out her five or so years in Jersey.

32. For a discussion about *intra*community boundary drawing, see Kai Erikson, *Wayward Puritans: A Study in the Sociology of Deviance* (New York: Wiley, 1966). Also see Fredrick Barth, *Ethnic Groups and Boundaries: The Social Organization of Culture Difference* (Prospect Heights, Ill.: Waveland, 1998).

33. See Gilbert Osofsky, *Harlem: The Making of a Ghetto, Negro New York, 1890–1930* (New York: Harper & Row, 1965); Roger Waldinger, *Still the Promised City: African Americans and New Immigrants in Post Industrial New York City* (Cambridge: Harvard University Press, 1996); and Mary C. Waters, *Black Identities: West Indian Immigrant Dreams and American Realities* (Cambridge: Harvard University Press, 1999).

34. See Sherry Ortner, *Making Gender: The Politics and Erotics of Culture* (Cambridge: Beacon, 1996), for a discussion of "serious games."

35. I instinctively referred to many of my older informants (fifty and older) by their last names, especially if they didn't make an explicit point of correcting me, an ingrained gesture of respect.

36. Here, Sheila refers to the murder-suicide of Roland Smith Jr. at the Freddie's Fashion clothing store in December 1995. Seven employees died in a fire. The assailant allegedly entered the store, shot four whites inside, told blacks to leave, set the place ablaze, and then shot himself. This is supposed to have been in retaliation for the Jewish store owner's attempt to evict a black-owned record store beside him in a scheme to increase his store's floor space.

37. For more examples in a U.S. context, see Brett Williams, *Upscaling Downtown: Stalled Gentrification in Washington, D.C.* (Ithaca, N.Y.: Cornell University Press, 1988); Rhoda Halperin, *Practicing Community: Class, Culture, and Power in an Urban Community* (Austin: University of Texas Press, 1998); William Hawkeswood, *One of the Children: Gay Black Men in Harlem* (Berkeley: University of California, 1997).

38. Countee Cullen's poem "Heritage" is an imagistic distillation of this same place-based question, a question that African Americans have asked since slavery. While teaching college courses in Harlem, one of my students handed in her own brief, hand-written take on Harlem, a take that included a small poem and a short paragraph about Harlem's symbolic worth: "Harlem is where it's at. Harlem is a place for rats and cool cats; Harlem is where it's at." She had been moved to compose that poem as a sixth grader and could still retrieve it from her memory these many years later. The paragraph she included with the piece was also suggestive: "I think of Harlem as home, and throughout my travels I will always return there. As a Black American I often feel left out when I hear Puerto Ricans or Jamaicans here in America talking about their homelands. I dream that Harlem will always remain the Black capital of New York, and centuries from now my great, great, great, great grandchildren can refer to Harlem as their homeland."

39. Paul Stoller, "Places, Spaces, and Fields: The Politics of West African Trading in New York City's Informal Economy," *American Anthropologist* 98, no. 4 (1996): 776–88. See also Sharon Zukin, *The Cultures of Cities* (Malden, Mass.: Blackwell, 1995), especially chapter 5.

40. Most recently, Mart 125 vendors are being displaced again as the city seeks to privatize the space.

41. The gathering was organized by the Patricia Lumumba Coalition, a pan-Africanist group headed and founded by activist Elombe Brath in the 1970s—and named after the first prime minister of the independent Republic of Congo, a man assassinated in 1961.

42. The text underneath the photo reads as follows: "THE POLITICS IN OUR COMMUNITIES are controlled from the outside, the hospitals in our communities are controlled from the outside, the economics of our communities are controlled from the outside, the schools in our communities are controlled from the outside, and WE OURSELVES are controlled by the racist/fascist police who come into our communities from the outside and occupy them, patrolling, terrorizing and brutalizing our people like a foreign army in a conquered land. Our black communities are colonized and controlled from the outside and it is this control which must be smashed, broken, shattered, BY WHATEVER MEANS NECESSARY."

43. For a discussion of these "old heads," see E. Anderson, *Streetwise*.

44. The official name for the backers is the New York Black Power Organizing Committee, a group with ties to another political activist organization, the December 12th Movement, named after a march in support of Tawana Brawley on that date in 1987. Like the Black Panther iconography that some vendor protesters used, Muhammad's New Black Panther Party was an overtly self-conscious invocation of 1960s and 1970s militancy.

45. See Damaso Reyes, "The March Is On!" *New York Amsterdam News,* 27 August–2 September 1998, 1. For internal squabbles within black Harlem over

the march, see Peter Noel, "At Each Others' Throats: Political Retribution in Harlem in the Wake of the Million Youth March," *Village Voice,* 6 October 1998, 48–50. The following year's Million Youth March can be read for similar community conflicts; see Peter Noel, "By Any Means (Unnecessary): A History of the Confrontational Politics That Led to the Assault on Councilman Bill Perkins by the Bully Boys of the Million Youth March," *Village Voice,* 7 September 1999, 51–53.

46. Older residents remember a 1960s Harlem rally against police violence that ended in about one hundred injuries, five hundred arrests, and at least one death. This was often a not-too-distant subtext for discussions about potential clashes in the 1998 rally.

47. I do believe Muhammad owned a brownstone in the area (or was about to buy one at around the time of the rally), but there were issues concerning how much that was just a gesture aimed at feigning solidarity with the community. Moreover, which community was more important in that context? What did *community* mean? Did it refer to the "black community" or most specifically to the Harlem residents who actually resided in upper Manhattan?

48. See Andrea Peyser, "Idiot Judge Will Be to Blame if Chaos Erupts," *New York Post,* 2 September 1998, 6.

49. One candidate for a local community school board election held within a year of the Million Youth March distributed pamphlets to local residents that linked these different levels of community quite explicitly. The slogan on the front stated that she had "a Proven Track Record On Community School Board 5, in the Harlem Community and in the World Community of African People." Even a local school board election facilitated movement across vastly different geographical economies of scale.

50. A young man had been shot in Brooklyn only a week earlier when New York City Police mistook his toy gun for a real one.

51. It is important to remember that the Garveyite flag is a kind of Americanist African reconstruction that doesn't represent any particular country in Africa but rather the idea of Africa at large as an African American homeland. This is an important distinction. The subjecthood and racial citizenship formed under the tricolored flag of red, black, and green (colors that symbolize blood, people, and land, respectively) map a different spatial geography than any actual nation-state on the continent itself. This speaks most directly to what the newest strands of cultural geography would highlight about the geographical and psychological co-construction of subjectivity through mobilizations of spatiality. See Steven Pile and Nigel Thrift, eds., *Mapping the Subject: Geographies of Cultural Transformation* (London: Routledge, 1995).

52. Muhammad maintains that no vehicles within the vicinity of the march were allowed to leave the area and that he did not flee the scene in a white Mercedes-Benz as many journalists claimed.

53. See Michael Herzfeld, *A Place in History: Social and Monumental Time in a Cretan Town* (Princeton, N.J.: Princeton University Press, 1991); Eric Hobsbawm, *On History* (New York: New Press, 1997); Greil Marcus, *The Dustbin of History* (Cambridge: Harvard University Press, 1995). Moreover, Foucault's arguments about knowledge, power, and discourse are operative here. See Michel Foucault, *The Archeology of Knowledge* (New York: Pantheon, 1972),

Discipline and Punish: The Birth of the Prison (New York: Vintage, 1979), *History of Sexuality* (New York: Vintage, 1985), and *Power/Knowledge: Selective Interviews and Other Writings, 1972–1977,* ed. Colin Gordon (New York: Pantheon, 1977).

Chapter 2

1. For example, see Lorene Cary, *Black Ice* (New York: Vintage, 1991); Nathan McCall, *Makes Me Wanna Holler: A Young Black Man in America* (New York: Vintage, 1994); Janet McDonald, *Project Girl* (New York: Farrar, Straus and Giroux, 1999) as examples of racialized rags-to-riches offerings.

2. See Jennifer Hochschild, *Facing Up to the American Dream: Race, Class, and the Soul of the Nation* (Princeton, N.J.: Princeton University Press, 1995), for a look at how African Americans of different classes buy into the prospects of upward social mobility in the United States. Sarah J. Mahler, *American Dreaming: Immigrant Life on the Margins* (Princeton, N.J.: Princeton University Press, 1995), examines recently arrived Salvadorans' beliefs in the potential for success in the United States. Also see Studs Terkel, *American Dreams: Lost and Found* (New York: Pantheon, 1980).

3. I remember thinking that the phrase "dirty gentleman" sounded quite interesting to my ears, a kind of overly affected and cleaned-up rhetoric of homelessness. There are always interesting questions about how "informants" parrot back to researchers what it is they think the researchers want to hear, the way they think researchers want to hear it. You want to feel that as a good ethnographer, you are sensitized to those self-consciously obliging responses. Of course, that isn't always the case. You can just hope that you've collected enough data that these kinds of moments don't unduly influence your findings—and that too many don't flit by you without your even noticing.

4. One can undoubtedly go on and on with citations of Marxism's basic tenets. I'll just list a few of the texts that were most helpful to me in this regard: Anthony Giddens, *The Class Structure of Advanced Societies* (New York: Harper & Row, 1973); Reeve Vanneman and Lynn Weber Cannon, *The American Perception of Class* (Philadelphia: Temple University Press, 1987); E. P. Thompson, *The Making of the English Working Class* (New York: Pantheon, 1963); John Roemer, *A General Theory of Exploitation and Class* (Cambridge: Harvard University Press, 1982); Nicos Poulantzas, *Classes in Contemporary Capitalism* (London: New Left, 1974); and Georg Lukàcs, *History and Class Consciousness* (Cambridge: MIT Press, 1971) among many others.

5. Marx's class bifurcation has two anchoring poles: those who relate to production as workers and those who own the means of production. Surely, he also recognized a lumpenproletariat (arguably, an agrarian version of the hypermarginalized "underclass" demonized today) and a petite bourgeoisie, but the motor of historical change is the inevitable conflict between the workers and the owners, the working class and the real bourgeoisie. Even before the capitalist mode of production took shape, Marx believed that societies were always already carved up into classes in terms of the people's relations to the means of production. The seminal social relations were those contingent on people's roles in the production process and the division of labor. It was a

"structure of doing" that led to a certain class-based "structure of feeling" (in Raymond Williams's sense), and that underpinned Marx's class analysis: you did work or you didn't; you labored or you exploited. Certain actions distinguished classes of people in terms of their function in the production process. Class was at the core of truth for all identities; the other facets of people's social realities were considered more provincial, partial, and inconsequential than the purer, harder fact of class position and property ownership. Class identity and the conflicts inherent therein would link all the world's workers together by common experiences of exploitation in a global fight against capital. People's lives are grounded in the classes to which they belong (a class membership specifically contingent on people's relation to the production process, says Marx; contingent on property, power, and prestige, says Weber; based on one's relation to the modes of consumption, says Baudrillard). For Marx's theoretical arguments, see *Capital* (New York: Vintage, 1976); *Pre-Capitalist Economic Formations* (New York: International, 1964); *The 18th Brumaire of Louis Bonaparte*, trans. C. P. Dutt (New York: International, 1963); and, with Friedrich Engels, *The German Ideology* (New York: International, 1947). For Weber, see H. H. Gerth and C. Wright Mills, eds., *From Max Weber: Essays in Sociology* (New York: Oxford University Press, 1958); *Economy and Society*, trans. Guenther Roth and Claus Wittich (1921; reprint, Berkeley: University of California Press, 1978) and *The Protestant Work Ethic and the Spirit of Capitalism* (New York: Charles Scribner's Sons, 1958). For Baudrillard, see *Simulations* (New York: Semiotexte, 1983); *America* (London: Verso, 1989); and *Cool Memories* (London: Verso, 1991).

6. For example, minoritarian communities rewire Marxist discourse to fit the mandates of a racially inflected class struggle. John Hall, ed., *Reworking Class* (Ithaca, N.Y.: Cornell University Press, 1997); Paul Gilroy, *There Ain't No Black in the Union Jack: The Cultural Politics of Race and Nation* (Chicago: University of Chicago Press, 1985); Cedric Robinson, *Black Marxism: The Making of the Black Radical Tradition* (Chapel Hill: University of North Carolina Press, 1983); Robin D. G. Kelley, *Race Rebels: Culture, Politics, and the Black Working Class* (New York: Free Press, 1994); and David Morley and Kuan-Hsing Chen, eds., *Stuart Hall: Critical Dialogues in Cultural Studies* (London: Routledge, 1996) are good places to find the outlines for such arguments.

7. One can always go back to certain canonical texts when thinking about this issue: Simone de Beauvoir, *The Second Sex: The Classic Manifesto of the Liberated Woman* (New York: Vintage, 1974); bell hooks, *Ain't I a Woman: Black Women and Feminism* (Boston: South End, 1984); Gayatri Chakravorty Spivak, "Can the Subaltern Speak?" in *Marxism and the Interpretation of Culture*, ed. Cary Nelson and Stan Grossberg (Urbana: University of Illinois Press, 1988). Also, Mary Jackman and Robert Jackman, *Class Awareness in the United States* (Berkeley: University of California Press, 1983), provide a well-organized overview of the issues that are relevant to such a context. Independent filmmaker Lizzie Borden's film *Born in Flames* dramatizes the projected insufficiency of a revolution that deals with class and ignores gender. Such a revolution, she argues, would necessitate a second gender-based revolution in its wake.

8. Lucius Outlaw, *On Race and Philosophy* (New York: Routledge, 1996) and Marshall Sahlins, *Culture and Practical Reason* (Chicago: University of Chicago

Press, 1976) are two methodologically distinct and discipline-specific places to begin such a discussion.

9. See David McLennan, *Marxism after Marx: An Introduction* (Boston: Houghton Mifflin, 1979); Seymour Martin Lipset and Gary Marks, *It Didn't Happen Here: Why Socialism Failed in the United States* (New York: Norton, 2000).

10. See Theda Skocpol, *Protecting Soldiers and Mothers: The Political Origins of Social Policy in the United States* (Cambridge: Harvard University Press, 1992) for a very rich historical and analytical overview of these kinds of governmental protections.

11. These workers can also be racist and xenophobic. See David Halle, *America's Working Man: Work, Home, and Politics among Blue-Collar Property Owners* (Chicago: University of Chicago Press, 1984); Anthony Gronowicz, *Race and Class Politics in New York City before the Civil War* (Boston: Northeastern University Press, 1998); David Roediger, *The Wages of Whiteness: Race and the Making of the American Working Class* (London: Verso, 1991). Marx himself dismissed the rural population's revolutionary potential; however, the only major revolutions under the Communist banner have come from those very same rural places and peoples, allowing some to urge that Marx's class theories have worked least well in large industrialized countries such as the United States— the only noteworthy cases of class revolt taking place in rural, agrarian nation-states during preindustrial and early industrial capitalism. See Jeffrey Paige, *Agrarian Revolution* (New York: Free Press, 1975); Friedrich Engels, *The Origin of the Family, Private Property, and the State* (New York: International, 1972).

12. Reeve Vanneman and Lynn Weber Cannon, *The American Perception of Class* (Philadelphia: Temple University Press, 1987), offer an interesting critique of what they call the "psychological reductionism" of social scientists' assessments of America's working-class politics: the basis for other critics' discounting of class-consciousness in the United States owing to the lack of any substantive working-class revolutionary movements or political parties. To the contrary, Vanneman and Cannon maintain that workers in the United States are, in fact, class-conscious but are powerless to impose their wills on a significantly more powerful owning class. And that, they argue, is why there have been no major class-based social movements in the United States.

13. The legal scholar Patricia J. Williams puts it this way: "So malleable is the black middle class in the cultural imagination that 'most' blacks are middle class when the analysis is convenient: the fully employed, better-off-than-ever, demanding, insistent, arrogant. . . . Then in a flick of an eye, 'most' blacks are underclass: underemployed, better-off-than-the-poor-anywhere-on-earth, demanding, insistent, arrogant." "Inside the Middle Class," *Civilization* (1994): 42. The point is that both of these categories are often utilized toward the same discursive and political ends, as different as their starting points may be. Also see Herb Gans, *The War Against the Poor* (New York: Basic, 1995) and Lillian Rubin, *Worlds of Pain: Life in the Working-Class Family* (New York: Basic, 1976).

14. See Erik Olin Wright, *Class Counts: Comparative Studies in Class Analysis* (Cambridge: Cambridge University Press, 1985) and *Classes* (London: Verso, 1985).

15. Henry Shyrock and Jacob Siegel, *The Methods and Materials of Demography* (Washington, D.C.: Government Printing Office, 1975). Many studies use the

terms "middle-class" and "underclass" yet use those terms differently. Two recent ethnographies on the black middle class, Mary Pattillo-McCoy, *Black Picket Fences: Privilege and Peril among the Black Middle Class* (Chicago: University of Chicago Press, 1999) and Karyn Lacy, "Negotiating Black Identities: The Construction and Use of Social Boundaries among Middle Class Blacks" (Ph.D. diss., Harvard University, 2000) discuss two very different black middle classes in terms of strict demographic considerations.

16. See Melvin Oliver and T Shapiro, *Black Wealth/White Wealth: A New Perspective on Racial Inequality* (New York: Routledge, 1995) and Dalton Conley, *Being Black, Living in the Red: Race, Wealth, and Social Policy in America* (Berkeley: University of California Press, 1999).

17. See Paul Siegel, *Prestige in the American Occupational Structure* (Ph.D. diss., University of Chicago, 1971).

18. See Sarah Boxer, "Professors or Proletarians? A Test for Downtrodden Academics," *New York Times,* 26 January 1999, B7; and Barbara Ehrenreich, *Fear of Falling: The Inner Life of the Middle Class* (New York: HarperCollins, 1990).

19. See St. Claire Drake and Horace Cayton, *Black Metropolis* (New York: Harcourt, Brace, 1945); E. Franklin Frazier, *Black Bourgeoisie* (New York: Free Press, 1957). Ulf Hannerz, *Soulside: Inquiries into Ghetto Culture and Community* (New York: Columbia University Press, 1969) has an interesting extended discussion of lifestyle differences within the black class structure of an urban ghetto.

20. Status is not exclusively contingent on economic factors. See Ralf Dahrendorf, *Class and Class Conflict in Industrial Society* (Stanford, Calif.: Stanford University Press, 1959); Gerhard Lenski, *Power and Privilege: A Theory of Social Stratification* (New York: McGraw-Hill, 1966); Ray Gold, "Janitors vs. Tenants: A Status-Income Dilemma," *American Journal of Sociology* 58 (1952): 486–93.

21. For example, the "conspicuous consumption" arguments of Frazier, *Black Bourgeoisie,* as borrowed from Thorstein Veblen, *The Theory of the Leisure Class* (New Brunswick, N.J.: Transaction, 1991).

22. Oliver Cox, *Caste, Class, and Race: A Study of Social Dynamics* (New York: Modern Reader, 1948).

23. John Leggett, *Class, Race, and Labor: Working Class Consciousness in Detroit* (New York: Oxford University Press, 1968); James A. Geschenwender, *Class, Race, and Worker Insurgency* (Cambridge: Cambridge University Press, 1977); and Vanneman and Cannon, *American Perception of Class.* It is class-consciousness that helps define the working class and allows for its collective mobilization against the owning class that would exploit it.

24. See Robert Bellah et al., *Habits of the Heart: Individualism and Commitment in American Life* (Berkeley: University of California Press, 1996).

25. Passages in quotation marks are actual phrasings from informants themselves, gathered during tape-recorded interviews or jotted down immediately upon utterance.

26. This film was still playing in first-run movie theaters at the time. We were watching a bootlegged copy that Daniel had purchased on 125th Street.

27. See Mary C. Waters, *Black Identities: West Indian Immigrant Dreams and American Realities* (Cambridge: Harvard University Press, 1999) and Roger Waldinger, *Still the Promised City: African Americans and New Immigrants in Post Industrial New York City* (Cambridge: Harvard University Press, 1996) for

some historical and cultural context for the experiences of first- and second-generation West Indians in the United States.

28. This is a very different racialization of "the undeserving poor" from the one found in the literature. See Michael B. Katz, *The Undeserving Poor* (New York: Pantheon, 1993). For a discussion of street life, specifically a racialized and classed homelessness, in the context of whiteness, see Brackette F. Williams, "The Public I/Eye: Conducting Fieldwork to Do Homework on Homelessness and Begging," *Current Anthropology* 36 (1995): 25–39. For a recent ethnography on New York's homeless community, see Gwendolyn A. Dordick, *Something Left to Lose: Personal Relations and Survival among New York's Homeless* (Philadelphia: Temple University Press, 1997).

29. Extreme class isolation is just as atypical of black neighborhoods as is complete income integration. Paul Jargowsky, *Poverty and Place: Ghettos, Barrios, and the American City* (New York: Russell Sage Foundation, 1997), maintains that the concentration of poverty in black urban communities has increased significantly in recent years even though poverty rates have not changed all that drastically. This is an important point, and he uses it to offer a new geography of racial poverty that has been mobilized to buttress arguments about the estrangement and distance between poor and middle-class blacks. Jargowsky's work is vital to charting the specific geographical patterns of poverty and wealth, but I would argue that a growing spatial concentration of poverty is not synonymous with (or reducible to) utter and complete class isolation—and does not necessarily mean that African Americans have no contacts across class lines.

30. See Katherine S. Newman, *No Shame in My Game: The Working Poor in the Inner City* (New York: Knopf and Russell Sage Foundation, 1997); Mark Granovetter, *Getting a Job* (Chicago: University of Chicago Press, 1995); and Mercer Sullivan, *"Getting Paid": Youth, Crime, and Work in the Inner City* (Ithaca, N.Y.: Cornell University Press, 1989).

31. See Bart Landry, *The New Black Middle Class* (Berkeley: University of California Press, 1987) for a discussion of these issues. There is this idea that because of the relative poverty of contemporary black America vis-à-vis white America, the notion of middle-classness for blacks needs be more inclusive than the one used for whites.

32. Sudhir Alladi Venkatesh, *American Project: The Rise and Fall of a Modern Ghetto* (Cambridge: Harvard University Press, 2000) does a good job of looking at, say, drug dealers and gang members within the context of their full integration into the rest of their community—a kin project, in some respects, to the kind of diversity I'd like to underscore here. Drug dealers and gang members aren't segregated in some underclass hinterland; they are a part of the same vibrant and active communities where working-class and middle-class urban residents live their daily lives.

Chapter 3

1. See Sarah Lawrence-Lightfoot, *I've Known Rivers: Lives of Loss and Liberation* (Reading, Mass.: Addison-Wesley, 1994); Lawrence Otis Graham, *Our Kind of People: Inside America's Black Upper Class* (New York: HarperCollins, 1999); Mary

Pattillo-McCoy, *Black Picket Fences: Privilege and Peril among the Black Middle-Class* (Chicago: University of Chicago Press, 1999). See also Sam Fulwood, *Waking from the Dream: My Life in the Black Middle Class* (New York: Anchor, 1996).

2. See Bart Landry, *The New Black Middle Class* (Berkeley: University of California Press, 1987); Joe Feagin and Melvin Sikes, *Living with Racism: The Black Middle Class Experience* (Boston: Beacon, 1993); Ellis Cose, *The Rage of a Privileged Class* (New York: HarperCollins, 1993).

3. The notion of the "culture of poverty" was given one of its first comprehensive articulations in Oscar Lewis's 1959 work on poverty in Mexico. Lewis argued that behaviors associated with life in poverty-riddled areas (alcoholism, violence, crime, male desertion, hypermasculinity, female-headed households) could be explained by two very distinct kinds of causes. The initial or ultimate causes of these behaviors, he claimed, were "macrostructural" constraints on the poor, constraints linked to unemployment and underemployment. Lewis then added to this formulation by suggesting that these macrostructural conditions give rise to a poor people's "culture" that perpetuates and promotes the kinds of behaviors initially molded by structural constraints. This "culture," he concluded, is a more immediate cause of the deviant behaviors emerging from the depths of poverty, a kind of transgenerationally learned model for living with a stability, persistence, and agency independent of the ultimate source (those macrostructural conditions) that originally created it. This culture of poverty is thus considered to be a kind of ready-made "cultural repository" for a new generation's expedient learning of an older generation's deviant ways. See Oscar Lewis, *The Children of Sanchez: Autobiography of a Mexican Family* (New York: Vintage, 1961) and *The Culture of Poverty* (New York: Scientific America, 1966). Once created, this culture becomes a self-sustaining cause of persistent poverty across generations. Important to point out with respect to Oscar Lewis and his model of the culture of poverty is the fact that he did, see macrostructural constraints as key ingredients in the formation of this so-called deviant ghetto culture. However, in recent discussions utilizing Lewis's notion, this macrostructural side of his equation disappears almost entirely. See Charles Murray, *Losing Ground: American Social Policy, 1950–1980* (New York: Basic, 1984); George Gilder, *Wealth and Poverty* (New York: Basic, 1981). In these versions of the culture of poverty, links between cultural patterns of behavior and macrostructural conditions are downplayed and even dismissed. Ghetto residents' moral shortcomings and deviant cultures alone are said to produce their social problems, and the only solutions offered in the wake of such perspectives seek to intervene with culturally and psychologically based remedies to save the poor from themselves and their self-destructive activities. Social analysts took the policy recommendations a step further by maintaining that welfare, one of the government's major attempts to assist the urban poor, merely fortifies and endorses their deviance and cultural depravity. They claim that the "liberal welfare state" adversely affected the incentives governing the behavior of poor people with its overly permissive welfare policies. These policies, they say, resulted in even greater degrees of poverty and cultural pathology because the regulations governing welfare made marriage and menial labor undesirable while promoting unwed childbearing and laziness. In one of the most popular and often-cited articulations of this perspective, Charles Murray argues that

the welfare policies developed during the War on Poverty made it profitable for poor people to behave in the short term in ways that were detrimental and self-destructive in the long run.

A major problem some critics have had with the culture of poverty argument has to do with its rather uncritical pathologizing of a vast number of inner-city behaviors—some of which, detractors argue, may not be pathological at all. See Annette Weiner, "The False Assumptions of Traditional Values," in *The Family on the Threshold of the 21st Century: Trends and Implications,* ed. Solly Dreman (London: Lawrence Erlbaum and Associates, 1997). For instance, what is so "wrong" with the inner-city family structure (female-headed households, and so on)? Is the nuclear family (with father, mother, child, dog, and a white picket fence) any more valid than some of the family structures pathologized by culture of poverty proponents? Moreover, are these inner-city families in poverty simply because they haven't learned how to defer immediate gratification for more long-term goals? Carol Stack, *All Our Kin: Strategies for Survival in a Black Community* (New York: Harper and Row, 1975), offers an oft-cited answer to these questions. She claims that the black family and its extended kinship organization are an extremely "rational" (not pathological) response to societal constraints. In the inner city, with its ever-present economic hardships, one could not survive, she argues, without the extended family kinship network, a network that not only requires frequent injections of one's own funds (for the benefit of others in the network) but in return provides social bonds that allow each and every participating member a social safety net during exceptionally rough economic times. It is this social group that does not allow for the growth of individual and personal wealth, but it is also these very individuals, she says, who provide much-needed financial support when one of their lot faces economic hardships. Furthermore, these networks conduct vital services that would be unaffordable otherwise—child care being a prime example. Stack even goes so far as to argue that the child-raising units in poorer black families are often not domestic but interdomestic, communal (or trans-generational), existing over many households and sharing parental rights, duties, and responsibilities for children among several members. But this, Stack maintains, is not necessarily deviant and pathological. Instead, she paints it as a vital strategy necessary for survival against the material constraints of an economically marginalized inner-city existence.

4. Ulf Hannerz did a good job trying to show this in his 1969 ethnography *Soulside: Inquiries into Ghetto Culture and Community* (New York: Columbia University Press, 1969). He makes it quite clear that not all people living in the ghetto are the same. Hannerz makes this case with respect to "lifestyles," arguing that some residents of the ghetto are "mainstreamers," others "swingers," others "street families," and still others "streetcorner men." Here, Hannerz's four social categories are based, fundamentally, on differences in behaviors—sharp distinctions in what people do and how they behave. The mainstreamers "conform most closely to mainstream American assumptions," "are home owners," "are employed," "married and living in nuclear families with a quite stable composition" (pp. 38–39). The swingers "have not yet married" and "spend relatively little of their time just sitting around at home alone or with the family. Weekday nights and particularly weekends are often spent going

visiting" (p. 42). Streetcorner men are the ghetto dwellers who "return day after day to the same hangout. There they talk and drink, play cards, shoot crap, or just do nothing.... There is continuous drinking.... If they are not yet alcoholics, they are well on their way" (p. 54).

Hannerz unequivocally affirmed that ghetto neighborhoods were not just home to black poverty or deviance. He recognized a black middle class residing there, a fact other social analysts had a harder time seeing. There were "better-off" residents ("mainstreamers") around as well as those deviant, do-nothing, soon-to-be alcoholic streetcorner men. However, Hannerz's job as a researcher was to explain the causes of black poverty, and these mainstreamers were, therefore, not as relevant to his research as the streetcorner men, especially if the underlying question had to do with the extent to which black poverty was unlike white poverty. Hannerz was being a social problems researcher, and the black middle class simply wasn't a social problem that merited study. Still, Hannerz at least recognized class-based differences within black communities.

As the burgeoning body of literature on ghetto communities (so-called pockets of poverty) increased steadily, it decreased the value of social scientific discussions about black Americans whose actions were other than indicative of ghetto difference. For Hannerz, the point was not necessarily to look to black "mainstreamers" but to the blacks behaving in supposedly ghetto-specific ways associated with black poverty. "There are people in the ghetto who have good, stable jobs," he offers, "help their children with their homework. Eat dinner together at a fixed hour, make payments on the car, and spend their Saturday night watching Lawrence Welk on TV—to their largely mainstream way of life we will devote rather little attention" (p. 15). Hannerz notices class heterogeneity based on actions (everything from television watching to making payments on automobiles) but focuses our attention on what he offers up as ghetto-specific behaviors: "[A]ll ghetto dwellers will not get equal time here. There are many who are in the ghetto but not of the ghetto in the sense of exhibiting much of a life-style peculiar to the community" (p. 15). Hannerz delineates the behaviors setting black ghetto residents apart from other blacks not behaving that way (and ultimately separating them, as the other-older binary social model would have it, from white Americans as well). The mainstreamers behaved too much like middle-class Americans to be of interest to most poverty researchers, and it was through poverty studies that a substantial portion of the social science discourse on black America took root. These same emphases on what some black ghetto residents did (how they acted) justified the foregrounding of culture (shared actions and beliefs) and the mobilization of culture of poverty arguments as a means of solidifying assumptions about black racial difference in the growing social science discourse on America's race problem. Behavior was mistakenly reduced to a proxy for culture, and that conflation opened the floodgates for one of the most popular and destructive explanatory models of poverty ever argued.

5. *Peops* is a derivative of *peop(l)e,* meaning very close friends and relatives. It's a commonly used term among many of the folks I spoke with in Harlem.

6. It is also important to note that a binary model of class differences within black America (the very same binary that I have taken great pains to challenge in earlier chapters) rears its dichotomous head here. This time, however, it is

not an "etic" analytical category that social scientists impose on subjects from above. Instead, it is an "emic" articulation of the social world based on Paul's own subjective understandings of class differences within his social networks. One cannot simply rail against Paul's conception as wrongheaded and mistaken; one must understand why this binary folk-analysis exists as a categorization in the first place—and try to understand the cultural work it achieves.

7. Pattillo-McCoy, *Black Picket Fences,* and Douglas Massey and Nancy Denton, *American Apartheid: Segregation and the Making of the Underclass* (Cambridge: Harvard University Press, 1993).

8. The anthropologist's relationship is often a precarious one in terms of class dynamics that serve to structure his or her interactions in the field, even if a "native." Some of my informants would categorize me as a friend, others as an acquaintance, and often class would rear its ugly head either way. The first time Dexter introduced me as his "ace" (at a house party another one of his friends threw on Long Island), I thought he was being funny or trying to exaggerate our relationship to make me seem like more a part of the in-crowd to his friends than I actually was. This was early in my fieldwork, and I had only known Dexter about a month. Eventually, I began to accept that Dexter was not as burdened by the need for objectivity and scientism as a pretext for our social interactions as I was, and genuinely found our conversations (with or without tape recorders) as wonderful opportunities to get to know one another as friends. And I only began to believe that I was really engaging in fieldwork and becoming an anthropologist when I was able to view our interactions in the exact same light. Furthermore, I have found that my socioeconomic position makes me useful on a great many levels to the people whose views are included in this book. For example, I've loaned money and resources to Zelda many times—always getting it back whenever a check comes in. I've tried to connect Dexter with a Columbia professor when he was expressing interest in medical anthropology. And I even helped a few people get jobs with verbal and written recommendations. Some of these exchanges between informant and ethnographer are class-marked sites of social interaction. Class is still important when dealing with more clearly middle-class, professional and upwardly mobile residents. My status as a doctoral student signified class similarity among many of them and helped me to enter certain spaces that might have been closed to me otherwise.

9. Katherine S. Newman, *Falling from Grace: The Experience of Downward Mobility in the American Middle Class* (New York: Vintage, 1988) looks at intergenerational downward mobility within the white middle class. For a quantitative look at class permeability, see Erik Olin Wright, *Class Counts: Comparative Studies in Class Analysis* (Cambridge: Cambridge University Press, 1997).

10. For a discussion of telephones as technologies of transnational conversation and community building, see Roger Rouse, "Mexican Migration and the Social Space of Postmodernism," *Diaspora* 1, no. 1 (1991): 13. For an analysis of how these cross-cultural conversations transform the relationships people have with their closest neighbors, see Deborah A. Thomas, " 'Tradition's Not an Intelligence Thing': Jamaican Cultural Politics and the Ascendance of Modern Blackness" (Ph.D. diss., New York University, 2000).

11. See Keyoung Park, "Use and Abuse of Race and Culture: Black-Korean

Tension in America," *American Anthropologist* 98, no. 3 (September 1996): 492–99, for a discussion of these issues.

12. See Elijah Anderson, *Streetwise: Race, Class, and Change in an Urban Community* (Chicago: University of Chicago Press, 1990).

13. See Mark Granovetter, *Getting a Job* (Chicago: University of Chicago Press, 1995) for a discussion about the importance of "weak ties" in the transformation of social capital into more than just lateral occupational movement.

Chapter 4

1. Richard Sennett and Jonathan Cobb, *The Hidden Injuries of Class* (New York: Norton, 1972) attempt a relocation and rearticulation of class conflict such that it can be said to take place not only between individuals but also within them. They posit an "internalization of class conflict" (located in the hearts, minds, and souls of blue-collar workers and birthed from, among other things, what they consider to be our society's narrow conception of "human dignity"). This internalized conflict pits the individual worker against himself. One part of a person's ideological makeup wages a kind of psychological warfare against the other, and this harmful bifurcation complicates the worker's attempt to find, realize, and live the American Dream. Sennett and Cobb's recognition of a possibly self-destructive division in the mentality of the working class seems to be a useful hypothesis when rewired and reconfigured to analyze something akin to what W. E. B. Du Bois canonized as "the souls of black folk" in 1903. In a fascinating example of what one might call the *internalization of racial and class conflict,* Todd possessed what seemed to be two egregiously conflicting and mutually exclusive views about the obstacles facing blacks in America. On one hand, he seemed optimistic about the prospects of any determined African American to succeed. However, he also voiced sentiments saturated with a profound kind of race-based pessimism.

2. Conspiratorial thinking often transcends class and race, as discussions of the trilateral commission and illuminati fill the discourse of various white militia groups as well as black extremist groups. See Patricia Turner, *Heard It Through the Grapevine: Rumor in African-American Culture* (Berkeley: University of California Press, 1993); Mark Fenster, *Conspiracy Theories: Secrecy and Power in American Culture* (Minneapolis: University of Minnesota, 1999). Obviously, African Americans do not corner the market on conspiracy theorizing. See Richard Hofstader on "populist paranoia" in *The Age of Reform* (New York: Knopf, 1955).

3. Nicholas Dirks, Geoff Eley, and Sherry B. Ortner, eds., *Culture/Power/History: A Reader in Contemporary Social Theory* (Princeton, N.J.: Princeton University Press, 1994). In this context of structuring agents and agential structures, see Sherry B. Ortner, *Making Gender: The Politics and Erotics of Culture* (Cambridge: Beacon, 1996). Bourdieu's notion of habitus is a useful point of entry into discussions about class, race, and their internalization. For Bourdieu, habitus operates as a kind of pre-behavioral starting point for any and all individual actions within a given social system. See Pierre Bourdieu, *Outline of a Theory of Practice* (Cambridge: Cambridge University Press, 1977); *Distinctions: A Social Critique of the Judgment of Taste* (Cambridge: Harvard University Press, 1984); and *The Logic of Practice* (Stanford, Calif.: Stanford University Press,

1990). Habitus allows people to reproduce their social order through practices and discourses that have mostly been uncritically internalized. Positions in the social structure lead to particular dispositions toward the social world. In this sense, one can find fuel for a kind of strictly structuralist argument about human behaviors within a macrostructural matrix that conditions (and to a certain extent predetermines) the very behaviors and discourses individuals use to negotiate it. Moreover, this structural precondition of human action would imply that the actions prefigured by habitus serve to replicate the habitus through a reproduction of the social system it permeates. For a Bourdieu-based engagement in contemporary Harlem, see Philippe Bourgois, *In Search of Respect: Selling Crack in El Barrio* (Cambridge: Cambridge University Press, 1995), where he uses social reproduction theory in an ethnography of crack culture in East Harlem. Some readings of the practice theorist Michele de Certeau, *The Practice of Everyday Life* (Berkeley: University of California Press, 1984), marshal his work to take issue with such a formulation of the relation between structure and agency. De Certeau's walks through the city are often invoked to frame an analysis of actions ("tactics") as potential sites for resistive, countercultural, or individualized responses to structural constraints. De Certeau's social actors seem to possess more power to transform their sociostructural realities through particular practices that redefine, reformulate, and reappropriate what the social structure provides for their negotiation. In this version of human behavior and its relation to structural constraints, actions have the disruptive force to halt and challenge society's structural imperative to reproduce itself ad infinitum. The relation between class and race offers an interesting guidepost for exploring debates about behavior as either social reproduction or viable resistance to social constraints. I want to explore specific social practices and folk discourses concerning class in Harlem to investigate some of the ways in which these actions and ideas are made meaningful in people's everyday lives. Moreover, I seek to inject these findings into a discussion about the contradictory and conflictual interpretations of race and class found in a contemporary black America grappling with the interconnections between structure and agency in personal histories and stratified social networks.

4. See Charles Murray, *Losing Ground: American Social Policy, 1950–1980* (New York: Basic, 1984) and Dinesh D'Souza, *Illiberal Education* (New York: Free Press, 1991) for widely disseminated versions of this argument.

5. See William Julius Wilson, *When Work Disappears: The World of the New Urban Poor* (New York: Vintage, 1996); Cornel West, *Race Matters* (Boston: Beacon, 1994); Micaela di Leonardo, *Exotics at Home: Anthropologies, Others, American Modernity* (Chicago: University of Chicago Press, 1998); and Stephen Steinberg, *Turning Back: The Retreat from Racial Justice in American Policy* (Boston: Beacon, 1995).

6. People have an impact on their class positions that is considered to be more obvious and clear-cut than in the case of race, gender, and ethnicity—and certainly more lauded by the ideologies of the land. Of course, class location also gets passed on from generation to generation. See Nelson Aldrich, *Old Money: The Mythology of America's Upper Class* (New York: Viking, 1988).

7. St. Clair Drake and Horace R Cayton, *Black Metropolis: A Study of Negro Life in a Northern City* (Chicago: University of Chicago Press, 1945) also make

this point. In some ways these class distinctions have gone on forever. In other ways, they have taken on new forms in a post–civil rights context where black middle-classness is less restrictively tied to the rising and falling of less-well-off blacks.

8. See Karl Marx, *Capital* (New York: Vintage, 1976); *Pre-Capitalist Economic Formations* (New York: International, 1964); *The 18th Brumaire of Louis Bonaparte,* trans. C. P. Dutt (New York: International, 1963); and, with Friedrich Engels, *The German Ideology* (New York: International, 1947).

9. Seymour Martin Lipset and Gary Marks, *It Didn't Happen Here: Why Socialism Failed in the United States* (New York: Norton, 2000); Marshal Berman, *Adventures in Marxism* (New York: Verso, 1999).

10. David Halle, *America's Working Man: Work, Home, and Politics among Blue-Collar Property Owners* (Chicago: University of Chicago Press, 1984).

11. For example, should a middle-class categorization be based on an annual income between $55,000 and $85,000 or between $25,000 and $45,000? And why? One can look at any number of qualitative and quantitative studies and find differing equations used to determine class composition along trajectories of income, education, occupation, or some combination thereof. For some of this variation on how the black middle class and underclass are defined, see Thomas J. Durant Jr. and Kathleen H. Sparrow, "Race and Class Consciousness among Lower- and Middle-Class Blacks," *Journal of Black Studies* 27, no. 3 (1997): 334–51; Sean-Shong Hwang, Kevin M. Fitzpatrick, and David Helms, "Class Differences in Racial Attitudes: A Divided Black America?" *Sociological Perspectives* 41, no. 2 (1998): 367–80; Arthur Lewin, "A Tale of Two Classes: The Black Poor and the Black Middle Class," *Black Scholar* 21, no. 3 (1990–91): 7–13; Thomas J. Duranti and Joyce S. Louden, "The Black Middle Class in America," *Phylon* 47, no. 4 (1986): 253–63; Sharon M. Collins, "The Making of the Black Middle Class," *Social Problems* 30, no. 4 (1983): 369–81.

12. Kevin Gaines, *Uplifting the Race: Black Leadership, Politics, and Culture in the Twentieth Century* (Chapel Hill: University of North Carolina Press, 1996). See Daryl Michael Scott, *Contempt and Pity: Social Policy and the Image of the Damaged Black Psyche, 1880–1996* (Chapel Hill: University of North Carolina Press, 1997) for discussion of the disparaging and contemptuous assessments of the black poor sometimes carted into these uplift sentiments.

13. The theoretical differences between the way Du Bois and, say, Booker T. Washington dealt with the black masses have been outlined in many places. For example, see Thomas E. Harris, *An Analysis of the Clash over Issues between Booker T. Washington and W. E. B. Du Bois* (Ann Arbor, Mich.: University Microfilms, 1981); Manning Marable, *Black Leadership: Four Great American Leaders and the Struggle for Civil Rights* (New York: Penguin, 1999); Louis R. Harlan, *Booker T. Washington: The Wizard of Tuskegee, 1901–1915* (New York: Oxford University Press, 1983) and *Booker T. Washington: The Making of a Black Leader, 1856–1901* (New York: Oxford University Press, 1972); David Levering Lewis, *W. E. B. Dubois: Biography of a Race, 1868–1919* (New York: Henry Holt, 1993).

14. For instance, they create separate clubs, blue-blood organizations, and secret lodges. See Lawrence Otis Graham, *Our Kind of People: Inside American's Black Upper Class* (New York: HarperCollins, 1998); E. Franklin Frazier, *Black Bourgeoisie* (New York: Free Press, 1957).

15. See Harold Cruse, *Crisis of the Negro Intellectual* (New York: Morrow, 1967) for a critique of black middle-class leadership in the 1960s.

16. See Eli Ginzberg, *The Middle-Class Negro in the White Man's World* (New York: Columbia University Press, 1967) for a specific study of these black middle class views.

17. See W. E. B. Du Bois, *The Souls of Black Folk* (New York: Bantam, 1989) and *Dusk of Dawn: An Essay Toward an Autobiography of a Race Concept* (New Brunswick, N.J.: Transaction, 1968).

18. See Bart Landry, *The New Black Middle Class* (Berkeley: University of California Press, 1984).

19. Historically, the black middle class has championed civil rights and the needs of the black poor. But many more blacks are making the ideological move to the right as their class position begins to trump racial solidarity. See Cornel West, *Race Matters* (Boston: Beacon, 1993) for a popular reading of this trend.

20. See Peter J. Wilson, *Crab Antics: A Caribbean Case Study of the Conflict between Reputation and Respectability* (Prospect Heights, Ill.: Waveland Press, 1995).

21. Nelson Aldrich, *Old Money: The Mythology of America's Upper Class* (New York: Viking, 1988). Most recently, Lawrence Otis Graham has written on the black upper class, examining how they view themselves, their behaviors, and their relationship to both the black poor and the white world in *Our Kind of People.* Part of Graham's point seems to be that wealthy blacks behave very differently from the black masses, in ways that purposefully differentiate them from the masses. Again, not only do they know that, they actively promote it through certain social organizations (lodges, fraternities, sororities, Jack and Jill, and so on).

22. In December 1995, a gunman killed seven people by burning down Freddie's Fashion Mart on 125th Street. The assailant was part of a local activist group that believed the store's owner (1) didn't employ enough African Americans and (2) was conspiring to evict the black-owned record shop next door in an expansion scheme. Two years later, a different store owned by that proprietor was picketed again by some of the same protesters for insensitivity to the local community.

23. For a discussion of streetcorner men, see Ulf Hannerz, *Soulside: Inquiries into Ghetto Culture and Community* (New York: Columbia University Press, 1969) and Elliot Liebow, *Talley's Corner: A Study of Negro Streetcorner Men* (Boston: Little, Brown, 1967). For a long time, these streetcorner men were the hegemonic social scientific models for understanding black masculinity in an urban context, a masculinity disconnected from the female-headed households of the black poor. William Hawkeswood, *One of the Children: Gay Black Men in Harlem* (Berkeley: University of California Press, 1996) levels a compelling critique against this disconnected notion of black male familial involvement—and against heteronormative presuppositions about what black masculinity entails.

24. See William Labov, *Language in the Inner City* (Philadelphia: University of Pennsylvania Press, 1972); Joey Lee Dillard, *Black English: Its History and Usage in the United States* (New York: Vintage, 1973). See also John Baugh, "A Survey of Afro-American English," *Annual Review of Anthropology* (1983): 335–54; Marcyliena Morgan, "Theories and Politics in African American English," *Annual Review of Anthropology* 23 (1994): 325–45.

25. Various grammatical and phonological characteristics are attributed to black English. On the grammatical front, the absence of the copula ("he crazy"), the lack of number inflections ("he is fifteen year old"), and the invariant *be* ("He be talking all the time") are all read as indicators of black English's syntactical uniqueness. Phonological properties of black English are also considered indicative of its distinctiveness: alveolar stops (*d* and *t*) for interdental fricatives (*th*); the absence of the postvocalic *r* ("I need mo' sugar"); the loss of unstressed initial syllables ("I am 'bout to go"); the consonant cluster reductions ("They already lef'"); and the substitution of labiodental fricatives (*v* and *f*) for interdental fricatives ("Take it out of your mouf"). Indeed, one of the key issues for an anthropologist writing with a sensitivity to African American Vernacular English has to do with how that English is to be represented on the printed page, what linguists call "eye-dialect." I have tried to keep my eye-dialect to a minimum, especially with respect to phonological attributes. So, for instance, if a speaker says "mouf" for "mouth," I am writing "mouth," unless that difference has some specific importance in the context of the utterance or seems to imply particular social significance at the time of enunciation. In this book's quoted passages, I have tried to use very little eye-dialect to catch the phonological specifics of the people quoted. I have retained the syntactical structure of the sentences.

26. For a playful reading of the issues of spotting class in everyday situations, see Paul Fussell, *Class: A Guide Through the American Status System* (New York: Simon and Schuster, 1992).

27. See Kathy Russell, Midge Wilson, and Ronald Hall, *The Color Complex: The Politics of Skin Color among African Americans* (New York: Doubleday, 1992).

28. For a discussion of blackness, hair, and stylistic choices, see Ingrid Banks, *Hair Matters: Beauty, Power, and Black Women's Consciousness* (New York: New York University Press, 2000) and Kobena Mercer, *Welcome to the Jungle: New Positions in Black Cultural Studies* (New York: Routledge, 1994). Bourgois, *In Search of Respect*, argues that poor Latinos in East Harlem don't have a middle-class sense of what proper attire is because of their marginalization from mainstream society and that the poor have a different understanding of aesthetics.

29. See Erving Goffman, *The Presentation of Self in Everyday Life* (New York: Penguin, 1959) and *Stigma: Notes on the Management of Spoiled Identity* (Englewood Cliffs, N.J.: Prentice-Hall, 1963).

30. This speaks to a question about the biographical limits of class as behavior. That is, how much does personal biography have to match particularly class(ed) behaviors? The assumption is usually that one's self-representation is accurate. Once it is proved false, the behaviors in question are reinterpreted as phony and insincere.

31. See Elijah Anderson, *Streetwise: Race, Class, and Change in an Urban Community* (Chicago: University of Chicago Press, 1990).

32. Likewise, speaking as if one is "from the street" can jeopardize a middle school teacher's authority in "the hood" but can also increase an urban anthropologist's sociocultural cachet among certain informants.

33. I was the butt of many, many jokes about not fitting in at various points in time during my fieldwork.

34. In 1937 the Apollo Theater was a union shop, but during the past five

NOTES TO PAGES 154-157

decades it has not been. The theater is too small a venue (approximately 1,500 seats) to compete with other theaters for top entertainment acts. Therefore, it was only operating part time with part-time workers.

35. Percy Sutton purchased the Apollo in bankruptcy court in 1980 for about $250,000, attempted to renovate it, but decided to turn it over to the foundation in 1992. Again, the theater's relatively small audience space couldn't attract the kind of business that would have made the Apollo a viable private investment. The ICBC received a five-year licensing agreement to tape *Showtime at the Apollo,* with a provision that the ICBC pay the foundation $2,000 per taping or 25 percent of the net profits, whichever was greater. During this probe, the ICBC was accused of underpaying the foundation, and the foundation leadership was alleged to have purposefully allowed that to happen because its chairman, Congressman Rangel, was a friend of Sutton.

36. The Economic Development Corporation's Request for Proposals on the Harlem Piers area has spawned many new project applications, include floating piers, a grand hotel with a museum devoted to Harlem's history, entertainment and sports complexes, and ferries to New Jersey and the World Trade Center downtown. See Nina Siegal, "Pier Developers Look Toward Harlem: A Neglected Riverfront Stretch Brings Forth Visions," *New York Times,* 25 October 1998, 4, 29. The Department of Parks and Recreation is constructing "Cherry Walk" as a walkway and bikeway along the edge of the Hudson as part of the Hudson River Valley Greenway System, which links Harlem to Battery Park City and Troy, New York. There is also a handbook on area development, "Harlem on the River: Creating a True Community Vision. Community Design Workshop Handbook, April 10, 1999, a Collaborative Planning Project of West Harlem Environmental Action, Inc. and Manhattan Community Board 9. Hosted by City College School of Architecture."

37. There were also many diasporic proposals suggested by the HUDC, proposals that explicitly linked the fortune and future of Harlem to economic connections among African Americans, Caribbeans, and Africans. For example, the HUDC had been trying to construct the Harlem International Trade Center for several years before Pataki pulled the plug on the organization and its plans. The Harlem International Trade Center was to be a place where African and Caribbean leaders could stay when doing business in the United States. In 1999, several Harlem arts establishments, including the Apollo Theater Foundation, the Boys Choir of Harlem, the Dance Theater of Harlem, and the Studio Museum in Harlem, used a renewed tourist impulse to create what they labeled a "strategic cultural collaborative" whose member organizations share responsibilities in increasing public outreach and audience attendance for their events. Again, these organizations are able to leverage Harlem's cultural notoriety as a mechanism for channeling tourist interest in the arts.

38. Many local activists and residents fight the dislocation that has already occurred in the area. Renewed commercial interest in Harlem combines with skyrocketing rental prices as the city privatizes its Harlem property. Organizations such as the West Harlem Coalition and ACE (Action for Community Empowerment) mobilize low-income tenants to defend themselves against the threat of eviction and displacement.

Chapter 5

1. For a broader context, see Steven Gregory and Roger Sanjek, eds., *Race* (New Brunswick, N.J.: Rutgers University Press, 1994); Ruth Frankenberg, *White Women, Race Matters: The Social Construction of Whiteness* (Minneapolis: University of Minnesota Press, 1997). For a discussion of cultural thievery, see George James, *Stolen Legacy: Greek Philosophy Is Stolen Egyptian Philosophy* (New York: Philosophical Library, 1954).

2. See Erik Olin Wright, *Classes* (New York: Verso, 1985). For other forays into this particular topic, each from different starting points, see Saskia Sassen, *The Mobility of Labor and Capital: A Study in International Investment and Labor Flow* (Cambridge: Cambridge University Press, 1988); Kofi Buenor Hadjour, *Another America: The Politics of Race and Blame* (Boston: South End, 1995); Robert Smith, *Racism in the Post–Civil Rights Era: Now You See It, Now You Don't* (Albany: State University of New York, 1995).

3. For the fault lines of this debate, see Kwame Anthony Appiah and Henry Louis Gates, *Identities* (Chicago: University of Chicago Press, 1995); Lucius Outlaw, *On Race and Philosophy* (New York: Routledge, 1996).

4. See R. C. Lewontin, Steven Rose, and Leon Kamin, *Not in Our Genes: Biology, Ideology, and Human Nature* (New York: Pantheon, 1984); Lee D. Baker, *From Savage to Negro: Anthropology and the Construction of Race, 1896–1954* (Berkeley: University of California Press, 1998).

5. See Alexander Alland, *Human Diversity* (New York: Anchor Books, 1971); Carleton Coon, *The Origin of Species* (New York: Knopf, 1962) and *The Living Races of Man* (New York: Knopf, 1965). See also William Stanton, *The Leopard's Spots: Scientific Attitudes Toward Race in America, 1815–1859* (Chicago: University of Chicago Press, 1960); George Stocking, *Race, Culture, and Evolution* (Chicago: University of Chicago Press, 1982).

6. See Audrey Smedley, *Race in North America: Origin and Evolution of a Worldview* (Boulder, Colo.: Westview, 1993); Reginald Horsman, *Race and Manifest Destiny: The Origins of American Racial Anglo-Saxonism* (Cambridge: Harvard University Press, 1981); Michael Blakey, "Skull Doctors: Intrinsic Social and Political Bias in the History of American Physical Anthropology," *Critique of Anthropology* 7, no. 2 (1987): 7–35.

7. See Roland Barthes, *Mythologies* (London: Vintage, 1993). Also, Emile Durkheim and Marcel Mauss, *Primitive Classification* (Chicago: University of Chicago Press, 1963), argue that we carve the world up as our social world is structured. These are not arbitrary constructions but are truly social down to their core. Also see Peter Berger and Thomas Luckman, *The Social Construction of Reality: A Treatise in the Sociology of Knowledge* (New York: Anchor Books, 1966).

8. For very different historical takes on pre-racialization, see Deborah Poole, *Vision, Race, and Modernity: A Visual Economy of the Andean Image World* (Princeton, N.J.: Princeton University Press, 1997); Frank Snowden Jr., *Before Color Prejudice: The Ancient View of Blacks* (Cambridge: Harvard University Press, 1983); Pat Shipman, *The Evolution of Racism: Human Differences and the Use and Abuse of Science* (New York: Simon and Schuster, 1994).

9. See Emile Durkheim, *Sociology and Philosophy* (New York: Free Press, 1974).

10. Barbara Jeanne Fields, "Slavery, Race, and Ideology in the United States of America," *New Left Review* 181 (1990): 93–118, maintains that if there is no such thing as "race" in any transhistorical and natural sense, then one cannot mobilize race quickly and easily as a catch-all explanation for other sociohistorical phenomena. Kwame Anthony Appiah, *In My Father's House: Africa in the Philosophy of Culture* (Oxford: Oxford University Press, 1992), raised an intellectual stir by arguing that Du Bois, the father of black sociology in the United States, was guilty of essentializing race even though he has been championed by many as the forefather of nonessentialist, antiracist discourse in African American studies. Walter Benn Michaels, *Our America: Nativism, Modernism, and Pluralism* (Durham, N.C.: Duke University Press, 1994), levels some of the most scathing critiques at this idea of race as a social construct—especially as it has implications for contemporary anthropological notions of culture. Michaels argues that social constructionism uses notions of society and culture as a mask for what are at bottom still biological arguments about race hidden behind an invocation of the cultural. Michaels, a literary critic, looks at early nineteenth-century fiction to show how visible class differences within black America, as represented in fiction, cleared the way for racial identity to be compromised by class position.

11. Randall Kennedy, "My Race Problem—and Ours: A Consideration of Touchy Matters, Racial Pride, Racial Solidarity, and Racial Loyalty—Rarely Discussed," *Atlantic Monthly*, May 1997, 55–66. Kennedy has been attacked by various writers, and from many different angles, most notably in Paul King, "A Matter of Pride: To Reject Racial Kinship Is to Embrace Self-Hate," *Emerge*, October 1997, 62–65. King, chairman of UBM, Inc., a black-owned construction firm in Chicago, invokes the 1970s term "mentacide" to maintain that Kennedy's position is both a "cultural suicide" and a "psychological assassination." King insists that blacks "embrace racial kinship because it is necessary for Black survival."

12. Michaels, *Our America*, p. 129.

13. James Clifford, *The Predicament of Culture: Twentieth-Century Ethnography, Literature, and Art* (Cambridge: Harvard University Press, 1988), p. 338.

14. Ibid, p. 341.

15. Michaels, *Our America*, p. 177.

16. Issues of cross-cultural power dynamics get short shrift in Michaels's work. He brackets out questions about what and who causes the kinds of cultural changes in question: capitalist exploitation, colonialism, neocolonialism, racism, and so on.

17. See Michaels, *Our America*, p. 30 for a discussion of Zora Neale Hurston's dilemma in writing race and class.

18. Frances Cress Welsing, *The Isis Papers: The Keys to the Colors* (Chicago: Third World Press, 1991).

19. The passage of local laws have made it possible for vendors of "written materials" to remain on sidewalks in Harlem and the rest of the city, provided they abide by certain restrictions with respect to location and table placement. See Mitchell Duneier, *Sidewalk* (New York: Farrar, Straus, and Giroux, 1999) for more discussion on these laws and on street vending in general.

20. For interestingly gender-specific notions of race, see Signithia Fordham,

Blacked Out: Dilemmas of Race, Identity, and Success at Capital High (Chicago: University of Chicago, 1996).

21. See Ellis Cose, *The Rage of a Privileged Class* (New York: HarperCollins, 1993); Joe R. Feagin and Melvin P. Sikes, *Living with Racism: The Black Middle Class Experience* (Boston: Beacon, 1993); Jennifer Hochschild, *Facing Up to the American Dream: Race, Class and the Soul of the Nation* (Princeton, N.J.: Princeton University Press, 1995).

22. See David Lionel Smith, "What Is Black Culture?" in *The House That Race Built,* ed. Wahneema Lubiano (New York: Vintage, 1997).

23. See Signithia Fordham and John U. Ogbu, "Black Students School Success: Coping with the Burden of 'Acting White,'" *Urban Review* 18, no. 3 (1986): 176–206; Signithia Fordham, "Racelessness and Private Schools: Should We Deconstruct the Racial and Cultural Identity of African-American Adolescents?" *Teachers College Record* 93, no. 3 (1991): 470–84; John U. Ogbu, *Minority Status and Schooling: A Comparative Study of Immigrant and Involuntary Minorities* (New York: Garland, 1991); Prudence Carter, "Balancing 'Acts': Issues of Identity and Cultural Resistance in the Social and Educational Behaviors of Minority Youth" (Ph.D. diss., Columbia University, 1999).

24. See W. E. B. Du Bois, *Dusk of Dawn: An Essay Toward the Autobiography of a Race Concept* (New Brunswick, N.J.: Transaction, 1984), p. 148 for a rumination on a very racialized "delicious chuckle." He writes: "This [black] race has the greatest of the gifts of God, laughter. It dances and sings; it is humble; it longs to learn; it loves men; it loves women. It is frankly, badly, deliciously human in an artificial and hypocritical land. If you will hear men laugh, go to Guinea, 'Black Bottom,' 'Niggertown,' Harlem. If you want to hear humor too exquisite and subtle for translation, sit invisibly among a gang of Negro workers. The white world has its gibes and cruel caricatures; it has its loud guffaws; but to the black world alone belongs the delicious chuckle."

25. See Mary Douglas, *Purity and Danger* (New York: Routledge, 1992).

26. See Robin D. G. Kelley, *Yo Mama's Disfunktional: Fighting the Culture Wars in Urban America* (Boston: Beacon, 1997). Also, for a discussion of white influences on the Harlem Renaissance, see George Hutchinson, *The Harlem Renaissance in Black and White* (Cambridge: Harvard University Press, 1995).

27. For elaborate analyses of this threat, see Mamadou Chinyelu, *Harlem Ain't Nothin' But a Third World Country: The Global Economy, Empowerment Zones, and the Colonial Status of Africans in America* (New York: Mustard Seed, 1999); Dorothy Pitman Hughes, *Wake Up and Smell the Dollars! Whose Inner City Is This, Anyway? One Woman's Struggle Against Sexism, Classism, Racism, Gentrification, and the Empowerment Zone* (Los Angeles: Amber, 2000); Neil Smith, *The New Urban Frontier: Gentrification and the Revanchist City* (New York: Routledge, 1996).

28. There is a long history of anthropological and cinematic discussions of visuality and the ethnographic gaze, including Rosalind Morris, *New Worlds from Fragments: Film, Ethnography, and the Representation of Northwest Coast Cultures* (Boulder, Colo.: Westview, 1994); Fatimah Tobing Romy, *The Third Eye: Race, Cinema, and Ethnographic Spectacle* (Durham, N.C.: Duke University Press, 1996). Film theorists often invoke Lacanian insights to ground discussions of the camera's gendered and gendering gaze. See Elizabeth G. Traube,

Dreaming Identities: Class, Gender, and Generation in 1980s Hollywood Movies (Boulder, Colo.: Westview, 1992). For a highly touted ethnographic engagement with cross-cultural gazes as mediated through the textual reality of ethnographic monographs, see Michael Taussig, *Shamanism, Colonialism, and the Wild Man* (Chicago: University of Chicago Press, 1987).

29. For the well-known discussion of this veil, see W. E. B. Du Bois, *The Souls of Black Folk* (London: Dover, 1994).

30. See bell hooks, *Black Looks: Race and Representation* (Boston: South End, 1997).

31. Michael Omi and Howard Winant, *Racial Formation in the United States: From the 1960s to the 1980s* (New York: Routledge, 1986), p. 61.

32. John Hartigan Jr., "Locating White Detroit," in *Displacing Whiteness: Essays in Social and Cultural Construction,* ed. Ruth Frankenberg (Durham, N.C.: Duke University Press, 1997), p. 182.

33. See France Winddance Twine, "Brown-Skinned White Girls: Class Culture and the Construction of White Identity in Suburban Communities," in *Displacing Whiteness: Essays in Social and Cultural Criticism,* ed. Ruth Frankenberg (Durham, N.C.: Duke University Press, 1997); Jonathon Warren and France Winddance Twine, "White Americans, the New Minorities: Non-Blacks and the Ever-Expanding Boundaries of Whiteness," *Journal of Black Studies* 28, no. 2 (1997): 200–218; and Matthew Frye Jacobson, *Whiteness of a Different Color: European Immigrants and the Alchemy of Race* (Cambridge: Harvard University Press, 1998).

34. See John Hartigan Jr., *Racial Situations: Class Predicaments of Whiteness in Detroit* (Princeton, N.J.: Princeton University Press, 1999).

35. For the philosopher J. L. Austin, performative speech acts have to do with utterances that don't simply describe actions but are the actions themselves, that is, constitute the act during the very moment of speaking (for example, "I christen this here ship!"). See J. L. Austin, *How to Do Things with Words* (Cambridge: Harvard University Press, 1977). As scholars have used the notion of performatives to write about the construction of identity, they have argued that various performances of, say, gender and sexuality do not only index essential identities but also constitute them. Certain performances of identity not only reflect an ontological status that is precultural but fashion that identity in the performances themselves, performances that are read as constitutive and not merely indicative of the identities they index. Judith Butler makes an important distinction between performances and performativity (the former about actions that can change the world, the latter more related to the world's power over our actions) that is indicative of the intricacies of this discourse. See Judith Butler, *Gender Trouble: Feminism and the Subversion of Identity* (New York: Routledge, 1990). In *Bodies That Matter: On the Discursive Limits of "Sex"* (New York: Routledge, 1993), Butler refines this argument. In *The Psychic Life of Power: Theories of Subjection* (Stanford, Calif.: Stanford University Press, 1997), she offers a more interiorized version of these arguments, explaining the psychological underpinnings of her performative arguments, examining how the performative construction informs the production of the individualized self. (The question of what the "self" means for performance theory is one that I plan to think about a great deal in the future, per the compelling advice of

Naomi Quinn.) Also see Rosalind Morris, "All Made Up: Performance Studies and the New Anthropology of Sex and Gender," *Annual Review of Anthropology* 24 (1995): 567–92 for a more general overview of the literature on performance and its use in anthropological theory. The intersection between race and performativity is also a debate about essentialism. In "Real Men Eat Like Us: 'Racial' Categories in New Ireland," *Anthropology Newsletter* 39 (February 1998), Steven Jackson, who has conducted fieldwork with the Sursurunga in Papua New Guinea, argues that when racial identity is seen as performative, as it is for the Sursurunga, it is a nonessentialist categorization. According to Jackson, there are two types of performative criteria for social difference among the Sursurunga (one type based on what one knows, the other on the kinds of food one eats: real food, "from one's own efforts" and labor, vs. "non-real food," from a can or machine). Jackson maintains that these differences are "non-essentialist" and "non-primordial" because "they are malleable and qualitative in the sense that they can be altered." And a performative racial typology, he argues, is therefore an improvement over essentialist racial notions found in the Western world. "How remarkable," he writes, "and enlightened it seems to think of 'race' as what you do rather than what you are." I would argue that a "white Harlem," particularly Cynthia's white Harlem (one, she says, I should be careful not to "write"), is a land where racial categories and racial identities are refracted through this very same prism of performativity, but in ways that do not necessarily escape the essentialist ties that bind.

36. This becomes an ethical issue, as well. Is one misrepresenting oneself for the sake of ethnographic rapport and good data?

37. For the latest entry into this debate on the implications of anti-intellectualism among black youngsters, see John McWhorter, *Losing the Race: Self-Sabotage in Black America* (New York: Free Press, 2000).

38. This is a decidedly gendered notion of achievement, one that connects quite well to Signithia Fordham's work in a Washington, D.C., high school, *Blacked Out.*

39. For historical takes see Theodore Allen, *The Invention of the White Race,* vol. 1, *Racial Oppression and Social Control* (London: Verso, 1994); David Roediger, *The Wages of Whiteness: Race and the Making of the American Working Class* (London: Verso, 1991); Jacobson, *Whiteness of a Different Color;* Robert Young, *White Mythologies: Writing History and the West* (London: Verso, 1990); Fred Pfeil, *White Guys: Studies in Postmodern Domination and Difference* (London: Verso, 1995). For more ethnographic studies of whiteness, see Hartigan, *Racial Situations;* Ruth Frankenberg, *White Women, Race Matters: The Social Construction of Whiteness* (Minneapolis: University of Minnesota Press, 1997). Also see Brooke Thomas and Helán Page, "White Public Space and the Construction of White Privilege in U.S. Health Care: Fresh Concepts and a New Mode of Analysis," *Medical Anthropology Quarterly* 8 (1994): 109–16.

Chapter 6

1. Much of this employment rhetoric hit a snag early on when community residents complained about the lack of African American construction workers on the site. Organizations such as Harlem Fightback demanded a larger black

presence in these construction jobs—and argued that this early exclusion didn't bode well for the extent of future diligence about employing local black residents. Many residents scoff at these jobs, labeling them dead-end jobs with few benefits or chances for advancement.

2. Many local businesses complained about the threat of eviction in the wake of such change, and some were even casualties of skyrocketing post–empowerment zone rents.

3. This is often classed, since televisions may be less likely to be turned on the further up the occupational ladder one goes.

4. When aired on network television, the sign was changed to "I hate people," a choice that worked against the film's central racial impulse.

5. *The Siege* (1998) was such a film. The discussion of anti-Arabian racism within the film destroyed the box office returns by provoking protesters to picket the movie.

6. See Robyn Wiegman, *American Anatomies: Theorizing Race and Gender* (Durham, N.C.: Duke University Press, 1995).

7. This "vapid fetishization of the visible" is indicative of the changes in black-white interaction and integration throughout society more generally. Following Michelle Wallace's lead, this can be labeled a move from "invisibility blues" to "hypervisibility rhapsodies." See Michelle Wallace, *Black Macho and the Myth of the Superwoman* (New York: Verso, 1990).

8. For a discussion of these stereotypes, see Donald Bogle, *Toms, Coons, Mulattoes, Mammies, and Bucks: An Interpretive History of Blacks in American Films* (New York: Continuum, 1994).

9. In his comments on black urban living more generally, John Jeffries also claims that "race" has become both invisible and highly conspicuous at one and the same time. See "Toward a Re-Definition of the Urban: The Collision of Culture," in *Black Popular Culture: A Project by Michelle Wallace,* ed. Gina Dent (Seattle: Bay, 1992). For a discussion of the black press and its constructions of blackness as related to the portrayals and policing of AIDS in the black community, see Cathy J. Cohen, *The Boundaries of Blackness: AIDS and the Breakdown of Black Politics* (Chicago: University of Chicago Press, 1999). Cohen discusses the public invisibility of black AIDS patients.

10. Herman Gray, *Watching Race: Television and the Struggle for "Blackness"* (Minneapolis: University of Minnesota Press, 1995), p. 125.

11. See Bart Landry, *The New Black Middle Class* (Berkeley: University of California Press, 1987).

12. Wiegman, *American Anatomies,* p. 145.

13. In a post-Tarantino context, even *Lethal Weapon's* last installment introduced an overtly racialized discourse through the comedian Chris Rock and his play on racist assumptions of black criminality.

14. John Singleton foregrounds the symbolic importance of naming in this origin story by having the young teacher very grudgingly and self-consciously correct her term "Indian" with "Native American."

15. The wooden pointer and the pink Africa also hint at the layered gendered components to this discussion of identity. This is especially true given the filmmaker's choice of having the young black girl answer Tre's query about Africa. Moreover, it is almost as though this talk about Africa mirrors "the talk"

daddies have with their sons about sex and where babies come from—where all babies come from being analogous to Tre's argument about where all black people come from.

16. On a certain kind of "homeboy cosmopolitanism," see Manthia Diawara, *In Search of Africa* (Cambridge: Harvard University Press, 1999).

17. To chart this discussion see Melvin Herskovits, *The Myth of the Negro Past* (New York: Beacon, 1958); E. Franklin Frazier, *The Negro Family in the United States* (Chicago: University of Chicago Press, 1966); Sidney Mintz and Richard Price, *The Birth of African American Culture: An Anthropological Perspective* (New York: Beacon, 1976).

18. Jada Pinkett and Quentin Tarantino, "Setting It Off: Jada Pinkett and Quentin Tarantino on Real Estate, Romance, and Race," *New World,* November–December 1996, 38–45.

19. Ibid., 34.

20. Ibid., 35.

21. This song is titled "Waitin' in School" by Gary Shorelle.

22. Gwendolyn Dubois Shaw, "The Lactation of John Brown" (paper presented at Harvard University's W. E. B. Du Bois Institute, Cambridge, Massachusetts, October 2000) offers a masterful transracial and trangendered reading of Caroline Walker's John Brown imagery, a reading that resonates with this cross-racial reading of Hollywood buddy films.

23. Gray, *Watching Race,* writes about televisual attempts to rigorously depict complicated multiple claims on blackness while taking gender and class differences seriously. His argument is that the class-homogenous representations of black life (from the middle-classness of *The Cosby Show* to the decidedly underclass housing projects of *Good Times*) can be challenged by shows such as *Roc, Frank's Place,* and *In Living Color*—all of which, for better or worse (and not perfectly), problematize easy integrationist or color-evasive renditions of black America. For a network-specific discussion of black television's evolution during the 1980s and 1990s, see Kristal Brent Zook, *Color by Fox: The Fox Network and the Revolution in Black Television* (Oxford: Oxford University Press, 1999).

24. See Jean Baudrillard, *Simulations* (New York: Semiotexte, 1983). Further spins on contemporary society's fabricated kernels (what I'm calling Harlemworld) are unpacked in Ian I. Mitroff and Warren Bennis, *The Unreality Industry: The Deliberate Manufacturing of Falsehood and What It Is Doing to Our Lives* (New York: Birch Lane, 1989); Bill Nichols, *Blurred Boundaries: Questions of Meaning in Contemporary Culture* (Bloomington: Indiana University Press, 1994).

25. For a discussion of the primitive as anthropological fiction, see Adam Kuper, *The Invention of Primitive Society: Transformations of an Illusion* (London: Routledge, 1988).

26. See Johannes Fabian, *Time and the Other: How Anthropology Makes Its Object* (New York: Columbia University Press, 1983); Eric Wolf, *Europe and the People without History* (Berkeley: University of California Press, 1982).

27. Many ethnographic works are sensitive (explicitly or implicitly) to this dilemma; for a few of the most recent examples, see Michael Jackson, *Minima Ethnographica: Intersubjectivity and the Ethnographic Project* (Chicago: University of Chicago Press, 1998); Linda Green, *Fear as a Way of Life: Mayan Widows in Rural Guatemala* (New York: Columbia University Press, 1999); Kathryn Marie

Dudley, *Debt and Dispossession: Farm Loss in America's Heartland* (Chicago: University of Chicago Press, 2000); E. Valentine Daniels, *Charred Lullabies: Chapters in the Anthropography of Violence* (Princeton, N.J.: Princeton University Press, 1996); Marjorie Shastak, *Return to Nisa* (Cambridge: Harvard University Press, 2000).

28. See Bronislaw Malinowski, *The Sexual Life of Savages* (New York: Harcourt, Brace and World, 1929); Margaret Mead, *Coming of Age in Samoa: A Psychological Study of Primitive Youth for Western Civilization* (New York: American Museum of Natural History, 1973); Zora Neale Hurston, *Tell My Horse: Voodoo and Life in Haiti and Jamaica* (New York: Harper & Row, 1990) and *Their Eyes Were Watching God* (New York: Harper & Row, 1990).

29. See James Clifford, *The Predicament of Culture: Twentieth-Century Ethnography, Literature, and Art* (Cambridge: Harvard University Press, 1988).

30. See Helán E. Page, "'Black Male' Imagery and Media Containment of African American Men," *American Anthropologist* 99, no. 1 (1995): 99–111.

31. See Faye Harrison, "The Persistent Power of 'Race' in the Cultural and Political Economy of Racism," *Annual Review of Anthropology* 24 (1995): 47–74.

32. See Arjun Appadurai, *Modernity at Large: Cultural Dimensions of Globalization* (Minneapolis: University of Minnesota Press, 1996).

33. See Paul Gilroy, *The Black Atlantic: Modernity and Double Consciousness* (Cambridge: Harvard University Press, 1993).

34. See Immanuel Wallerstein, *Africa and the Modern World* (Trenton, N.J.: Africa World, 1986) and *The Modern World System* (New York: Academic, 1974).

35. See Jacques Derrida, *Of Grammatology,* trans. Guyatri Spivak (Baltimore: Johns Hopkins University Press, 1998); Clifford Geertz, *Interpretation of Cultures: Selected Essays* (London: Fontana, 1993).

36. Smith relayed Washington's advice to reporters from various newspapers, magazines, and television shows many times while promoting the movie.

37. For the general fault lines of this debate see Tricia Rose, *Black Noise: Rap Music and Black Culture in Contemporary America* (Hanover, Conn.: University of New England Press, 1994); Gilroy, *The Black Atlantic.*

38. The hip-hop artist KRS-One explicitly centered his allegiances to the Boogie Down Bronx (from which his crew, Boogie Down Productions, got its name) and helped catapult hip-hop onto the national map with an early ode to place (a song whose mantra-like chorus emphasizes just that: "the South Bronx, the South, South Bronx, the South Bronx"). There was a kind of zero-sum game of rapping credibility that for some dismissed the very possibility of authenticity as a function of place. Queens, as some rival Queens-based rappers in Marly Marl's Juice Crew claimed, would rebut that South Bronx origin story for hip-hop long before academicians got into the mix. To this KRS-One triumphantly retorted, "Manhattan keeps on making it / Brooklyn keeps on taking it / Bronx keeps creating it and Queens keeps on faking it. . . . / The Bridge is Over, the Bridge is Over," the bridge in question being the Queensboro Bridge. The contest was focused, from the very beginning, around place. Queens or the South Bronx? Of course, this geographical "placing" could also be decidedly diasporic, as dance hall and dub musical genres informed the instrumental and vocal styles of hip-hop artists. For a particular example of Jamaican-American musical cross-fertilization, see Grant Fared, "Wailing Soul:

Reggae's Debt to Black American Music," in *Soul: Black Power, Politics, and Pleasure* (New York: New York University Press, 1998). Indeed, concerns of place were at the center of debates within the hip-hop community from its inception. For some important historical context for an understanding of hip-hop culture and its commercial rise, see Nelson George, *Hip Hop America* (New York: Penguin, 1998).

39. See Russell A. Potter, *Spectacular Vernaculars: Hip-Hop and the Politics of Postmodernism* (Albany: State University of New York Press, 1995); George, *Hip Hop America;* Mary Anthony Neal, *What the Music Said: Black Popular Music and Black Popular Culture* (New York: Routledge, 1999).

40. Tricia Rose, "Black Texts/Black Contexts," in *Black Popular Culture: A Michele Wallace Project,* ed. Gina Dent (Seattle: Bay, 1992), p. 225.

41. For some of Mase's and Puffy's history, see Minya Oh, "State of Mase," *Vibe,* June–July 1999, 101–8; Steven Daly, "The Real Rap on Sean 'Puffy' Combs: From Gangsta Life to Martha Stewart and Maybe Back Again," *Vanity Fair,* August 2000, 130–37, 163–69; Jeannine Amber, "Against All Odds," *Vibe,* December 1999–January 2000, 144–52. For explicit connections between hip-hop and Hollywood, see S. Craig Watkins, *Representing: Hip Hop Culture and the Production of Black Cinema* (Chicago: University of Chicago Press, 1998).

42. In 1991, Puff Daddy was involved in organizing an overbooked celebrity basketball game at City College's Harlem gymnasium, a game that ended in a stampede and the death of nine attendees.

Conclusion

1. Details about this new financial interest in Harlem can be seen in "Governor Pataki Announces Funding for Apollo Theater," a 2 November 1999 press release disseminated by the governor's office. Many critics and community residents view this renewed outside interest in Harlem's imagery with extreme suspicion.

2. For more details about these demographic changes in the Harlem community during the 1990s, see "Harlem Rising," *The KIP Business Report,* August 1998.

3. For a look at the different ways in which institutional and individual racism are assessed in American society today, see Robert C. Smith, *Racism in the Post–Civil Rights Era: Now You See It, Now You Don't* (Albany: State University of New York Press, 1995). For a legal theorist's description of contemporary racism's many subtleties, see Patricia J. Williams, *The Alchemy of Race and Rights* (Cambridge: Harvard University Press, 1991).

4. For a glimpse at the fault lines of this debate about the spatialization and racialization of poverty, see Paul Jargowsky, *Place and Poverty: Ghettos, Barrios, and the American City* (New York: Russell Sage, 1997); Douglas A. Massey and Nancy A. Denton, *American Apartheid: Segregation and the Making of the Underclass* (Cambridge: Harvard University Press, 1993). See Mary Pattillo-McCoy, *Black Picket Fences: Privilege and Peril among the Black Middle Class* (Chicago: University of Chicago Press, 1999), for an ethnographic take on the implications of this same debate for the lives and life chances of the black middle class.

5. In the Harlem case, many local residents argue that Disney used its lever-

age and corporate muscle to ring the death knell for area street vendors who had been threatened before but not successfully stopped. Disney's new Harlem store is only the most literal manifestation of that company's corporate influence on contemporary urban communities. New York's Times Square is one of the most explicit and recent re-*class*ifications of urban space for middle-class familial consumption à la Disneyland. For a discussion of contemporary urban renewal strategies as real-life theme-parkifications of urban space, see Sharon Zukin, *The Cultures of Cities* (Malden, Mass: Blackwell, 1995). Also see Samuel R. Delaney, *Times Square Red, Times Square Blue* (New York: New York University Press, 1999).

6. In November 2000, media conglomerate Viacom bought BET from Robert Johnson, offering its media clout to increase BET's reach and revenue.

7. See Ken Auletta, *The Underclass* (New York: Random House, 1982); Lawrence Mead, *Beyond Entitlement: The Social Obligations of Citizenship* (New York: Free Press, 1986); Charles Murray, *Losing Ground: American Social Policy, 1950–1980* (New York: Basic, 1984). For a general analysis of how behavior is used by theorists of poverty, see Adolph Reed, *The Stirrings in the Jar: Black Politics in the Post–Segregation Era* (Minneapolis: University of Minnesota Press, 1999), especially chapter 6, "The 'Underclass' as Myth and Symbol: The Poverty of Discourse about Poverty."

8. Katya Gibel Azoulay, *Black, Jewish, and Interracial: It's Not the Color of Your Skin, but the Race of Your Kin, and Other Myths of Identity* (Durham, N.C.: Duke University Press, 1997), p. 14.

9. See Paul Gilroy, *Against Race: Imagining Political Culture beyond the Color Line* (Cambridge: Harvard University Press, 2000), for an argument that links any and all invocations of race to the slippery slope of fascism. See Kwame Anthony Appiah, *In My Father's House: Africa in the Philosophy of Culture* (Oxford: Oxford University Press, 1992), for a critique of problematic references to Africa as an essentialist grounding for black racial identity and particularity. Walter Benn Michaels, *Our America: Nativism, Modernism, and Pluralism* (Durham, N.C.: Duke University Press, 1995), argues that any mention of race is biologically based. This argument is most explicit in his critiques of Adrian Piper's notion of passing and James Clifford's definition of culture.

10. See Howard Winant, *Racial Conditions: Policy, Theories, Comparisons* (Minneapolis: University of Minnesota Press, 1994), and Lucius T. Outlaw Jr., *On Race and Philosophy* (New York: Routledge, 1996) for slightly more redemptive articulations of race than those offered by Gilroy, Michaels, and Appiah.

11. W. E. B. Du Bois, *The Souls of Black Folk* (1903; reprint, New York: Dover, 1994), p. 1.

12. See Albert Memmi, *Racism* (Minneapolis: University of Minnesota Press, 2000) for an extended argument about the arbitrariness of the contents used to buttress racism's essentialist and hierarchical categorizations.

13. For a general outline of this debate, see Melville Herskovits, *The Myth of the Negro Past* (Boston: Beacon, 1990); E. Franklin Frazier, *The Negro Family in the United States* (Chicago: University of Chicago Press, 1939); Sidney W. Mintz and Richard Price, *The Birth of African-American Culture: An Anthropological Perspective* (Boston: Beacon, 1976).

14. See Thomas Kochman, *Black and White Styles in Conflict* (Chicago: University of Chicago Press, 1981).

INDEX

Italicized page numbers refer to photographs or illustrations. Material in notes that span multiple pages is indexed under the page where the subject/name actually occurs.

273